MORE THOUGHTS ON

TUCSON SALVAGE

"A true champion of the dispossessed and forgotten. Smith's one of the few journalists giving voice to the voiceless. We need this now more than ever. I can't recommend this book highly enough."
—**Willy Vlautin**, author of *The Motel Life*, *Lean on Pete*, and *Don't Skip Out on Me*

"These aren't stories of the movers and shakers of our world, these are stories about the rest of us, the lucky ones trying to hold it together under the daily grind and the not so lucky who have been crushed by all the moving and shaking. Brian Jabas Smith lovingly describes these people, their remarkable spirit and resilience and the city and desert they call home. Thank God or whatever deity may be out there that we have gifted writers like Brian Jabas Smith who have chosen to undertake the noble endeavor of telling these stories, and to remind us that these human beings who exist in the shadows are as much as those who live in the limelight."
—**Tom Hansen**, author of *American Junkie* and *This is What We Do*

"Brian Jabas Smith sees stories in the faces of people the rest of us don't notice, and he tells them in a way that's impossible to ignore. The writing is terrific, but it's the grace, the empathy, his reverence for humanity, that makes this work so beautiful and important that it takes my breath away."
—**Amy Silverman**, author of *My Heart Can't Even Believe It: A Story of Science, Love, and Down Syndrome*

"In this collection of essays Brian Jabas Smith empathetically captures the plight of the disenfranchised, the forgotten, and the misunderstood (often people of color) that comprise the backbone of the cultural landscape of urban Arizona. Read this book and try not to weep — ideally you will."
—**Pat Thomas**, author of *Listen, Whitey! The Sounds of Black Power 1965-75*, and *Did It! Jerry Rubin: An American Revolutionary*

"These are haunting, human stories written with an expert's eye for salvation. In his profiles of the overlooked, the forgotten, and the dismissed, in his ability to stop while others move on, Brian Jabas Smith has captured the spirit of Joseph Mitchell and set it to roam out here in the desert. If you think you know Tucson, stop and read this."
—**Thomas Mira y Lopez**, author of *The Book of Resting Places*

"I can't think of an American writer who captures place with as much empathy, precision, and grace as Brian Jabas Smith. *Tucson Salvage: Tales and Recollections of La Frontera* is as gritty as it is kind, and Smith's prose sparkles with insight and heartbreaking description. In these pages we encounter a gifted writer at the height of his powers. An enviably brilliant book."
—**Cal Freeman**, author of *Fight Songs*

"Whenever I want to hear about the truth about what's really going on in the world of the American Southwest and the particulars of that regional story, I turn to the writing of Brian Jabas Smith. Smith doesn't flinch or turn away from telling the truth exactly as it is, straight on, no chaser. His tales of lives lived hard but true take us inside the everyday struggles of what it means to be alive. The American Southwest may be a desert in the eyes of most, but Smith shows us otherwise: that this is a region infested with sharks, and these are true stories of people – artists, magicians, fighters, hustlers, bus-stop mystics – swimming to save their lives. Pick up this book if you don't mind your whiskey from the well and your habaneros dipped in the Rimbaudian fires of hell."

—**Peter Markus**, author of *The Fish and Not the Fish*, *We Make Mud*, and *Bob, Man or Boat*

"They say everyone you meet has a secret that would break your heart. In *Tucson Salvage*, Brian Jabas Smith meets with the discarded men and women among us and with an openhearted curiosity searches for the humanity in these secrets and finds it. Every. Single. Time."

—**Danny Bland**, author of *In Case We Die*, and *I Apologize in Advance for the Awful Things I'm Gonna Do*

"Brian Jabas Smith's street poet writings are quilted with a lean patchwork sewn up with extensive thread. It's poised work that allows the reader to walk away knowing someone they've never met. He is remarkable in such infiltration with the rare breadth of delivering poetics in prose, as opposed to cons. It feels like it's a matter of time until he scours the entire cityscape revealing all that lurks in shadow land, himself a beacon."

—**Howe Gelb**, singer-songwriter, Giant Sand

First published in 2018
by Eyewear Publishing Ltd
Suite 333, 19-21 Crawford Street
London, W1H 1PJ
United Kingdom

Graphic design by Edwin Smet
Cover image photograph by Brian Jabas Smith
Printed in England by TJ International Ltd, Padstow, Cornwall

Based on the column, "Tucson Salvage", which first appeared in the *Tucson Weekly*, 9/2015-Present. Used with publisher permission.

The editor has generally followed American spelling and punctuation at the author's request.

Set in Bembo 12 / 15 pt
ISBN 978-1-912477-19-7

WWW.EYEWEARPUBLISHING.COM

Briansmithwriter.com
Tucsonsalvage.net

BRIAN JABAS SMITH

TUCSON SALVAGE

TALES AND RECOLLECTIONS FROM LA FRONTERA

FOREWORD BY DAN STUART

Dedicated to Howard McDonald Smith

TABLE OF CONTENTS

FOREWORD

I-10 heading west travels pretty much a straight line from the Atlantic ocean to a point just south of downtown Tucson, where it takes a hard right north towards Phoenix and despair. To the left lies Mexico lurking like a huge Gila monster, one can feel its hot breath all the way from El Paso. It's a junction that acts as a vortex, an asphalt and concrete divining rod with the aquifer underneath shrinking by the day. Two imposing granite and pine partitions – the Catalina and Rincon mountains – form a natural shelter for the city, keeping past lives and disappointments at bay. An outpost for the lost and weary, a sanctuary for misfits, miscreants, and misers, Tucson is the town that refuses to be a city, even with a half million denizens that now call it home.

A friend of mine from San Francisco once asked me why Tucson has so many drifters and dreamers – this was right after a bartender jumped over our beers and knocked out a surly drunk in a dive called The Boondocks – and I replied that people trying to get to LA run out of gas or the radiator goes and they just wind up staying. They find a weekly rate hotel, get a minimum wage job, and put off the better life in California for the next month or so. Soon, however, their physiology starts to change, it's hot and dry and they become desert creatures, moving slowly from shade to shade and never *without* shades which could leave one blind. They morph into cactusheads and like a saguaro that only grows an arm a century become patient in spite of themselves. Without really trying, they soon develop a philosophy they can live with. It really is quite extraordinary.

Brian Jabas Smith knows these desert dwellers, *his* people, just like Studs Terkel knew his in Chicago. Born and raised in Tucson, a champion cyclist and fantastic punk frontman in his youth, he came and went a few times but finally returned for good when life and love became unbearable in a rust belt capital where the sun doesn't shine but a few months a year, and half as bright at that. To pay rent and keep the swamp cooler blowing, he put his hard-earned journalist chops to use and started writing a column for the local weekly. He called it *Tucson Salvage* and dedicated it to the kooks and crannies of a city that only a native can uncover and fully understand. It really was no different than his childhood hikes in the desert, turning over rocks and poking into holes to discover what others wanted no part of: strange and sometimes venomous critters to be treated with respect and wonder. A naturalist back in his element, he hit his stride in middle-age, the opposite of poor brilliant Joseph Mitchell hiding in his *New Yorker* office with nothing left to type. A collection of critically acclaimed stories soon arrived called *Spent Saints*, bittersweet tales about the demon meth and the endless 40's of nasty brew that used to sustain him night after night, before sanity returned like a favorite cat not seen in years. Mirroring his characters and subjects, Smith allowed himself to believe in the desert's power to bake the hurtful past right out of you, leaving only the sanctity of today, this moment right now. He replaced the racing bike of his youth with long rambles through town to see what's new, or more often, what has changed and will never return. It was the perfect match all around, writer and environment, and unlike crusty Edward Abbey, who aged about as well as mayonnaise left in the sun, Smith held onto his humanity like a shield and used empathy like a weapon, disarming all with his earnest queries and impish grin.

The portraits in *Tucson Salvage* are wide and varied, from legless gangbanging artists to Mormon baseball mascots to crime scene clean-up cowboys. Swap meets and tourist traps figure prominently, as do junkyards, dive bars and greasy spoons. Smith has the time and patience to duck into the places we all rush by and wonder about; or to stop and chat with a street "crazy" who is anything but. He never patronizes anyone, or worse, romanticizes life's hard knocks and cruel turns. Foot in door, his genuine curiosity and natural charm encourages his subjects to open up and share sweet joys and triumphs they haven't thought about in years, or reveal poignancies that are too hard to unload on families or friends, only a kind stranger will do. Brian observes, listens, then transcribes... a post-punk priest or travelling sin-eater he captures the stories folks didn't even know they had, and stitches them back into the communal quilt that makes us all stronger, safer, more human. It's holy work, no doubt about it, but done by a fallen altar boy who truly knows what it's like to feel completely alone and abandoned, all bridges burned, no direction home. Smith is happy to listen because it quiets his own internal voices that taunt and harangue, carnies looking for an easy mark. We can all learn from this, the basic grace of an open heart and mind that can deliver us from our own worst impulses, from *el mal* that waits like a coyote eyeing a toddler, grinning from ear to ear.

Lately I've grown weary of life in a megalopolis, and as I read over Smith's columns a second and third time I find myself dreaming about returning to the desert, to become a character worthy of his attention. I imagine working as a tight-lipped night clerk in a neon drenched motel on Miracle Mile, or maybe a happy-go-lucky pool cleaner sporting a huge Asian rice hat with arms as dark as coffee. I could quit drinking, lose twenty pounds, buy a potter's wheel, keep a pet snake, fall in love, read the *Bhagavad Gita*, stop trying so hard. Austin aside, Tucson is the original slacker town, and regardless of how many transplants from stress-bomb states arrive, that will never change. The desert welcomes pilgrims, but also shuns past conceits. Start over or leave, just too damn hot to carry around all that baggage, grab yourself a frozen Eegee's instead.

It's worth noting that many of Smith's interactions are with people who hold opposite views to his own: guns, the current president, immigration, etc. Smith doesn't argue, instead he'll bring up a point or ask a question that subtly prods his subject into acknowledging their own uncertainty, their own closely held deceits. He would make an exceptional diplomat, or cultural anthropologist, or the perfect bartender. His eyes see what we don't, what we've become inured to, the terrible truth of ordinary people trying to live with dignity and honor in a world that has gotten harsher and more polarized by the day. These pieces will stick around long after Smith and his menagerie have passed, and will stay with me until my own reckoning as well. Read and enjoy, but keep a tissue at hand, you're gonna need it.

Dan Stuart, singer-songwriter, Green on Red, author of *The Deliverance of Marlowe Billings* and *The Unfortunate Demise of Marlowe Billings*

Mexico City, March 2018

INTRODUCTION

In these pages, you'll meet a goat farmer who cleans up crime scenes. The cast of characters who pass through a smokeshop round about midnight. An AM radio legend, scraping by after spending his life stitching together voices and music. An old prospector, flat broke and full of yarns, true or not. Folks passing through a desert truck stop on New Year's Eve. A beat-up hero cop coming across a horrific suicide attempt while on patrol. A downtown hot-dog vendor, slinging her goods even as she mourns the loss of her daughter. And plenty of others, people rising, or down and out, or damaged, or forgotten, or never noticed at all.

Brian Jabas Smith tells these stories in the pages of my newspaper, the *Tucson Weekly*. He connects with his people in a way few writers do, penning vignettes that'll move your heart without falling back on sappy clichés.

Smith grew up in this dry desert town, in a much different time. He tried his damnedest to get out of here, moving to Phoenix and L.A. and Detroit. He survived many lives – bike racer, rock 'n' roll star, junkie, newspaper columnist, drunk, alt-weekly editor, author – and then ended up back here, living calm and sober, happily married with a young boy to look after.

And, having salvaged himself, he brings us *Tucson Salvage*. We're lucky to have him and, as you're about to find out, so are you.

Jim Nintzel
Executive Editor *Tucson Weekly*

Q-MART
FOOD MART

SUICIDES, MOTHERS AND SONS

Alcoholic ghosts with suffering faces – ruddy with busted capillaries – circulate the dirty corners and bus stops at the intersection of Alvernon Way and Grant Road, and I step around them on long nighttime walks of the city. I could've been, or maybe should be, one of them. Frightened into menace and floating around Circle K's coffee kiosk, guzzling the stuff by the gallon to ease the meth crashes, and counting out dimes at the Dollar Store for some sad shelf trinket to brighten a stalled, dreamless world that exists nearby between ugly cinderblock walls and bedsheet-covered windows. I could wind up in that place again one day, still, searching insanely in the wrong direction for the shiny and the new.

Whores in unflattering clothes move up Alvernon toward Pima Road and bicker fantastically to themselves. Hoot things at me too, like, "Hey, Yip Yaw, woo-hooooooo," before they can see me. It's a gift how they sense men before they see them. Their entire beings wilt or rage in direct proportion to the level of meth or catastrophe in their systems, but in the watery streetlight, they're nearly translucent, their roadside sashays and random hip-grinds seem weightless. They became the focus of so much longing, and I relive it all later, over and over in solitude inside my safe little house near Tucson Boulevard. Their children and mothers, their fathers and brothers and sisters. I count tombstones.

The young mother who lived next door years ago, the last time I'd lived in Tucson. How she committed suicide at the now-abandoned filling station at Pima and Alvernon. How she pumped gasoline over herself and sparked a lighter. How she left behind two little daughters. How before she died, I'd read to her girls out in the sun in my front yard, and they'd stare back at me with eyes all big and curious, faces candy-sticky. Sometimes the littler one would climb onto my back and yank pieces of my hair.

My brilliant running bud Doug Hopkins and how he'd stay with us in our casita over on Camilla Street. He'd blow in from Phoenix, sometimes on a freight train, and we'd kill nights in Tucson, and in Nogales, like we did when we lived in Phoenix. I wanted to die too when he committed suicide. His big-footed, see-beauty-in-everything drunken self still stumbles all over this low, dusty town. His sweet pop songs are on the radio, still.

My mother, born on Halloween, died too young not long ago, and she wasn't ready to go. She circulates. From the downtown Lawyer's Title building to old midtown bars to eastside card-game tables. I see her still in her green damask apron, in a dusty stream of depressing afternoon sunlight in our old kitchen on Kenyon Drive. She's looking straight down into my four-year-old eyes, her hand on my cheek, giving me access to the one world that's safe and dreamy, and I'm trying to articulate a sensation I was too young to grasp, but soon understood as the dull ache of inescapable melancholy. I swear she sometimes brushes hair off my forehead when I sleep, her hand smelling of rose water and cigarettes.

The ghost of my father, who two years ago died from cancer. He's everywhere. I'll hear his tenor sax ostinatos and gentle guitar runs, like he's next to me playing with a passion only he could get lost in. He could never be disconnected in that place, and I learned about musical transcendence from watching and listening to him. I think of gigs he did when I was a little boy – from living room rehearsals to the old Pioneer Hotel to the Westward Look Resort. This is my Missouri-born dad who, long before I was born (the fourth of five), brought television to Tucson at KOLD-TV, literally: He was Tucson's first TV cameraman, and he helped bring the nighttime sparkle and shimmer to those towers atop Mount Bigelow, and I feel him when I look up there, 8,000 feet up along the high ridge of the Catalina Mountains. He turned down job offers in bigger TV markets because Tucson was now in his blood, and because he was always searching for a kind of peacefulness, which he found. This was his Tucson.

I was hardly a fan of my pop when I was a kid, and left home at a tender age. I later understood, of course, that he suffered (quietly) as much as anyone, if not more. After my parents divorced he found and married a whip-smart Texan who saw the kindness in him, and there was a shift. Through long conversations in the few years leading up to his death, I got a grasp of his fierce intelligence and empathy for the world. He'd answer personal questions – the kind that could never be asked – involving his life, loves, and fears. I saw him vulnerable. I confessed things that were far too shameful to otherwise admit out loud to anyone. He inspired and awed and I did not want him to go. He died a soldier of the gentle class.

Sometimes I spot him watering plants in front of his house where he died, around the corner from where I now live.

★ ★ ★

This city is crammed full of memories and nostalgias that are my own and not my own – the bus route straight up Broadway, the sweet-screech orchestras of summer cicadas, the low-stakes quality of its place in the world. I returned here from Detroit – a busted, haunted city if ever there was one – because my heart was shattered. (I began to believe that all I had in life to show her was the worst that my world had to offer, until we were living in a house built on sadnesses and sorrows, like all my houses. She didn't deserve that.) Was already in a state of untenable brokenness after my father died, a death that slowly became so cataclysmic it divided my history into the before and the after.

And it was like there was nothing else in the world for me to do, and nowhere to go, except, maybe, to Tucson, the one place I swore I'd never return. It's inviting when you're broken, if you're getting by on longing, like anything informed by potent boyhood memories and distance. All hallowed and womb-like. I was born here and there's family and all those chemistries beyond DNA and bloodlines. So I split Detroit late spring.

I live in a beautifully ragged neighborhood in the middle of town. It's full of chain-link and yucca-fenced front yards of gravel and dirt and decorated with home-crafted sun gods or sun-rotted swings or Egyptian-looking cacti. The shut-in next door keeps abandoned trucks under a magnificent pine tree. I wanted in to this milieu, among ghosts of hard-working family men who built lives on seemingly futile struggles. Like how my dad did. It inspires me more than any gentrified barrio or artist's enclave or block teeming with moneyed beardos riding fixed gears. And Tucson's dusty mesquite and walled-in mountain safety – where overhead jets pierce the quietness, where stupid saguaros wave like they're always happy – reveals a place that will always be lost and found, and haunted. The first thing I remembered upon arriving here again was how the heavy desert scents and weirdly saturated colors after rains heal. It's autumn now and it's so well done. The burnt light softer, the shadows taller, harsh edges at the end of the world gone.

October 29, 2015

YOU DIE TRYING

A dust devil charges down the swap-meet walkway and stirs the shop's neatly displayed sunglasses, silver trinkets, and daisy-happy pillows. A fleeting hippy prism half obscured by dust refracts from a store across the way, and it's gone. Cosmic kitsch on a bizarrely warm January day.

Shop proprietor Abelardo "Abe" Caraasco hurries from behind his counter to retrieve sunglasses flung to the squall. "Yesterday I had three sunglasses stolen," he shouts. "What are you going to do?"

A moment later, Abe's conversing effortlessly in Spanish and English, counting change for a customer's new necklace, surrounded by a wall of hats, perfumes and umbrellas. In the last two hours, a few dozen customers of assorted sizes, ages and nationalities strolled in, obliged mild curiosities, and left. A precious few spent cash.

Abe's manning his storefront at the Tanque Verde Swap Meet. He began here five years ago selling things on a single table he hauled from home, then two, and "it grew from there." Now it's a shop stocked of sparkly goods purchased from a California wholesaler or brought from his Oaxaca, Mexico homeland. His prize ponies are the real silver chains and several handmade rugs.

It's not an easy business, especially now that swap-meet culture is slowly dying. The shop suffers further in summer months and the rent is tough to make, but monsoons offer salvation. A leaky roof here, a snapped tree there. People call him. He fixes and builds things. "I have three kids and a wife," he says, straightening sunglasses on a rack filled with them.

"But I try not to think about my future."

He shrugs.

"Sometimes I think I am very blessed."

Earned wisdom from someone who learned to make himself valuable in a city where he's been mostly unwanted and ignored since arriving penniless in 1996. He's a Mexican national with a green card awaiting U.S. citizenship.

A 2011 arrest saw Abe nearly deported for not having his green card, yet the paperwork for said card had been filed. He spent two weeks in jail and his family suffered. Trump's anti-humanist position and racist ICE policies fill Abe with worry and tension, but it's a familiar feeling. "They're always watching me," he says. "They know everything about me, my identity, personal history, the taxes I pay. I can't lie about anything. It's like they want to catch you in a lie so they can kick you out of the country.

"And in this country," he adds, "you can't be late on your bills. You can't be late on anything."

★ ★ ★

Guided by his young cousin, then 17-year-old Abe left his tiny village in the state of Oaxaca, Mexico and made the bus ride to Mexico City. He'd never seen a metropolis before. Abe's family was one of maybe 20 in their tiny village near Tamazulapam del Espíritu Santo. The Mexican capital was dirty, loud, terrifying, and he felt alone in the world for the first time. When night came, they got robbed.

Stuck in Mexico City, they starved, slept where they could, and hustled masonry work for cash.

You don't go home, Abe told himself. *You die trying*.

Two months later he'd saved 150 pesos (less than $100 U.S.), enough to get to Nogales, Sonora, and to begin the journey into the Arizona desert. The checkpoint police between Mexico City and the bordertown frightened them, especially in Sinaloa cartel country. They pegged Abe, with his darker skin and shorter stature, as Central American, not Mexican, and made their hatred known. The racism was "worse than here," Abe says. "We had to always prove we were Mexicans, otherwise they abused us."

They arrived in Nogales, the top of Mexico, at sunup, 36 hours on the bus. Next stop: the border fence. Abe's 21-year-old cousin had real-life experience, he knew where to cross.

Their first attempt was hijacked by a border gang and saw Abe stripped naked at knifepoint, searched and stabbed, but not seriously injured. They spent six weeks in the bordertown attempting to get over the fence for good. "Every time we crossed we had an incident with gangs," he says. "We were scared but we always fought back. If they had knives we had rocks."

Border patrol caught and arrested Abe five times, and each time he was sent back to Nogales, where he told them he lived. The sixth border-crossing attempt was the charm, so to speak.

Abe grew up with no shoes. His parents and grandparents were born into abject poverty. From generation to generation the poverty was like disease. A dirt-floored adobe hut with a tree-branch door served as the family home, built by his father. He was 11 years old when electricity arrived. Forget plumbing; trees doubled as outhouses, rivers as baths ("there's a certain dirt that made your hair soft," Abe says). He'd learned to work, hard, pretty much from the day he slipped from his mama's womb, and helped raise six younger siblings. He quit

school in 9th grade to help.

Planting and harvesting, the family lived solely on food they grew, or that from their cow and chickens. Hunger (and logic) taught Abe to live with no money, taught survival habits. He hunted with rocks, mostly rabbits and doves, but there was the occasional bobcat. ("You don't know how mean they are when they are hurt. But we never ate coyotes"). The one-room poverty showed his mother's pains – from menstrual cycles to miscarriages. "She couldn't afford pads. I saw her lose babies. A kid my age, I thought she was dying."

He imagined young a world where his siblings wouldn't starve, a place with running water, and maybe a refrigerator. A refrigerator would be riches.

You don't go home. You die trying.

Abe didn't die the first time he crossed over to Arizona, but came close. He collapsed in the desert south of Tucson, crippled by dysentery and dehydration. The group who crossed the mountains and desert with him left him to die like so many before and after him. But his cousin stayed, and saved his life. "I walked almost seven days in the desert, ran out of water after three days," Abe says, adding, "It gave me a good lesson."

If he could make it to Tucson he'd have a place inside a toolshed in someone's yard, where king snakes hunt mice, where his bed would be a blanket and a plywood board atop dirt, alongside other undocumented migrants. He'd have hard-labor jobs no one else would do. If he could just make it to Tucson.

You don't go home. You die trying.

He and his cousin made it to a Circle K on Tanque Verde Road on foot, Nogales to Tucson. And for three years Abe lived with others in that tiny windowless toolshed. He paid $2 a day for it. He bathed in a bucket, pooped in a Porta Potty.

"Wintertime was tough," Abe says. "Summertime was OK, we'd be in our underwear. We slept on plywood. Earned $2 an hour to landscape, lay concrete, build fences, do odd masonry work."

Harder than that, he says, was not knowing the language. "I'd have no idea where to go or who to ask for help. I was so scared. People would get sick or hit on their bicycles, and their bodies would be shipped back to Mexico. I was scared. So I learned English. I'm still learning." His English is percussive, formal and attentive; concentration in lieu of verbal theatrics. He's more confident speaking Spanish. His wide brown eyes convey what words don't, they're expressive, kind even.

Abe learned in those toolshed years the rules of construction and craftsmanship: "If somebody said, 'Put a wall here,'

I'd put a wall there. When I started welding, it was one man who said, 'Oh, I'll teach you,' and then I learned to weld." Learned plumbing, electrical, construction, driving tractors and forklifts. The autodidact learned "how to just work with people," especially wealthy ones, who'd see nothing wrong with hiring dirt-cheap Mexican labor, work their asses off, offer no raises or even tips, all the while micro-managing, pulling out digital levels to measure their work, and so on.

Abe crossed the border illegally, then legally when things improved. His siblings now all live in Arizona, his mother too. He recently purchased a house, works and barely supports his family with the shop and occasional masonry side gigs; hard work as a show of love. The antiquated heroic American dream, down to family/work binaries.

★ ★ ★

The family home is clean, bright and comfortable, familiar-feeling, nothing arranged for show, aside from many framed family photos. A laundry room with washer and dryer, spacious backyard – modern conveniences in off-whites and beiges. Two cars outside, a small trailer for hauling things. A newly purchased modular home in central Tucson.

"Sometimes we're down to beans and rice," Abe says. "That's good enough for us."

Their three children, all born in Arizona, have decidedly English – and German-sounding names, "so they can move around easy here," Abe says.

Leo, their 4-year-old, is bilingual and shy, instinctively speaks to me in English, shows off his plastic dinosaur and shark pillow. Their autistic middle daughter Brittany is off at the International School of Tucson. The eldest, Emily, is a sophomore at Salpointe Catholic High School with a 3.97 GPA.

Abe crushed on his wife Yadira back in middle-school, but was too poverty-shamed to talk to her. She had shoes, pretty dresses, an only child whose father had a government job. Abe hardly stood a chance. Once he migrated to Arizona, he returned home to collect family members. He discovered Yadira had been widowed, with a daughter. Her husband was a cop, murdered on the job. Abe had a little confidence now, so he wooed her, and won her. But her parents didn't want their only daughter (and granddaughter) living in the states.

"Her parents weren't happy with me bringing their daughter through the desert," Abe says, his expression softened by a thought that maybe the crossing was, after all, pretty damn dangerous. He adds quickly, "she was never hungry crossing over, and she didn't have to run from the Border Patrol."

Yadira nods. Never dreamed of leaving Mexico. Crossing, she adds, "took two days. No border patrol. And no bad guys."

That was 2001, and Yadira's daughter stayed behind, which wasn't easy either. "I see her as my daughter," Abe says. "It's her and our three kids." The family visits Oaxaca every year, spending as much time as possible. Gives Abe opportunity to show his children the penury from which he rose. "I think that they think that even having a TV is a normal thing," Abe says. "I want them to see how it can be."

Yadira cooks meals culled from family recipes, passed down. The couple hope to open a restaurant, small, "maybe breakfast and lunch." There's no way they could raise the capital to start anew, they'd have to take over a restaurant that's gone under. Anyway, they point out, their special-needs daughter requires extra parenting and time.

Yadira's beautiful dark features show knowing calm, like she could assess everything about you without saying a word. She has flowing black hair and is often mistaken for Filipino, Native American, "or Asian. It's funny." Abe too gets mistaken, like his days traveling penniless in Mexico. He's been hassled by border patrol in Tucson but let go because they figured him Native American.

Abe speaks of his dad, who's 76, in terms of drinking and fighting. "He still drinks and gets in fights, because he still thinks he's young." Dad lived in Arizona and in California but chooses Mexico. Abe and his siblings send money home, though he's not sure where dad's living exactly, maybe with a woman. "He's the kind of man who didn't mess with his kids' lives. He always said we'd always find food."

He knows he can drink like his old man, the only family member who could, he says. As a kid, he cut agave plants for the juice, to ferment. ("That's how we get into alcohol as kids.") Abe's boozing about blew his family apart, he cowers slightly talking about it. Says the AA rooms saved him. "I don't go to church," he adds, "I did when I was a boy. I'm not a very religious guy, but sometimes I pray. I should be more thankful. Sometimes I say, 'Thank you, God.' Sometimes I get mad and say mean things to my wife. I don't want to. I want to be a better man.

"I know that you help those who need it, and the more you give, the more you get. We never got food stamps or anything like that, and I really appreciate that I can work and provide."

He lingers.

"It makes me sad that people here think that Mexicans just take."

He and Yadira work long swap-meet hours. It was all new and so the couple enrolled in business classes to learn book-keeping, marketing. But Abe's worried he's losing the life skills, the purity of tasks of basic human survival. "I get too much into this robotic world," he says. "I'm scared of that. I'm going to be 40. I could be left in the middle of nowhere and still feed my family, but I don't feel like I can do that now. The survival skills – climbing, hunting, navigating lands and waters, animal care, surviving with my hands. When I had no shoes there were thorns and sharp rocks, and we never got poked or hurt. Now if I walk outside with no shoes I'd get poked and hurt. See? Now I worry about having enough money for everything, all the time.

"But I don't want anyone to go through what I went through," he adds, pulling his cap off. His fingers part his thick black crewcut to reveal a rosy, pinkie-length scar, which he traces with a hint of pride. "A horse kick," he says.

"Crossing now," he continues, "it's different, harder. I'm legal now, but it's still not easy. The poverty in Mexico is not going to stop unless the government steps in. The trees are disappearing too, the wood-cutting… Thank God we still get rain there."

Abe and Yadira walk Leo to his preschool, a few blocks away. Yadira keeps the boy close to her hip along the street. I try to imagine what part of this Abe is sensing. The rippling songs of wind chimes, the pleasing brick duplexes and rectangle ranch-style homes, the great palm trees, and still the promise of sweet possibility. It's what's in this damn light.

February 8, 2018

STILL LIFE AT THE CHATTERBOX

You walk into the bar on a Monday night and at first it's one like any other. You recognize its sorrow-killing aspects: the overly saturated reds and greens, the pedestal of booze bottles behind the bar, the gently humming loneliness – a place once populated with drunken inmates just like you. Inmates who used to be older but now they're not, or they're dead. This bar is empty of customers tonight, how you like it these days – emptiness as a living, breathing thing. You recall how you'd visit these spots with regularity like atonement.

The swamp cooler is blowing hard enough to rustle the hair on your arms, and it's comforting, like how Tucson summers are time-stamped to your childhood, and so it feels like the moment is forever slipping away. That motion.

A youngish street urchin of 33 or so steps in off the dark street and hits up the bartender for matches. You notice the street-corner Army green, and mean eyes trying hard to be kind, and wonder how long it has been since he bent out of the shape of someone who could be loved. He makes you sad because you might've been him in some other time. He turns and looks right at you and his face shows warning, and he mumbles something but it's overpowered by the cackle of the basketball game on one of two flickering TVs. He ambles out of the bar in a hazy glow of real or imagined menace and steps out into the night. You figure he would've stayed longer if you weren't there. He would've kept his gaze on the bartender because he obviously regards her like you do in that quiet sunken way that withdrawn people do around anyone who is beautiful.

Louie, an employee from Luke's Italian Beef restaurant next door, wears a kitchen apron and moves with slow tired ease, like maybe he carries the tragic nature of some universe on his sloped shoulders. You think maybe he does carry such weight because he's black and he's a legend on this tiny stretch of Alvernon just south of 22nd Street – he's cooked at Luke's for 30 years. He totes in food for Chatterbox bartenders – a long-standing, recurring gesture of kindness – bread and salad and things, all wrapped up. Sometimes he brings crossword puzzle magazines and pizza and candy.

You notice the bartender's name penned in cursive on the dry-erase board hanging in light near the bathrooms: Isabel. Louie chats with Isabel about water dripping through a keg-sized hole in the ceiling. Isabel places a bucket in the center of the floor to catch it.

You know of the lady who was living in her car with her Chihuahua who Isabel befriended. Then she'd come into The Chatterbox and plug in her rice cooker and drink free soda until one day she was gone. Just like that.

Without a goodbye, Louie the Legend moves like an apparition through the open door, and heads south, back to his home of 30 years.

Isabel looks at you and looks up at the hole in the ceiling. She giggles. Says, "Like I said, this place is a hole."

You wouldn't want it any other way. Not the lovely Chatterbox, a bar that's been around since just after World War II, and has been owned by the same guy since '74. It's had some glory years, serving well the neighborhood regulars and unemployed machinists and broken newlyweds and alcoholic liars and the hit-upons and best friends and anyone you can personally name who'd manned a stool here. It's had some downner years and you guess it's probably in the middle of a downner year or five right now. It makes you happy that there are no craft cocktails here, and no preeners who look like an unfortunate cross of Garth Hudson (circa '69) and Haircut 100. It smells of wet concrete and warm beer, not the hygienic pong of new money and fresh interior design. Only marketing here: glowing Bud and Coors signs.

In this moment, there's no one here but you and the bartender. There's no jaded air of drink-slinger responsibility about her; you understand how she's comfortable in her skin in that way people are who've not let life punishments erode trust and curiosity in others.

She extends her hand to show you the ring her man David Anthony Doc Holliyday Lopez gave her three days ago. Its many diamonds shimmer. You're not lying when you tell her it impresses. You marvel at her fiancé's name too. She tells you his parents give their children names after western heroes, complete with spelling variance.

You learn the 37-year-old began working in the bars at 18, and has worked in every local dive you can recall, The Buggy Wheel, Home Plate, The Buffet, The Silver Room, Lazy V, Alfie's Pub, The Runway, The Office and others. She's been at the Chatterbox on and off for at least a decade.

You understand how bars helped lift Isabel from what she terms "a rough childhood." You learn of the book she composed in third grade, the one that landed her on local news, the true account of how her uncle killed her pregnant (eight months) aunt and wounded her five-year-old cousin and then committed suicide. The uncle was a "drunk, and that runs in the family," she explains. That family devastation devastated the extended family.

Her dad drank, hard, he was never around. He had another family. A tattoo on her shoulder tells of familia solidaria, depicting Isabel and her sister.

Drive-by bullets sprayed her government-subsidized childhood Tucson homes often and her brother is lucky to be alive even though he's in prison. He went to the big house at age 16. He got out for a few months and now he's back in. Lifer.

She always wanted to be a writer, but life has a way of getting in the way. Sometimes she writes when she's alone in the Chatterbox. She'd earned young author awards at Wakefield Junior High and Pueblo High. She says she learned what not to do by watching others in her family.

In all your whiteness, you think of this woman with the rose and heart tattoos, jeans and tight top, as a tough Latina, in the best way possible, hard and beautiful and with a soft, quietly beating heart. You think of how lucky bar patrons have been over the years to have had her do the pouring. You figure none had much idea.

You wonder if she's ever frightened to be behind the bar here alone at night, this bar near 22nd Street and Alvernon, with the "tweaker zombies" as one patron put it one night.

"No. Not really," she tells you. "Except the young gangbanger kids, with the rags on them. They make me more nervous than anyone else."

That's when she reaches below and pulls out a glimmering Taurus 1911 .45 pistol. You know very little about guns but even you can see it's formidable and could take your own head off. She tells you how David, her fiancé, "wants me to be prepared for anything."

She shows you pictures on her phone of her man's huge gun collection. She knows them well. A Glock 26 that holds up to 200 rounds, a pair of AR-15s, a 12 gauge, and so on. The bartender's fiancé David comes around often and in him you sense at first a lazy kind of agitation, see how she's hyper attentive to his needs. He leaves for an hour, drives off in his shiny big pickup, and then he comes back around. You consider him hovering danger, tattooed machismo moving in an inflexible bubble of jealousy. You watch close and soon learn how you're judgmental, and wrong. There's no domestic crisis in the air, or tension, but you sense his burden of Isabel working alone in a beat bar after dark.

Then he leaves. Returns an hour later with a brand-new chainsaw. Opens the box and admires its contents on the bar.

Got a deal on it, he tells her. She admires it too. The display of domestic tenderness sort of aches.

David was a tattoo artist who had his own shop and now he's a bootmaker too (a rising apprentice working for the Osuna custom boot family), a rodeo star (they both wear his championship belt buckles), and he co-owns a mesquite-shaded ranch in South Tucson called Rancho Bravo where he boards horses and other barnyard animals. There's chickens and goats and a goose they rescued after its beak had been cruelly clipped. The ranch is done up with found objects, from bull skulls to water tanks. David's got street entrepreneurial skills. A powerful presence.

He shows you pictures. Of his old Southside tattoo parlor called AZ Ink Tattoo, with the stripper pole and come-hang couches and liquor store located across the street. The parlor closed because David was getting hassled by cops after it became a destination for lowrider clubs. David grew up around Arizona ranches. His knowledge and love of animals is obvious.

You now see David as a protector. You're no fan of guns and he shows you Facebook videos of himself shooting automatic weapons in the desert. You see he lives by codes, rules of safety, which carry over to his life, his fiancée, his 18-year-old son, his ranch, his rodeo riding.

He talks of touching people's lives, through art (tattooing), through animals (his ranch) through kindness ("It's about helping people get to the next place"). You hate yourself because you are surprised. You know you would likely worry too if she was your fiancée. He tells you she loves dive bars. You can't tell anyone where to work. "What are you going to do?"

Their first date found them delivering a baby horse on that very ranch, three years ago. David had a crush on Isabel for years, but she was with someone else. That same someone else once snapped her back and he let her suffer on the floor for hours before calling an ambulance. A show of boundless brutality and terror, and it's a wonder she wasn't paralyzed for life. Still she suffers heavy back pain, needs one more operation so as not to wind up in a wheelchair. That's why David doesn't let her lift heavy things. You watch him help her at The Chatterbox. He tells you how he met her working on the tattoo on her neck that spelled out the name of the man who broke her back.

Still you marvel how Isabel is not lost to chaos. Because you are, still. She has her code and so does David. You walk out of there. You tally the ways how the two people are nothing like you, and you suddenly care about them so much it surprises you. At the Chatterbox on a lonely Monday night in June in Tucson.

June 15, 2017

WAR ON VETS

"All hands on deck!" soars like a battle cry. Prompts all sweaty homeless residents, men and women, armed and unarmed, minus the infirm, to hustle through the Bravo Base entrance to a waiting mini-van in the parking area. This bustle, fueled mostly on an exaggerated sense of duty, is to unload some donated water and food, quickly and efficiently, and store it back in camp. That's it. The June sun burns into the hundreds. Jaded war vets in wheelchairs roll eyes.

Then they relax some in the shade. Funny stories exchanged. There's been lots happening lately here, so relaxation is relative, especially for the "base commander" – a spindly Nam vet (three Marine tours) with thick white hair and burnt, seen-it-all eyes, and his "co-commander," Scott Powers, a tough, compact man of 60. Both of whom are under "high stress."

See, this is Veteran's On Patrol (VOP), led by vet's advocate Michael "Lewis Arthur" Meyer, who founded this non-profit back in 2015. An arm of that, "VOP Alpha Co – Team Pulaski" had days before overdramatically claimed a child-trafficking camp existed in the desert near West Valencia Road and I-19. Local TV news broadcast the findings with sensationalistic bents, and it all went viral. Indeed, said campsite, with its underground plastic septic tank littered with kid's toys, looked wrong, like how unnatural things in the Sonoran Desert can appear deviant and creepy, especially on video.

In short, Tucson cops and U.S. Immigration and Customs Enforcement found zero evidence of child trafficking, and cop cadaver dogs found no dead bodies, and it was widely report-

ed. Days later, VOP found a skull in the desert near Marana and claimed it was a child's. It wasn't.

This child-trafficking red-alert crisis was brigaded by tens of thousands online, including bogus news sites like Alex Jones' InfoWars.com. Wacked online conspiracies surrounding the (debunked) child-trafficking campsite raged, claiming ties to everything from the Clinton Foundation to Mexican cartels.

Note that Arthur has cameoed at notable militia standoffs in the past, such as the 2014 Cliven Bundy's Nevada ranch, and the 2016 Oregon Wildlife Refuge debacle. To his defense, he scaled a Surprise, Arizona lightpole in 2015 to draw attention to veteran suicide. That got him arrested.

One recent Facebook video shows him motoring in the desert investigating "rape trees" and delivering "supply drops" for his "boots on the ground" outside of Tucson. He refers to himself in the third-person, responding to naysayers, "Lewis Arthur has never claimed to be a vet, so you don't have to worry about stolen valor there, never once. And there are hundreds of veterans who come out here and step up because they know who I am."

His videos grow tedious, especially those featuring sermons on how their "guns aren't pointing at no Americans. They're pointing at the bad guys."

His is militarized cult-speak, ideology trumps fact. But on video, Arthur is tireless, smart and self-assured, charismatic and dusty good-looking enough to titillate his numbers with ghoulish militia fervor – the anti-government screeds, talk of militant stand-offs and how God's on his side (even working "miracles" in the desert for his cause) couched in virtuous endeavor, such as rescuing children and the homeless. There's a veneer of erudition and sympathy masking essential designs of conflict. It's a trickle-down Trumpian above-the-law mindset, and it appeals to factions prone to mollycoddle outrage and even war, particularly that's based on false news. It's so ridiculous now it's fish-in-a-barrel. But many Americans love hard assurances, love finding threat and intention in every rumor, and Arthur's following is growing.

To hear some VOP folk talk of these things, you'd think they found the child molesters and the children and even tortured dead bodies. They never let facts get in the way of Arthur. They believe in Arthur surely as Arthur believes in himself.

I'd first heard of this veteran's homeless camp after learning how some had patrolled Santa Rita Park on 22nd Street to rid it of drugs and dealers and how cops were cool with it. I'd also heard for months they were doing worthy work to help find, house and save homeless vets and non-vets. I go to meet Arthur, but he was gone, they said, on patrol. Anyway, "high stress, no time to talk." That's when I'm introduced to base co-commander Scott Powers. He'll give me a tour.

Bravo Base is a separate "division" of the VOP; different from Alpha Co's "high stress" recon and well-publicized call to arms. Bravo Base isn't us and them. This is really more about the holy trio of necessity: food, clothing, shelter.

★ ★ ★

There are no living green things at Bravo Base – "Camp Conklin." Except for the few women staying here, there's nothing feminine either. The air tastes like dust and dirt, and the rubber of walls built of myriad truck tires.

The entire area, which could fit inside a Walmart, looks

like what you'd imagine a desert combat command to look like in, say, Iraq. The grounds are organized into modular and geodesic military tents of assorted sizes, hued in camo, war green and dirt tan. They're fashioned into living quarters (some sleep 20 on cots) and supply huts – the vet tents over here, civilian tents over there, a med tent, a pantry, women's quarters, a reception area. Outside of a couple of those tents, private quarters are strung up in nooks in shadows, blankets for shade, which one homeless vet calls "Thunderdome."

One open tent flap reveals whiffs of man-sweat and old potatoes. Inside, a couple open-shirted old-timers with concave chests decorated with faded war-time tats lie stretched out and face-up on cots. Beards tinted yellow from years of nicotine. Squint and they could be unclaimed bodies arranged neatly in morgues, lost to a frigid society. They're not. They're saved.

The med tent today shows a woman being treated for heat exhaustion.

One vet couldn't live in four walls, ever, not after Nam. Veterans On Patrol built him a little house – volunteer high school kids from PPEP YouthBuild Tucson did the heavy lifting – that sits in the center of camp, christened Mercy Huss House. The little wooden abode is symbolic too. An on-site show of putting homeless in homes. Here he's surrounded by Army tents and dirt and squalor and death and drugs and booze problems, and the train, which rumbles by morning and nights, loud as thunder. He's happy. Beats the underpass in monsoons.

Meet Fred. He doesn't offer his last name. Just Fred. He was the first vet housed here. The Gospel Rescue Mission pulled him out of the rain, literally, and dropped him here. He's never leaving, one of a few who call Bravo Base permanent. Fred rolls, mostly, in a wheelchair. But when he walks, his slow, unnatural movements make it easier to imagine his pain. He's wearing a sleeveless denim vest, late-60s vintage, with individual patches spelling out ARMY, and a smaller one that reads, "Jane Fonda American Traitor Bitch." No shirt, heavy belt buckle, dirty jeans. Rail-thin. Fred looks to be in his 70s, easy. Must be. His face looks ghostly older. Long-faded tats on thin, rucked skin.

He's no fan of prying strangers, but he does tell me he's from Michigan. I ask if he ever saw the MC5 back in the day, and he gazes back at me, shrugs and looks away. His silence commands in that way that makes him easy to respect. Like anyone who's been off to battle, in the gory war fields, in the years of feral homelessness, with the bottle, with the speed. Fred's roommate here, Bill Wardel, from Utah, only nods. Yes, Fred commands respect. Wardel and others call him the camp patriarch. Says Fred experienced things in Nam that no human should ever have to. Ever. Says Fred got blown up too.

I imagine, above all else, in this minute, that Fred is uncomfortable with any moments of tenderness. The terrifying insides of his mind.

★ ★ ★

Bravo Base is surveilled in shifts by armed vets 24-7. A lookout platform rises above walls of truck tires stacked high in the front, facing south toward Santa Rita Park. Stands tall 660 hand-waveable American flags representing the number of vets who commit suicide each month. A giant canvas sign readable from 22nd Street declares, "Veteran suicides 22 per day."

The camp sits on 20th Street, cattycorner to Santa Rita

park on the southeastern edge of the gentrified Armory Park neighborhood. Gas-fueled generators provide Bravo's electricity now, and, soon, solar panels – everything off grid. Water and food are donated, including the water for the outdoor shower. The Bravo Base "Camp Conklin" Facebook callouts are many, and people and businesses respond in kind with gift cards and gas. Don't accept cash. Hardware and Metal Specialists next door provides the land, and they even donated water and power until a few months ago. They hope to again once their business picks up. Today locals donated pizzas and ice cream, and days before that Bravo provided a massive spaghetti dinner and fed the homeless at Santa Rita park.

I hear co-commander Powers' voice in my ear rattling details of Bravo Base. The camp is run military-like because that's who they are as people, how they've been shaped. It's like there's little else in life for Powers. He was homeless and rescued. Commander Harrison was homeless and rescued. So many vets homeless and rescued here since 2015. Hundreds.

"It is a base," Powers says. Military run, at least run in a military manner. It's not affiliated with the U.S. Armed Forces in any way. VOP is self-governing. Powers himself says he's off the grid. But where there are no checks and balances, who oversees those who seem to operate above the law? So far, VOP have been working in tandem with the cops, who sometimes bring homeless folk to the camp, along with other veteran outreach groups, rehab centers, and health organizations like Community Bridges Inc.

A medical marijuana card allows you to "smoke on base," in a designated area. No other drugs allowed unless you're on methadone. "Meth heads get kicked out," Powers says. "If you're caught stealin' and lyin' and cheatin', you're out. All that good shit."

Addictions or no, this isn't rehab, and Powers asserts they aren't babysitters. He calls it a staging area for the next phase of a homeless vet's life, and that includes helping with housing, rehab and personal responsibilities. "We got drug abusers, alcohol problems, mental dysfunctionality, mental illness, physical infirmities. They're safe here, even if they fall off the wagon. If the vet has a case worker, it's up to us to make a report as to their behavior."

So the main missive at Bravo Base is suicide prevention and awareness, and saving lives of vets. They don't necessarily turn anyone away, either, but one must show interest in helping themselves. He says they verify military backgrounds and check records of incoming so as not to let in "child molesters or anyone with serious arrest warrants. We do a psych eval too. We have doctors who come and donate time."

Right now, in early June, they're housing more non-vets than vets, 62 people total. But they're not all here today. Powers explains that "some got their benefits checks, so they're out there playing. Spreading their legs, feeding their addictions, whatever."

It's easy to understand the allure of the armed forces code – unit, corps, God, country – for the broken and the lost whose backgrounds are enhanced by military, PTSD and fragmented childhoods, these living homages to bloody-booted military ideals that shaped them.

Conversations with many here reveal talk of courage and patriotism and duty, and other easily digestible platitudes as rules for success. The military family idea that all families serve as one. Even if Bravo Base and Veterans on Patrol offers everyone – including and especially the commander and co-commander – a chance to continue living an antiquated logic, a kind of delusion, they're still advancing a greater good. Some of these people would be dead without them.

At one time, some of these vets were true warriors, heroes. Now, acting in the very same paradigm under a much different, peacetime context, they're vigilantes. Chasing drug dealers from Santa Rita Park while armed is a form of vigilantism. So's tracking down child-traffickers in the desert. Powers prefers the militia-ready buzz term "oath keepers" over vigilantism.

"This is the wild west, man," Powers says. "You got the bad guys out there killing people? By God, we're gonna take care of that. We're keeping our oath to this country against all enemies, foreign and domestic, and now I don't care if it's my next-door neighbor dealing drugs to kids... he's hurting innocent children. Man, I will take care of that in a most expedient manner, and it doesn't always have to be violence."

Hard to believe but Powers is compassionate. He's been homeless. He got out of the service 30 years ago, and he's been homeless off and on since. He was married. He has two daughters, 36 and 20. "But where I'm at now – my future's already set. I'll be fine, so it's not the money thing. I'm still serving my country. Still doing it. Full-time job. This is being responsible. This is how you do it."

He's fastidious, attentive to hygiene; fingernails, facial hair. He's fit. "I'm in top shape. I take nothing. I'm healthy, I don't take no pills, no medications, no aspirin. Drink lots of water. Don't drink alcohol. I keep myself healthy and clean."

He's part Sergeant Hulka and part that guy you'd want on your side if the shit comes down. And that's just it. These guys, vets like Harrison and Powers, the sense is all they want is to make the world better, and to believe in something greater than themselves, but it's like the government used them up and threw them away.

Born in Alamogordo, New Mexico to Native American dad and Scots-Irish mom, Powers started martial arts at age five. By 17 he was third-degree black belt. His mom was an alcoholic, he says, and more than happy to sign the enlistment papers, so Powers found himself on active duty two days after he turned 17.

"I chose to be a Green Beret when I was a kid," he says, "1968. John Wayne. Green Berets. I was too young for Nam – I wanted to go to Vietnam. I went in in '76 – November 24, 1976."

The guerilla warfare came later, Nicaragua, Panama, El Salvador and Colombia. "We were chasing Pablo Escobar around Colombia; I was Special Operations Command." He points to his cap. "That's what the patch is – Special Forces. Class 482. I've got all my benefits. Never went to jail. Never got arrested. DUI, 1990; I was guilty and I paid all my shit, and I was done, that's it."

Then came meth.

Makes sense how soldiers are attracted to the drug. It's a way to manufacture head-crank adrenalins, simulate rapid-fire dramas. "After 12 years in the military, I was teaching martial arts at two schools: one in Phoenix, one in Mesa. This guy brought me something, and it kept me up for four days going, 'Ooh *ooh*, I like that.'"

Four years later, he fell apart. Lost everything, and he was in deep. "But I was smart enough to not get arrested," he adds. "I was smart because of my military training. I knew where they were going to hit me two days ahead... they stashed half an ounce of cocaine in my truck. The cops." He pauses. "This is back then, my drug years."

Powers also spent two years as a deputy sheriff in Las Cruces, New Mexico, and has a brother who's a bishop in a Tucson Mormon church.

★ ★ ★

Jim Harrison (not the same Harrison as camp commander James Harrison), or "BBQ Jim," is part of a four-person overwatch committee at VOP, above the commanders. People who volunteer big to VOP.

There's no money. Jim met the Bravo folks while donating food from Holy Smokin' Butts BBQ, where he sometimes cuts meat. "I have a pension," he says. "I don't *need*." The unarmed gent has a big presence, ultra-confident, reveals little of himself, but seems considerate. He's a cancer survivor – a ruptured tumor in his head nearly killed him. ("People ask why I'm so happy. Well, I've already seen death twice.")

Harrison is retired law enforcement. Today I watch him co-lead a group meeting with the 40 or so residents gathered. He has an air of responsibility about him, commands respect. Residents – the vets and "civilians" – are talked at like prisoners and soldiers, or children. ("Is it not better than the park, than the tunnel? When you get your own house out there, you're gonna have to clean up after your ass.") Talk ranges from Agent Orange poisoning to trash cleanup to assuming personal responsibility.

Some are told to stand and be recognized for the work they're contributing, like the wood floors inside a newly erected vet's tent. Takeaways from this weekly gathering? You don't sweat, you don't eat. Everyone contributes something, unless you sit in a wheelchair.

Harrison later tells me about the cognitive thinking workshops he'll lead for the homeless here, basic programs to influence decision making, things he worked on with prisoners in the past. "If we don't teach them how to cope, who will? That's why I'm here. I can help build a life."

There are lots of volunteers, more coming now than going, I'm told. One woman, 37, who doesn't want her name used, says she's got four years clean from heroin, and she just started a job in public health service, a badly needed job. Had nowhere to go. Her teen daughter had run away, and VOP folks aided in finding her. She's been a VOP volunteer for 13 months. There are many other volunteers, she says, in Bravo Base and Alpha VOP Co. who wish to remain nameless.

⋆ ⋆ ⋆

Resignation to an existence with others whose only commonalities are military or homelessness or both. Sometimes that isn't much. But it makes Bravo, as homeless vet G. Cross tells me, a family. Evenings are often spent around a fire, people conversing, old school.

Cross has been here eight days. It's 107 degrees, he's overweight and he's wearing a thick, oversized white wool sweater. It earns him ridicule on the grounds. He keeps the sweater wet to stay cool. He's all about survival tactics. If I had to guess, I'd say he's one of few who lean to the left here.

He walks me over to the tent he shares with a dozen or so others. Talks about the service, working on nuclear missiles. He arrived at Bravo Base after camping out at Santa Rita Park. He'd been living in Sonora, Mexico and had come to Tucson seeking medical treatment, and for depression. Hit the VA hospital here, because, he says, it treats veterans much better than the one in Phoenix, "where you could die waiting."

Cross is kind, admittedly lost, pretty soft-spoken. I get the feeling he never mattered enough to anyone to be a focus of concern. He says, "How are you gonna get started if you have no one and no home? People don't hire people who are 58-and-a-half. What are my skills? I can drive. I can speak Farsi, Spanish."

He's hanging on until November, when his military benefits kick in. Until then he's got nada.

Says he'd moved from his Arizona home to Sonora because it was cheaper to live. Says lots of vets do that now. It's becoming a thing. Vets can't find work stateside so they go to Mexico. It's that or homelessness.

He leads to Bravo's outdoor "field shower." He'd just repaired it, easier flow for the water bag mounted above, and he'd made it more usable, extra room, added some waterproof flooring he'd found. He's proud of it. He talks about creating a garden in back, using shower gray water.

★ ★ ★

Joey Prouse is a handsome 19-year-old from Indiana who's been at Bravo Base eight days with his mother and 20-year-old brother. He wears a camo cap, Nike T-shirt and a silver crucifix around his neck, and he's the youngest Bravo resident. He's keeping watch on his hand-licking dog, a friendly shepherd mix called Savannah, while mom and brother work brand new jobs at Wendy's. His story unfolds: Dad was a vanishing drunk who found jail homier than freedom. Mom's job back home was good, they owned their trailer, but life was wearing on her health. They cashed out, packed up and moved to Tucson three months ago to stay with a relative, who last month kicked them out to the street. After blowing through all their money and landing in Santa Rita Park, sleeping in the car, mom saw the camp, walked over and asked if they could stay. Joey starts the following day working on fences for $10 an hour. Maybe, they'll soon have enough to move on and get a place of their own. Joey seems to think so.

★ ★ ★

I meet up with Powers again. He points to the platform in the front that overlooks Santa Rita Park. He says, "That's our high outlook up there. We can sit up there with a .50 cal if we want to, and watch the whole park. Yeah, we have a couple drones too. Most everybody, as far as all the vets, you know, we're on board, but civilians don't have a fucking clue."

Soon dusk creeps in over the little baseball game assembled across the stacked tires and American flags and military tents at Santa Rita Park, kids and parents and an air of festivity. The Union Pacific train passes on the camp's eastside and Cross goes to stand close to it in his big wool sweater. The train roars and thumps in an unsettling way. As unsettling as the tales of sorrow and distress inside the camp, the disturbing and the banal. The train slows to a crawl, and I think about how no one here ever bats an eye, as if we're all victims of the same damn conspiracy.

May 14, 2018

PLEASE RETURN
Shopping Carts
TUCSON

HUMBLE GLORIES ON 22ND

This white guy on the bus-stop bench is so pissed off. He caws, "Heygmm." It's threatening and mean in its way, and so the blood pressure rises and heartbeat quickens. Old fears fade hard – as if rooted in PTSD – but I remind myself that I no longer live in situations where I find myself constantly dreadfully fucked. Anyway it's been awhile since anybody howled horrible names at me on the street or threatened to beat my ass. I consider how things are actually OK these days.

I keep walking along 22nd Street.

"Heygmm," and louder this time.

So I turn around, walk back and stand there. He looks up at me, and says, "I'm Kilgore, Army Special Forces." Then he pats the bus-stop bench. "Have a seat."

Kilgore wears a backward trucker hat, but not in a street way, or a sexual statement way, or any silly way like that. Fits like he never leaves the house without it. He offers me a shot from his Sprite bottle but looks at it like he doesn't understand something. "Uh... shit, nothing in it." He pushes the empty back into the stuffed backpack at his feet.

Lights from passing cars reveal a thin face and glassy half-lidded eyes. Out of the blue, and just loud enough to hear over the traffic, he says, "You lost someone, and I don't think you're over it."

A woman with short, shagged blonde hair, dressed in black sits next to him on the other side. She rolls her eyes in that way that people do when they're damn tired of their partner being drunk but for some reason they can never leave them and wind up just being drunk, too. I know that look. My quick camaraderie with Kilgore is getting somehow dangerous, and she obviously doesn't want me around because maybe she senses danger, too.

"That's my lady next to me," Kilgore says. "Don't worry."

A long silent minute passes. He adds, "I'm Kilgore, Army Special Forces."

"Special Forces?"

"Damn straight."

His tone goes cryptic. The way he holds my gaze, a challenge. "You lost someone, and I don't think you're over it. Who did you lose?"

I grew up in this neighborhood, and when I walk miles on 22nd Street I think about people who died. I reoccupy shitty facts about my life. Offer up false hope. Swim in nostalgia. Own up to loneliness.

If you're walking at night down here near Kolb Road over near the Music Box Lounge, and EZ Money Pawn, and that tired car lot, across the street from tedious Starbucks/McDonalds commerce, it might be easy for someone to think you've lost someone and you're not over it yet. No one walks on 22nd Street at night. I love it.

I ask Kilgore where he and his lady are headed. Don't know why I asked, just did. Now I feel like a creep.

"Up to Country Club," Kilgore says.

The woman shakes her head in a way that shows even more disgust, and her face squinches up. She says to him, "Why are you telling him that? *Why*?"

Dusk is gone now and it's cool out. I stand to leave, and Kilgore goes, "Don't go, man. That's my lady. She don't bite." I hear Kilgore behind me as I move toward Palo Verde High School. "Heygmm!"

Smell fall's first chimney, the greatest smell in the world.

Darkness fills washes and sidewalk cracks and hides cats, and streetlights make scary shadows of big chollas rising over backyard fences. Giant towers look like ship masts and the electrical wires stretched between them hum when there's no traffic. Life beyond the few streetlights gets lost in its own blackness, and though the desert that surrounds the city can't be seen from this vantage, it feels claustrophobic here, and won't let go. The desert can do that.

This 22nd Street is historic and broken and real, therefore lovely, with no overpriced craft cocktails in sight. Up and down the street there's a peculiar assortment of mom-and-pops, and houses converted to businesses, with no nods to continuity or aesthetics, which is its own wondrous aesthetic: A tiny church next to a resale clothing shop next to a mystic candle dealer next to Cricket Wireless, next to a self-serve car wash. The Tucson I adore.

Rose brick and cinderblock homes fill area subdivisions, mid-century boxes and converted carports repeat one end into another. Long ago purchased by ex-G.I.s or Hughes Aircraft employees during the second burst of post-WWII growth, these houses don't look identical now. Too many heartbeats have passed through. I could live in one of these pretty houses again. Celebrated my first seven Christmases and eight birthdays in one nearby.

I keep walking west.

I watch a woman push a stroller whose one rear wheel thumps like it's got a flat and I guess it's probably uncomfortable, or maybe fun, for the baby on board. Four kids walk with her, two out ahead, looking down and not curious, like routine. Mom balances plastic bags filled with groceries. A guy in a wheelchair waits for kindness in front of the Mercado Y Carniceria La Mexicana grocery. There's no one else here on 22nd at 8:30 p.m.

The Taqueria Y Raspados Jason food truck glows in wan gray-blue light on a big dusty lot past Wilmot Road, elaborate with a colorful wall-sized menu, picnic tables and sturdy overhang. There are a few boys and girls bounding between tables, and tired parents eating on the benches. Luis Gamez is one of four people working here tonight; he cooks the dogs off to the side. It's family run; cousins, brothers, sisters, wives ... and business has been kicking, Gamez says. Naturally he says that. Walk-up traffic is rare. It's the second night working the order window for the owner's daughter, a girl named America. A high-school kid whose buoyant interactions make the littler kids here feel at home. America's learning the family business.

Food is home prepared, the salsa, beans, rice etc., and they're open every day. Whole deal wraps up at 10 p.m., and they park the RV-like truck at a nearby house. I don't eat hot dogs but I'm told they're Tucson's best Sonoran dogs, and they're cheap. Gamez, whose wife works here with him, sometimes makes hundreds of dogs in a day, even in summer when it's 110 degrees. No big deal, he says.

A thick swath of stars slices the sky all the way down to the shock-lighted UnHoly Ink Tattoo and Piercing shop, which abuts Tucson's longtime Mike Pierce Insurance in a little strip a few blocks west of the food truck. Like Denny's, UnHoly doesn't close, it's Tucson's only round-the-clock tat salon. It's clean inside, hospital bright. Flash art and tat designs decorate its green and black quasi-industrial interior. They're all bright-faced and happy here, which is disorienting, and the place smells of chocolate and vanilla. A trio of teen-girl customers huddle in the front, stirred by dramatics of their own conversations.

Jory Byerly is Unholy's lead artist. He's tremendously bearded, handsomely tatted and disarmingly approachable. He says he's worked the 10 p.m. to 10 a.m. shift and that's where you get the tweakers and "all kinds you can imagine." No robberies, though, because "everyone knows we carry."

Byerly grew up close by. Nods at 22nd Street, says with a know-all sigh, "it's still pretty ghetto, but it's not like it used to be." Still, he was surprised when a sixty-something guy came in for a full back tattoo. That's something.

Marcos Rios mans the counter at The Party House adult shop, which sits on 22nd between the sprawling Craycroft Baptist Church and the El Gordo Smoke Shop. He talks of "tweaker zombies" wandering further down 22nd Street and near that Walmart. He moved out of his nearby apartment because it was routinely robbed. It got tiring. He was robbed here too, once.

"I just started and it was the graveyard shift. A guy comes in here wearing a Green Hulk mask holding a revolver. I carry a knife now." He lifts a hammer from behind the counter. "There's this now." Two youngish-looking guys step in and out quickly, minutes apart, each purchasing boner enhancements offered behind the counter. A graybeard strolls an aisle filled with Evil Angel DVD titles. Another occupies one of 22 arcades in back. The cramped Party House has got to be the loneliest party in all of lonely Tucson. The affable Rios, early 20s, has been fulltime here for three years; that is, completely engulfed in porn 40-plus hours weekly in a windowless environment. Tonight, he's got Dave Navarro on some repeated reality show, for sanity.

He shrugs.

"Yeah, it can get lonely."

By nature, porn is lonesome. You only ever feel worse when you're done. It's seductive like meth or coke, similarly alters your brain chemistry and nervous system, depletes dopamine and fuels depression, and stays with you, demanding more. I once reviewed porn movies for a living and it nearly did me in. And who goes to adult shops anymore? Porn's free, as game as you want it.

"Well, some people think the government is keeping tabs on them, keeping a record of what they're watching on the internet," Rios says. "And maybe men don't want their wives or girlfriends knowing what they're doing, no computer trail."

"Any women come in?"

"Yeah. You'd be surprised. Four regulars a month I'd say."

A few hundred steps up from The Party House sits a tollbooth-sized truck called Churros El Rey, offering salvation in sugar. It's run by Isella Islas and her perpetually grinning elderly mother Sandra. They've located their mobile kiosk at various locations around Tucson, each time hoping for a better payday. Now it's 22nd Street.

"It's so dead, every night here," Isella says, "so very few customers so far." Just then an SUV rolls up and a Latino family spills out.

Mom and daughter handle orders in windowed isolation, practiced and efficient. The smell of fried dough and oily asphalt.

I walk more and meet up with a guy near Walmart. Next to him is a sturdy backpack and a rolled-up sleeping bag. Anthony Lewis Brown, he says. He's stick skinny, huddled with arms draped over knees, back against the Dollar Store wall, a gold hoop in each ear. I've seen him before, nights in the same spot. Says he's a rock star in hiding so he can't have publicity, something about witness protection, and he doesn't want to talk at all. Declines any handout or money. He's so alone. So I leave him. The best I can figure is he too probably lost some people he's not over yet.

October 20, 2016

CYFI GRAFFITI BOMB

When Beyoncé pimps your work on her socials and when Apple appropriates your imagery, you're into a heightened cultural pop lexicon.

It's what happened after muralist/graffiti artist Rock "Cyfi" Martinez created a Prince mural on red brick in Minneapolis last year and pics of it went viral. He'd said his purple-hued, white dove stunner – done in street-weaned spray-can art – was "a gift to Minneapolis." It certainly was. He remembers turning around at one point while he was working on it to a sea of people watching him, like some global DJ. Pop star on pop star. "It was insane."

Clearly Martinez is uncomfortable talking about this. Not the work – he grew up a Tucson b-boy, and Prince (and Michael Jackson) were two of his main musical figureheads as a kid – more the whole idea of a graffiti artist as a star.

Graffiti is about anonymity by tradition partially because it's mostly illegal. No matter how evolved an artist, or how much adoration is showered upon him, Martinez says emphatically that he "lets the art speak for itself. There are already way too many people with their bullshit selfies..."

He nods to the nearly completed mural he's working on down Stone Avenue in Tucson, which he calls Electric Desert, and explains his work in two simple sentences: "As a graffiti artist, letters are the most important. This is graffiti without the letters." It has the feel of something vital. Something that counts.

It's a Thursday afternoon and Martinez stands in a middle lane of Stone Avenue. There's a rare afternoon lull in traffic.

He wears Nikes, zip-up sweatshirt, jeans, a four-day growth and black-rimmed specs. The bright desert flora in his mural pulls his attention, how it's dulled in bleak afternoon sun, and he tilts his head slightly to some internal dialogue. He shakes the spray can, and says, "You're gonna flip."

He bounds back over the curb to the sidewalk and scales the ladder. With exacting precision, he sprays trails of gray tones onto the mural surface. The paint's all briny and sweet before the wind takes it. His work is rhythmic, he's consumed by it, yet he talks of grace of "long Arizona shadows," and how if you take time to discover them you'll see this city and desert differently. A minute later and he hops from the ladder, steps backward to the curb, and, as a city bus whooshes within inches of his head, he says, "See?"

I do kind of flip. The Spanish-colonial façade of this old flower shop built in the 30s, which is part of Plants for the Southwest nursery, is utterly transformed. It's illusionary; the shadows Martinez just added are unnoticeable unless you look specifically for them, but new depth is certain.

It's realism on a lovely, deliberate frieze. Such touches are Martinez hallmarks.

He darts across the street for another angle. "*Booyah*!" he shouts. Then he begins talking of triadic colors and personal palettes, which I ignore because the work gets me.

This colorful collage involves bright, psych-out desert succulents and flowers, a skull, a black widow, agave, saguaro, even peyote. Like other Martinez murals in Tucson, it offers spectacular little vortexes of light, or the impressions of light, which Martinez creates off stems and tentacles with shadows. They soothe yet sort of soar from the concrete three-dimensionally.

The heft and subtle strength shows why Martinez is so damn desirable, in Tucson and all over the country, and, lately the world. This particular mural was commissioned by the nursery, and co-owner Gene Joseph tells me they gave Martinez little guidance, because "they wanted *him*." Fans of his work.

People who don't know him fall in love with his art. He averages three commissions from each mural. Owners of the Shift Performance car tune up joint across from the nursery hit up Martinez while watching him work. They want a mural to grace three up-sliding industrial doors. Martinez is so busy he'll likely decline what would be a lucrative offer. The artist is flying to Philadelphia in a week, and then Paris and then North Dakota. He's got one due for the City of Tucson too, and an art show in Minneapolis, "inside where the Prince mural is." And, he recently returned from Mexico, where he was invited to represent the U.S. to paint graffiti there.

★ ★ ★

Martinez' work isn't "street art" – that overly branded, Madison Avenueized splash used to sell everything from burgers to cars – and he's careful to make the distinction. It's about the art, man. "That's why you have people pulling Banksy's off walls," he says. "I don't hate Bansky. I hate Banksy followers. Or some mural artist who puts his name on his T-shirt. That shit is the wackest fucking shit because you're promoting who you are, you're not promoting what you're producing."

His murals and the field of graffiti arts is similar to filmmaking. Because film studies have been around so long everyone's a genre expert. Highly literate auteurs are able to reference countless on-point filmatic allusions to the giants who've come before, but are also trapped by the rules – whether they follow or defy them – and recent releases are telling: *John Wick 2* with action, *Nocturnal Animals* with noir, *Split* with horror, *La La Land* with musical.

Martinez' work is rich in tradition: In the post *Exit Through the Gift Shop* world where Haring and Basquiat and Banksy are household names, graffiti artists face the kind of dilemmas of following or defying, or at least acknowledging in some way the innovators who came before. Martinez understands this, struggles with the illegal/ethical aspects of tagging but understands how it beautifies. Like Haring, Basquiat and Banksy, he struggles with the celebrity aspect.

Graffiti DNA is New York City and subways; it's black

America, not ancient Greece. His reveals bits of Mexican mural art too, tracing back to the 20s, when murals were created with messages to be understood by underprivileged populations. Martinez is a graffiti artist by tradition and proud of it. He knows the rules well enough to push beyond them.

The boyish 36-year-old has been graffiting long enough – and he's skilled enough – so he's not pretentious-sounding talking work. But he takes it seriously.

He's articulate in an autodidactic way. Super self-aware and picks up on my next question sometimes before it's asked. He listens closely, politely, never interrupts. Instantly likeable. He's too sincere to be called out on seriousness; dude's refreshingly unironic. He'd never be so gauche as to talk of his work as "his vision." Laughs and shakes his head at that thought.

His could be a workable antithesis to an on-demand, it's-an-all-me world, of social-media cacophony. Art defines us still, he believes. It must, "now more than ever." He pulls from the world *right here*. He sweetens harsh desolation, in desert wildlife and vegetation too, painting the feminine and the soft into unforgiving desert scenes and parables. There's conflict in some imagery; the skulls, black widows, peyote, UFOs (oh, the rich Arizona history). His are often about seeing the undersides, some other narrative not many others see or feel.

His crowning Tucson achievement is its largest mural, the 55-foot tall "Mayahuel (Goddess of Agave)" on Seventh Avenue on the west side of the historic Tucson Warehouse and Transfer building, part of Martinez' "Cactus People" series.

Another stunner: the 1,500-square foot Dia De Los Muertos mural of Frida Kahlo and Diego Rivera, south of Mercado San Agustin near Cushing Street.

The self-described perfectionist gravitated young to graffiti writing and art, came up spraying illegally. After getting popped once tagging trains and coughing up $11K in fines, Martinez had to rethink his program.

"I risked everything for my artwork," he says. "We're out there painting trains, we're out there painting billboards. But we're trying to produce something beautiful, not destroy anything. And if I didn't paint trains I wouldn't know how to do this.

"I might be old-school now," he continues, "some kids might not respect me, but I'm remaining relevant. I'm old-school because I'm using a spray can. I'm not using stencils or a straight edge. I have no projectors. This is all in the traditional way of painting, and murals. I remain true because I'm not trying to sellout a culture and seeing what I can get for it. I don't have to paint my name for somebody to pay me." He pauses. "If you didn't earn your stripes on the street, you'd get beat up."

If he suddenly disowned his earned traditions, it'd mess with his integrity, like a great singer resorting to Auto-Tune for the hit.

Martinez avoids talking his fees for legal murals, but says he no longer worries about food on the table and neither does his 12-year-old son Ezekiel. Martinez speaks of his son as often as he talks of his father, which is a lot. Fatherhood's a theme.

If his graffiti was all about getting into the most highly visible areas, he's now more particular about his locations, and what the images say to a city, to himself, as a father, and a son.

"If my son saw me in jail he would know it's because I was doing something I believed in," he says. "Tagging is expression. Is it wrong? Yeah. So is driving a car too fast. If I ever get busted doing graffiti, fuck it, I'll take it like a man."

★ ★ ★

Martinez has certain pride: "I like that I'm deep-rooted Tucson," he says.

Tucson-born to a white mother and an Aztec and Yaqui dad, Martinez has six siblings, and three more adopted little ones. He credits his old man – a life traditionalist who works blue-collar for the City of Tucson – for instilling in him a work ethic. He's "the best Martinez there is – he'd give his shirt off his back."

Growing up in Hispanic neighborhoods, Rock (yes, Rock is his birth name) Martinez was mostly a nerdy breakdancer who "drew pictures all the time." Picked on often, he once got tied to an ice-cream truck. "Look, I have a lazy eye, I wear glasses. Weirdos and freaks are my people."

Earlier in the aughts, Martinez brought local kids, gangbangers and nationally known graffiti artists together in Tucson for his yearly Winta Fresh fest (and sometimes corresponding Summer Fresh). Says the city gave him so much shit it wasn't worth it: "I was bringing all these people together for one day to create art. Nobody got shot. Nobody got hurt. Know what I mean? I was doing it for the city of Tucson." Had his own shop too, Art Terrain, and it moved locations before shuttering. One time a drunk driver smashed into it and he never saw a dime. He met artists there who pushed his boundaries, guys like Chris Rush, Titus Castanza, Luis Mena, David Tineo. He taught art to at-risk kids for years in a City of Tucson program. ("Those kids were awesome, and I learned through my teaching.")

He's done countless Old Pueblo murals – from tattoo parlors and flower shops and breweries and walls and sides of buildings. "When Michael Jackson died, I painted illegally on the Dunkin' Donuts/Baskin-Robbins location, I pulled my cans out of my trunk and wrote 'Who's Bad.'"

Then shit got bad. His business dried up, he split with the mother of his son, he got a DUI. He was depressed. With a son to raise and little interest in his art, Martinez bailed for Oakland.

Things changed quickly in Cali. He got a call to do a book cover in Los Angeles, which led to a tour, and soon Martinez was painting for High Times' Cannabis Cup. Soon he was painting murals in Boston, Baltimore, all over the east coast. The lucrative commissions began to roll in. He returned to Tucson and worked. Now he splits time between Minnesota (where his girlfriend Brandi Kole lives) and Tucson where Ezekiel lives with mom.

He's in constant travel mode, commission to commission. We talk Tucson arts and the little money available. City boosters say otherwise, but, in short, Tucson is busted. Martinez says he can't earn enough coin here, not like he can in other places.

He adds, "But I can paint the city. And the world."

★ ★ ★

On the first Sunday evening in March I stroll past Martinez' finished 20' by 40' mural on Stone Avenue. Ideas pop, images I'd missed too. The thing demands attention. A purposefully leaning saguaro of gentle jade calms. Shades of pink and red blend into tips of desert flowers, makes melancholy rise. A green skull tall as a five-year-old with purple shadowed eyes reminds me of Martinez' ideas of the circle of humanity and how his Tucson family lineage traces back to the 19th-century people of Fort Lowell. I think of these things now that I see them, even though I stared long and hard at this mural as Martinez was creating it – him moving with that kind of quickness that only inspiration can dictate.

March 9, 2017

HANGING OUT WITH RAY

Ramon "Ray" Encinas lifts his shirt to reveal the scar where his little sister used needle-nose plyers to wrench the bullet free.

"The blood squirted out with the heartbeat," he says, touching what looks like a smear of cookie dough on his gut, the scorched Benson Highway rolling past our window. "We call my little sister the ghetto nurse sometimes. She's done patched a few people from gang activities."

Ray had sold to another dope dealer's people. And over near 10th Avenue and 29th Street, he turned and saw a flash. He began running. "Then I looked and," he motions with his hand, "from here all the way down to my knees was blood."

His "sister freaked out" and couldn't sew the hole shut so Ray stuck gauze in it. He held on to it for two days before finally hitting the hospital.

He laughs. Jabs a finger to his belly. "My fat saved me."

We pull in and park at Earth's Dispensary. Ray climbs from the car and looms forward with robotic grace, in half-speed movements. He's got a sweet script today, and is psyched to roll a blunt when he finally arrives home.

The dispensary smells of fine weed, that kind of pleasantry only afforded others. Or afforded Ray, who's often crippled by physical pain. He sticks out too. In this drab, quasi-medical waiting area he's imposing in a black tee, NFL cap, calf-length shorts, earbuds, Reeboks, tats. He's big and tall and prosthetic legs help shape his posture.

This Native American son of a gangbanger mom and ex-Marine dad, both of whom died fairly young (2010 and

2008 respectively), lost his legs at the knees back in 2013. A toe scratch led to bone infection led to amputation – complications of diabetes.

"I should've been dead when I was 15," he says. "I've been jumped, stabbed, shot. I was dropped on railroad tracks, broken ribs. Been to prison three times. Got shot in one of my legs before I lost it too. I was done."

Chronic kidney disease gets this 34-year-old up at 4 a.m., three days weekly, for a trip to the dialysis center, where he sits plugged in to the blood filterer for four hours. The routine is more than two years old. Then he's on the city bus to work, cooking lunches at Café 54. He's been there about a month. Then it's back on the bus, either home on the Southside or off to the San Xavier Health Center on the Tohono O'odham reservation for myriad ailments. A check-up later today focuses on the deep eight-inch tear on his inner elbow, an infected fistula from dialysis, which – aside from the swelling, pain and unsightly wound – limits the use of a hand.

A bum hand isn't good, because it's his art that keeps Ray rolling, that and the small group of graffiti artists who populate their own church called Open Space. Headed by a kick-ass-named pastor, Lars Hammer, the Lutheran-based collective is, Ray says, "Bible with paint. An exploration of faith through art where no one judges you."

★ ★ ★

I first spotted Ray stepping off a city bus carrying a half-finished canvas. The work stood out, its colorful mashup of illustration, street whimsy and hints of Native American imagery. I actually followed him to a kidney disease center near downtown to ask to see it.

He told me he got into art watching his older cousins, using pen and pencil making giant Indian scenes. It saved his life.

And it doesn't matter to Ray where anyone stands on organized religions, he's been accumulating successes since meeting Hammer back in 2009. "I wanted to see what was out there beyond the streets of Tucson."

Ray is 100 percent Native American (Tohono O'odham), and his two sisters (and two younger adopted siblings) follow "all of our traditions" mixed with Christian ones. He shares this blend through Open Space. "I always think about being native. Natives are strong people. I always told myself, 'You're native. You can get up. You should be proud of who you are. Hold your feathers high.'"

But it took three stints in federal prisons to be reminded.

Ray acknowledges reality with an easygoing shrug, no self-flagellation or sneering. It is what it is. How he rolls. His stoicism dovetails Native American stereotypes – he preserves an enviable coolness, until you earn his trust, then mirth emerges and he goofs on himself often ("You're an Indian and you don't drink! What's wrong with you?"). Sometimes he disappears, even for a moment sitting in a car passenger seat, window down, or "with a backpack for days." To a quiet place "for strength," he says later, or, "I'm just tired as shit, *ha ha ha ha*. Yup."

* * *

The sun hangs above 12th Avenue, and Ray's squinting straight into it, telling how he spent nights bombing this town with spray cans, learning, honing graffiti skills. How he bounced through high schools so often he was finally asked to leave because he turned 21.

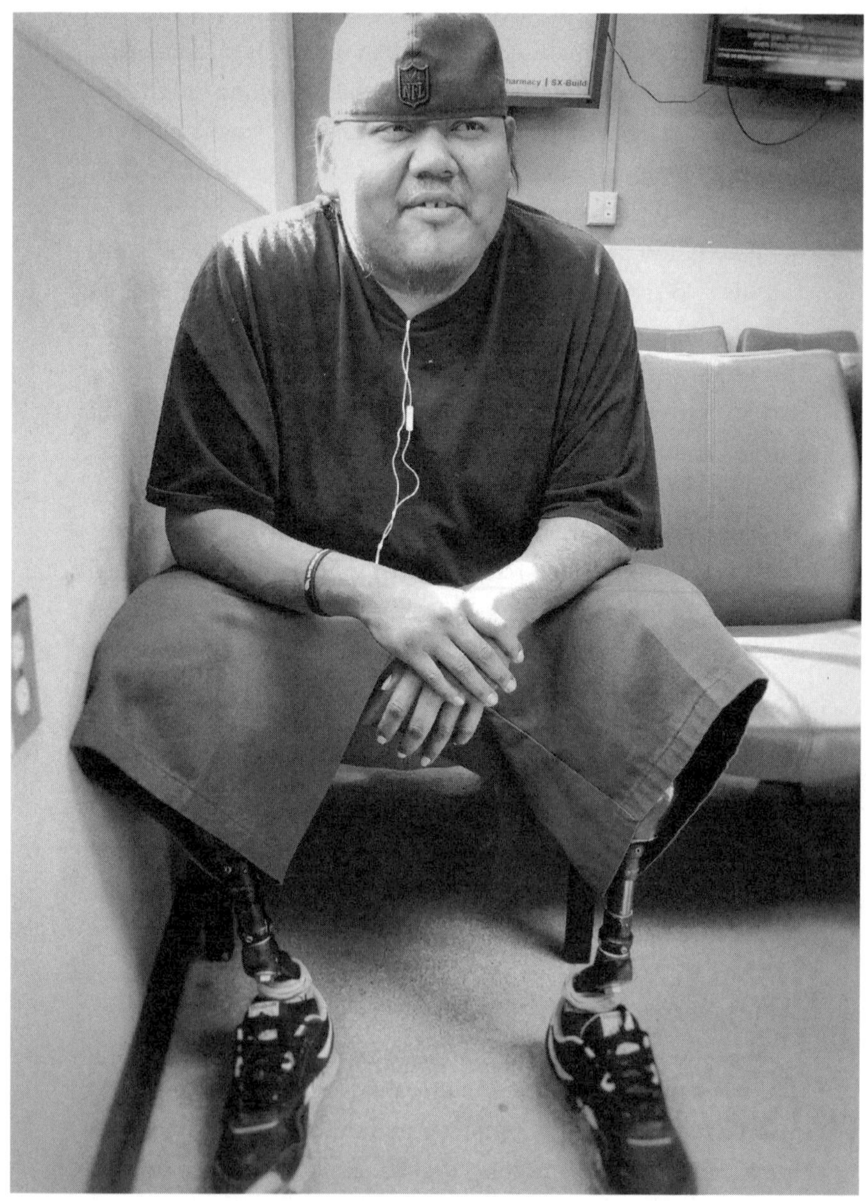
NFL
harmacy | SX-Build

How he slung drugs all over Tucson, to survive. "I would go everywhere in Tucson. If you had the money, just tell me what Circle K to meet you at. I mostly drove around but didn't have no license. Working street corners is the fastest way to jail. So we'd rent a smoker, a legal car from other crackheads, give them like four pieces, or you would have them drive you around, and that's how it worked."

We roll up to a dollar store on Oracle Road so he can load up on items for his girlfriend, who's in rehab for meth. The thoughtful, gentle way he selects the things she'd like. Brisk tea, Snickers, Reese's. He's flustered at the Doritos section because they don't have her flavor. He strolls the store aisles talking prison, and getting arrested on the reservation three times.

"First time I got popped with three $20 bags of crack and a gun, which is a lot to the tribe and the tribal police. They hate the drug thing. To them that's the worst thing you can do."

He was terrified of prison that first time. He thought, *Somebody's gonna kill me. They're going to jump me. They're gonna rape me.* Turns out it was nothing like the movies. "The only thing is, if you don't have self-respect, then you get your ass whooped. It's that simple."

The second time he got arrested hauling a truckload of undocumented immigrants. Third time he got popped leaving the reservation with more than 500 pounds of weed stuffed in a car. After seven years total behind bars, he got out for good in '09. "I'm like 'I'm done with this. I can't go home. I can't see my family. I can't fuck. What I am going to do with my life?'"

We pull into the Wayward Winds Lodge on Miracle Mile, now a Gospel Rescue Mission, where Ray's girlfriend is in rehab. He retrieves the dollar store bags from the back seat and makes the drop. He returns five minutes later, face alight.

"They let me see her – I got to see *her*. She wants to change her life. I'm all for that. I'm always there to help her."

As we ease the car on to Miracle Mile, he says, "I decided that my life was going to be about being a better person," he continues. "Either that or die." He interrupts the conversation to extol city beauties: An antiquated Harley on the road, a vintage El Camino in someone's gravel frontyard ("I would love to own that"), a sweetly distilled graffiti mural down on Drachman Street.

We all absorb certain ways of seeing the world, and maybe improve upon them after the chips are down. How to somehow exist with responsibilities, with warmth too, human or otherwise. A legless guy in a wheelchair pushes into a crosswalk on 12th Avenue, a slow defeated turn. Ray comments on that solitary, comfortless wheelchair life – the agonies of simple tasks and how the senses collect the worst of it, from avoiding car exhaust to finding a place to piss.

"I'd just roll myself around like that," he says. "I'd get picked on by drunks and stupid little kids. And you know how many times I've fallen in the middle of the street in my wheelchair? How many times I've just slept in my wheelchair in a park somewhere?"

Losing his legs left him suicidal. His mother had been gone a couple years. Huge depression mixed with homelessness lasted an entire year beginning at the end of 2013. He once tried to hang himself "but the rope snapped."

He wanted out of the chair, to at least create. "When I had legs, I'd go tagging or bombing all night," he says. "It was my whole life. The art. This wheelchair wouldn't let me."

Then he met a retired Marine, another Native, at physical therapy who'd lost his legs on duty overseas.

"He said that if I got up and walked, he'd give me his Purple Heart. A week later he passed away. I never got the Purple Heart. But that's when I started walking.

"It hurt. A lot."

★ ★ ★

Later in the day, Ray's leaning on a junked car in the chain-linked frontyard of the house he shares with his sibs. It sits in the shadow of massive electrical towers, near I-19. He's surrounded by his younger step brother and sister, a couple of cousins and a trio of excited pit bulls. He's leafing through books of his art, talks of inspirations and reminisces.

"My mom was a gangbanger," he says. "She wore makeup to cover her tattoos. But when she took off all her makeup? She had the Mi Vida Loca dots, a cross on her forehead, one on her lip. And then the dots on her fingers – they meant putting in work for your gang. My mom was certified for real. I never asked. [But] no matter how messed up you were, she'd always make sure you came inside and had something to eat. Friends, relatives, family members... We took care of her until her last day."

★ ★ ★

It's Thursday night and the Open Space meeting room is half-filled with folks from all walks – kids, adults. Like an AA meeting but youthful. Most are seated at long tables, painting. There's live music, one folkster offers acoustic renditions of *Sound of Music* chestnuts.

Church member Citizen Klown mans a table filled with

paints and canvases, free to use, donations accepted. Klown's a skilled graffiti artist who's genuinely happy to be here.

"This is a place to paint and create," he says.

We talk about Ray. Klown hints Ray's past sometimes returns to haunt him. "He doesn't see it," he shrugs. "He's been through a lot."

Ray learned painting skills from Klown. Were in the same graffiti crew, Lost Souls, LS. They've known each other years and Ray looks up to him. They both slung drugs too, back in the day.

Tucson might still offer Ray the trashed husk of his former life. His old leftovers, out there on 12th Avenue. He can't go back, so he says.

"Tucson may be a little butt-ass town," he offers, watching a pair of spindly graffiti artists spray boards out back. "But I love it. I know where I come from." He waves his hand and laughs a little. "I only hope some other person will look at me and say, if he can do it, I can do it."

Some time passes, and he says, "Look, I'm still trying to learn how to stay up on my legs."

March 22, 2018

MURDER, ACCEPTANCE, COMMUNITY

They swing open the glass door and step inside, sometimes in groups, or sometimes solo, and sometimes an hour passes and no one shows at all. There are stoner skateboarders and soon-to-be career drunks procuring St. Ides in the can and ex-cons with teardrop tats holding diapered babies. There are blue-collars pulling up in tool-stuffed pickups, the occasional white-collar driving a hybrid, and sweet-faced elderly folk. There are single moms with perpetual stoops who look older than their years with kids of varying sizes hopping up and down in tow. Over a few hours there are whites, Latinos, blacks, Native Americans, purchasing canned soup, or mac and cheese, or beer, smokes, soda, lottery tickets. Some have spouses, jobs, mortgages or school while others exist on government support. It's an unusual spectacle of classes, cultural diversity that well represents this part of Tucson, on the eastern edge of the Oak Flower neighborhood at Columbus Boulevard and Flower Street.

Observe long enough and an uncommon sort of social interaction unfolds like in some antiquated neighborhood tavern. The Patels, the Asian-Indian family who run this market could be the open-eared bartenders, greeting these folks by their first names, dispensing humor or listening to personal problems of their patrons with empathetic ears. You'll hear a middle-aged woman give an update on her long illness and how she's "out of the woods," or a lovely young mother offer a detailed response to a query about her newborn. This isn't exactly the discourse you'll find at, say, a Circle K, or Walmart or on a public bus. It's as if many of these folks visit the Patels for dinner.

One gray-headed woman, Sue Downey, purchasing a Pepsi on her way to a protest of Arizona's fave demagogue, Doug Ducey, has been hitting the Catalina Market for a decade. "It's the community," she says in a way that sounds like PR spin for the neighborhood. But her comment resonates; it's got nothing to do with any religion or ethnicity and everything to do with what it means to be a neighbor in a place where you give a shit about the area you happen to call home.

"I barely know these people," Downey adds, as she's stepping out the door, "but they're family."

Okay, the little Catalina Market, in all its hazy, ramshackle hominess – the hand-scrawled price tags and faint scent of cooked potatoes and fresh pipe tobacco – is so wonderfully backdated that the glorious Lucky Lager neon sign that still hangs above the tiny parking lot out front doesn't feel out of place, and corporate homogony is only visible on product labels that fill the three coolers or line the store's half-dozen aisles. The market's an anachronism in a world that revolves around shut-in online commerce and impersonal superstore marketing schemes. Ninety-eight percent of their customers, the shopkeepers say, are regulars.

And these shopkeeps, 68-year-old proprietor Jaynti "Jay" Patel, who lives with his wife in the shop's living quarters in the back, and his 46-year-old son Dharnesh "Danny" Patel, converse with each other in a piquant mix of their native Gujarati and English.

Time can tick by sluggishly here too, as delivery trucks and customers come and go. But there's no sense of that particular kind of wariness that's shared by many minorities, which is surprising considering the Patels suffer yahoo racists sometimes. That and Jay's brother was murdered here in 2010.

★ ★ ★

Jay's the family patriarch. He was working as a supervisor for the electric company back in his home city of Ahmedabad, the capital of Gujarat, an Indian state on the Arabian Sea, when he left his wife and three kids in 1985 for greener pastures in the United States. Some friends had done the same. Jay's other son, Saimi, says it was tough on his family and his mother when dad left India. "Of course," he says. "But somebody had to do something."

Now the actual "Patel" surname informs Jay's life. It has a long history in Gujarat, where there are roughly 12 million

Patels, about 20 percent of the state's population. The name originates from a complex caste structure in which a person's profession and social status was often decided by birth. Over generations, families became known by that status. In short, an early translation of "patel" is record keeper or village chief or landowner. In the mid-60s (in part thanks to the Immigration and Nationality Act) many Patels left Gujarat and gravitated to motel ownership (and other professions such as health and medicine) in the United States because they were pretty easy for families to operate, and housing was included. The AAHOA (Asian American Hotel Owners Association) reports that Asian-Indians, a high percentage of which are Patels, now own more than 40 percent of all hotels in America.

Jay says he didn't reject his homeland; he wanted something better for his family. He landed stateside with little money and a very slight grasp of the English language, first working at a motel in Atlanta, then as a security guard in Los Angeles and later as a partner in a Dunkin' Donuts in New York City. He wound up in Tucson in 1996 and soon purchased the Sunland Motel on the fading Miracle Mile, and then the Tiki with one of his two brothers. It took nearly 10 years before his wife could join him. "It was hard work," he says. "That's what it takes."

There's a deep reliance on the family system which includes, Jay says, "no-interest loans" available to Gujarat Patels from a large network of relatives, in-laws and friends. "There's no paper work. There are no contracts. Just verbal agreements, and no one cheats."

Jay says he quickly repaid the $100,000 loaned to him from the network to buy the Sunland Motel. After a few years he sold the motels and purchased the Catalina Market in 1998, and the family soon opened the Catalina Market 2 on Country Club Road. They own both properties free and clear.

Danny, who'd followed dad's footsteps, arrived in the states in '91, worked various jobs, and eventually came to Tucson to help run the market. Seven years ago, Danny purchased Charlie's Drive-In Liquors at Pima Street and Craycroft Road. He now has two teen sons attending the private Gregory School. His eldest is 17, and being courted by several Ivy League schools.

Common Hindu traditions (the Patels are devout followers of a modern sect of Hinduism called Swaminarayan) have survived the family's cultural transition too. The women do all the cooking, for example – dinners for 12 or more are prepared nightly in the kitchen behind this market – and there are expectations for all of Jay's grandchildren to enter into arranged marriages, just as their parents and grandparents did.

★ ★ ★

Yellowy newspaper obits taped to the walk-in beer cooler show how the Catalina Market has survived a lot more than the opening of a nearby Walmart and Fry's Food Store. Among tributes to deceased customers and a previous shop owner, there's the obit to Jay's brother.

Mahesh "Mark" Patel was behind the register when 25-year-old parolee, Bobby Francisco Lopez, stepped into the market and shot him in the heart. Lopez then took the cash register and ran out. He was tracked down two years later in Mexico, sent back to Arizona and sentenced to life in prison without parole.

"We got the cash register back but not my uncle," Danny

says, shaking his head.

David Stewart, a gregarious construction man who specializes in green, sustainable designs, befriended the Patels as a customer here a decade ago. He has accompanied them to their local Hindu temple and has spent time at their dinner table eating home-cooked Indian fare, which is strictly vegetarian. ("I'd be a vegetarian if I ate their food everyday").

Stewart remembers the community outpouring in the days and weeks after the murder, which shook the neighborhood, and the Patel family, to its core. "The love was everywhere in the neighborhood, and there was an outdoor memorial," he says pointing out across the parking lot. "It's probably why they didn't just close up the shop and move on."

The shop did close for 10 days after the murder.

"Feeling is in the heart," Jay says, gently touching his chest. "I know my customers. The killer was not from here."

Then there's the racism, which was especially hard after the September 11 attacks, even for a Hindu family from India. Danny says it never really amounts to much more than name-calling.

"I'm not afraid of anything," Jay says, adding that Indian conflicts between Hindu and Islam religions taught him a kind of fearlessness. "I grew up in India. I had a side business in an all-Muslim neighborhood. We don't scare."

Twenty minutes later a woman of about 35 steps up to the register. Her eyes are puffy, hair's unkempt, an ugly mood surrounds her. Before any words are spoken, Jay slides a pack of Camel Crush regulars out of its slot from behind the register and places it on the counter. He knows her brand, and he rings it up. He knows a lot about this woman.

"Why are you crying?" Jay asks.

"I'm not really crying," the woman says, not making eye contact.

"No? Is your boyfriend crying?"

"No, he's not crying."

Jay nods his head.

She hands cash over for smokes and Jay pretends to slide the pack into his pocket while doing a subtle two-step dance in place. A big fat grin on his face and he holds her with his gaze.

The woman begins to shake her head. She stands there, and then slowly, reluctantly, after several seconds, a smile finally cracks her mood.

December 3, 2015

THE BALLAD OF JOHN AND PEPPER

Pepper lifts her girlish red dress and with an arthritic finger traces deeply etched lines on her milk-white thighs. Ruddy scars form indecipherable words that could read "helter skelter." She lifts an arm, and the other, and her fingers find more old mutilations that look like coiled up caterpillars and puffed-out butterflies, on wrists, elbows, shoulders and torso.

She gently pushes fingers into her thick blonde mane, pushing along her scalp and hairline, and relates harrowing stories of unrestrained binges smoking way too much of the shit, which led to wounds on her head and a deep one below her chin and a permanently hoarse voice.

She has cut herself up in the past, others have sliced and burned her body too, and she's shot coke and dope so many times that her skin abscessed with such force the infections alone nearly killed her. In 2007 she was hit by a car in a crosswalk and about died.

Doctors say she's likely suffering congestive heart failure. Just another ailment aligned with her liver disease and blood flow problems, degenerative disc disease and diabetes, the spinal fluid collecting around her brain, the bad knees and holes in her feet.

She can only laugh.

"I swear I'm like Patches."

Her smile shows few askew teeth, defiant gravestones in a derelict cemetery.

Her grin seems effortless, there's no shame here. She's upbeat even, sometimes like a schoolyard girl ready for a future. It's strange, how little cynicism.

Pepper will say she loves life. Still. She'll tell you she loves people. Still. She'll tell you she's grateful to have a place to sleep at night, a floor under a roof and four walls.

Her man John hops down off the wall. Smells of dry sweat. His hunt for rolling papers proved futile. They kiss in the church parking lot shade behind the methadone clinic on 5th Street, where a half-hour earlier they picked up their daily doses. John collects the leashes for their dogs, a pit-bull/terrier mix named Deuce, and Chico, a bouncy, mirthful Chihuahua.

Pepper tenderly strokes the back of John's neck. Says, "I've never been loved like this in my entire life."

★ ★ ★

The next day Pepper collects trash, cups and wrappers and cigarette butts, from the front of a Circle K and tosses it into the receptacle. In a small way her actions contribute to a greater good, a self-defining deed as a way to not surrender. And a "cleaner world for my children."

John and Pepper occupy the same purgatory 24/7. They live and breathe each other's failures, chaos, and addictions, which are now limited to cigarettes and methadone. Like true lovers, they inhabit each other's fears. All life's punishments and ignominies and disappointments proliferate in a single union. The homelessness and loss and sickness and abject poverty and self-hatred. The shitty parenting, insane circumstances and molestation, and the horror of growing up with an increasing understanding that you're only a speck of some tiny existence the rest of the world wants nothing to do with. Wreaks daily devastation on the human psyche. They're terrified at all times.

And they greet each morning by vomiting hard.

They're sick. Their stomachs are distended because their livers are badly swollen and barely functioning. They each have Hep C. To get off heroin and provide relief from the physical pain and conditions they chose legal, state-funded methadone. They can't do illegal drugs and they're tested, and they've been dropping clean urine.

Methadone is the medicine, as man-made and harsh as it is. It's dated shorthand for heroin addicts with no other options, and it's harder to kick and more brutal than heroin, just ask any junkie. In fact, it's so wretchedly persuasive that if they lessen their doses they get violently ill. If you're as sick as Pepper and John, it's about impossible to wean off of. They've tried. John did it cold turkey once and perishes the thought. Pepper's got a dozen years on methadone, bore three babies on it.

They could use weed to ease the pain, but they're having trouble securing medical marijuana cards because they have no money. Government weed is pricey too when you're jobless and homeless. They can't buy weed on the street because whatever panhandled coin goes for dog food, bus fare and smokes. Packs of cigarettes are riches.

Deuce and Chico don't know the predicament they're in. They're happy; they play and they snooze. They've water and food and love.

So it'd be really easy to say Pepper Kenney and Johnathan Williams, who were homeless when they met last year at the methadone clinic, are experts at destroying their own forward momentums and livable actions through unconscious self-sabotage. But it's way more than that.

Each was doomed by the time they were six.

Buzz-cutted, sharp-boned 38-year-old John grew up in

Virginia. His coal-miner dad died in a mining accident when he was five. Mom never recovered. At 12 he was shooting up morphine, Dilaudid and such. He sold drugs and wrote bad checks and got popped, a lot. His record shows six felony arrests, and prison was home for 13 years of his life. In '05 John's wife suffered a freak aneurysm and died. Two of his children landed in foster care. He has a daughter living with his mother.

John's kind. It shows quickly once his suspicion of me recedes. The internal hurts are so obvious. And he's no idiot. He's worked jobs in warehouses, in sales, at car washes. He wants to work. He's hoping he lands the job at a pizza place near where they're staying, but nothing's easy "when you're a six-time felon." Nothing's ever easy in the afterburn.

Pepper's his recompense, and he can't live without her. And prefers to let her do most of the chatting.

"People have always said that bad things just happen to me," Pepper says, biting into a burger at Carl's Jr. "Like I have a dark cloud that follows me wherever I go..." In that moment she pulls a long hair from inside her food and drops her shoulders as if to illustrate her point. Her face goes sour. The hair isn't hers, it's black. John shrugs and takes the burger to the counter to get a new one made.

"I've been abused by men in some way my whole life," she continues. She looks to John at the counter. "But John is very old-fashioned. He the nicest man I've ever met. He doesn't call me a bitch. He doesn't call me a whore. I used to always have to walk catch-up behind my guys. John walks with me side by side. I mean he cares about me like I've never been cared about before. He carries the backpack and pulls the dog carrier, holds the leashes for both dogs, carries whatever groceries, the whole load, and still manages to hold my hand."

Pepper knows intimately street-life repulsions as much as the ugliness of negotiating governmental programs for the disenfranchised. How easily you can slip through cracks when you're trying to, say, get section 8 housing, or a place to stay. Or how shelters won't allow dogs, even though Deuce is Pepper's doctor-certified service animal. How there's no financial assistance available to them. How John can't get much help because he has felonies. The two are on AHCCCS but still wait months to see medical specialists after getting appointments, and Pepper still can't, for whatever reason, get the disability papers signed by her doctor. Loopholes loop, and there are many.

Born and raised in Southern California, Pepper had been raped multiple times by her sixth birthday, and beaten. Her biological dad yanked her from that living situation after discovering bruises, and took her to live with his parents. She discovered meth at 14, and that was the instant when things changed for good. She got pregnant at 15, which led to an abortion. ("I had nightmares for years after that abortion. It was *brutal*.") She bailed high school junior year – where she was enrolled in advanced classes. (Earned her GED in '01.)

At 17 she was a prostitute working Sunset Boulevard.

"It was that cliché. I was having sex with guys who were using me, I might as well get paid."

She talks of her "wife-in-laws" and downing 151 and Cokes everyday ("my only way"), and the guy who turned her out. "He was a light-skinned African-American. He was polite. He gave me his card; it said 'Goldies Treasures' on it. He told me how it all worked and how much I would make, and I did it. It was horrible."

She begins to cry. "At this point I had no morals."

She was raped and robbed numerous times at knifepoint and gunpoint. "Once I got in the car with this preppy college dude, I checked his body and I didn't feel any weapons. He took me up Laurel Canyon and he had a gun hidden in the car... He raped me and took everything."

She married one guy who helped get her life in order. A total *Pretty Woman*, as she calls it. A place in Malibu, a Vegas wedding at Circus Circus.

Pepper began working straight jobs in salons, radiology labs. The marriage didn't last. A series of unstable men, unexpected pregnancies, and a move to Tucson ensued. All of her five kids were delivered caesarean, all taken by Child Protective Services.

She'd begun to raise the first two, a boy and a girl, in a stable environment, which got dicey with the boy's anger issues. Pepper was late administering medicine to one of them. Someone called CPS. That's where it started.

She fought for those children with a court-appointed lawyer. Did parenting classes. CPS gives a parent a year to prove themselves, but bad things can happen in 12 months. Pepper lost her job in a radiology lab. Her new boyfriend had something for the pain. The heroin was instant addiction and she lost her kids. (She only recently established a relationship with that son, because he turned 18. She can't talk much about him or any of the others without weeping.)

They were homeless by 2001. She had the three other kids. She was arrested twice for shoplifting. Yet, in 2011, Pepper earned an associate degree in healthcare administration from the for-profit Brown Mackie College. No mean feat when you're homeless. Job interviews invariably go south.

"There are three reasons for that," she says. "A, my teeth. Who's going to hire someone with my grill? B, my voice; it goes out quickly, and, C, I get sick a lot and can't stand up for very long. I get migraines and the pressure in my head from the spinal fluid is unbearable."

To anyone whose life might parallel hers, the young junkies, the prostitutes, the abused and homeless, she offers herself as a cautionary tale. "If I can help anybody by my story, then it's worth telling. It wasn't until years down the road when the consequences of my life started coming back. If you don't deal with it, it all comes back."

John returns with a fresh burger. She bites in. She says, "Hey, I'm privileged to be alive. And I can say that some of the most wonderful people I've ever met are ones who have had the hardest, sickness-riddled lives – just these devastating lives, and some are happy to be here. But life isn't fair. The chick we're staying with right now is on disability. She had cancer as a kid. That's the hand she was dealt. Everyone's had a rough life. I've had a hand in how my life turned out."

Pepper and John get in at night and out in the morning of that one-bedroom place they're crashing in. They try to leave no trace they actually sleep there out of respect for their host, who's at the mercy of her apartment management company, which doesn't take kindly to pets, or the homeless. In exchange for a floor to flop on, the couple provides food stamps. They're an inch from the streets.

★ ★ ★

"I would stare at the sky for hours," Pepper says, sitting on an island-like swath of grass that separates Wetmore Road from the parking lot of a busy strip mall. "You ever see how many things move in the sky at night?"

Pulling and pushing, tired and hurting and there's no rest. Each day's primitive, a dreadful rotation of the others. There's no music. No books. No movies. No computer. No sleep. No bed. They're hopelessly and horrifically fucked.

She continues: "It's so scary living outside. I always covered my neck because I was afraid somebody would slice it."

You don't dream, she says, not when you're awake, not if you manage to sleep. You're too terrified about food and shelter, the basics, and your dogs come first. They say this is better than death, better than suicide.

They can't afford to wash their few clothes but they believe in god. She can see a world dying slowly daily, at least the part they're allowed to participate in. Wonder: what is the word of god, and who is that god, any god? Wonder: is death truly the opposite of life?

She tells me it's silly to even think of luxuries in this life. "I want simple things: I want a plant. I want to have a birthday party... I'm tired of being poor. And panhandling is so humiliating; two no's and I want to go away and cry. People have no idea what a quarter means."

"Don't get me wrong," she continues. "I love life. I love colors. I love happy. I'm happy when people get ahead. But where did our humanity go? Everyone is so *me me me me me me* now!"

Pepper leans over and pulls John's T-shirt up exposing a 10-inch knife wound over his ribs. Tells a horror story of John being attacked, involving the drunken, knife-wielding boyfriend of a friend. They filed a police report but nothing's happened. "And yet he's so calm," she says.

Her latest worry is that John now has liver cancer. She begins to cry. "Sometimes I feel like we're going to die out here. I don't want my kids to know that their mother died homeless."

John pets Deuce in long slow strokes, watching gleaming cars motor by on Wetmore Road. The dogs are now sleeping, in the shade and exhaust.

Pepper wipes her eyes, looks over at Deuce, his chest rising and falling. She says, "this dog is so judged. It's because he's part pit-bull." She hangs on the thought. "He's not judged by the content of his character," she adds, "but by his species..."

May 5, 2016

DEATH OR GLORY

Headed out for the usual long walk. One of those melancholy Tucson sunsets that color the sky, air and mountains a burnt orange. I walked first to a candlelit vigil in the parking lot of St. Mark's Presbyterian Church near Alvernon and Third Street, held for a 15-year-old boy named Sephaul Booker, shot dead a few blocks away. I'd heard this kid took a bullet, and man did it strengthen that inner Gordian knot, the fear and the sadness that falls over me like clockwork each afternoon. He was a mother's son with best friends and relatives and pets.

People loved him. There were about 30 folks at the church. Unusually heavy winds kept blowing the candles out.

The local TV news crews showed because a murdered boy is news alright. A few minutes of airtime filled with affected newscaster solemnity between ads and a titillating murder graphic. One coifed-up TV reporter's preeny face was lighted much of the time by her personal phone screen. Her indifference and the TV news presence diminished the remorseful stories folks were sharing of Booker, and how the essence of his murder absolutely devalued the neighborhood's soul, how it brought neighborhood folks to bended knees with sadness, regret. TV's polished-jackboot journalism and pushy faces amplified the fear the murder planted in hearts of those living in this neighborhood. TV goobs should've waited on the street.

I did learn of young Booker here, how he got into trouble, his arrest record. How his dad had walked out and how his single mom was in over her head. Another punk lost to Tucson street hassles? Nope. Booker had a brilliant side, quiet, funny, generous. True qualities, said those I talked with, and others who spoke at the vigil. Two of Booker's friends, 15-year-old Joel Beraca, and 19-year-old Jesus Lopez, were both crying.

"He didn't talk about what was going on with him lately," Lopez said. He'd met Booker five or six years ago playing basketball at the Boys and Girls club. "He'd just say 'It's all good.' But I could tell he was angry and sad a lot lately."

I was hoping to meet the boy's mother. It was too soon. She was too broken to even attend the vigil. Booker's cousin, Chelsea Kiki, spoke to everyone. Her voice and hurt soothed in the wild wind. "I wish I could've been there for him," she said more than once. She told how Booker influenced her own reading habits, calling him a genius.

Booker's tutor spoke too, said "beautiful" repeatedly to describe him. She was so shaken her voice was barely audible. One person pleaded to "put the guns down" and pastor Bart Smith offered soft words and a prayer.

The group was led in the gospel-tinged "We Shall Overcome," and the last refrain rose into the candlelit darkness, sung both tentatively and confidently, and in unison and harmony, by the white, brown and black folks: "We shall live in peace one day..." Never has that song worked itself into my bones like this.

When it ended I walked on. Sometimes I think walking saved my own life so I do it almost daily.

See, to begin a day is to begin one like the others. I often wake up in despair and then try to work until I eventually hate myself. Absolute relief comes on these ever-onward ambles through central Tucson neighborhoods. These escapes, which start just before sundown and last about 10 miles, stop whatever it was that sucked whatever life from me that day. Coincidences and curiosities become heightened. Contexts reframe. Sadnesses head south, resentments recede. The mystical connection to Tucson rises, the desert's edge-of-the-world magic. Renewal.

There's no way to absorb Tucson – the eclectic and seared neighborhoods and its people – unless traversed on foot. This is how Tucson unveils itself to me, anyway. I can stroll any street in any direction in neighborhoods that stretch out from my house – the working class to the working poor to straight-up poverty-riddled. And more than any other city I've lived in it feels like I'm home. The dogs know that. I've walked by many dusty pound mutts behind chainlink fences so often they quiet and wag tails as I approach instead of barking holy hell. I've given some names: Ezra, Jonesy, Mac and Cheese. Forget music or podcasts, it's the conversations with strangers. The countless stories live there.

So many sensations and images for the head to play with. I love the front-yards decorated with rusted wheelbarrows filled with dirt and prickly pear, and those populated with sagging pickup trucks or dilapidated motorcycles or sun-charred lake boats, machines turning to Earth.

The lime-colored adobes and mid-20th century cinder-blocks with gardens enclosed by chicken wire wrapped around PVC pipes. The tiny concrete porches where drunken couples bicker and laugh in the dirt-dry evening, with beer guts and cigarettes, on wobbly plastic chairs. I love the old ladies on their knees working on weeds in well-kept and loved yards of hacienda-style homes that see hummingbird feeders and octopus agave and sweet welcoming sunflowers.

I love the alluvial debris that collects where washes meet streets, and the rocky loam, silt and grass in the washes, which this time of year blooms into separate little ecosystems. The blankets strung up between Palo Verde and mesquite trees by homeless folks, wholly beautified by the bursts of virgin-white oleander blossoms, and sweet-smelling desert willow flowers that lift high over walls of abutting backyards.

Other things bring joy, like mailbox posts fashioned from cholla skeletons and the rare whiptail lizard scurrying for cover under creosote bushes or inside wall cracks. The piquant whiffs of home cooking from open-door casitas, laughter spilling out to the street, where people's lives, I like to surmise, sustain with some joy. I love the florescent yard-sale signs and overweight dog-walkers with bad hips and three-time DUI recipients with face tats careening shirtless on too-small bicycles down Flower Street. Always with a smoke. And how the heat generates a tinnitus-like hum that's finally mollified by the evening's faraway train whistle, or KLPX blasting AC/DC from a crappy stereo somewhere.

★ ★ ★

After the vigil I'd walked down First Avenue to Navajo and found a roadside altar, just south of the Boondocks lounge on the street's east side. A bicycle symbolically painted white with an offering box enclosed by little metal bars, like a tiny prison. Inside the box are delicate white rosaries, angels and plastic roses and paper cempasuchiles. Gilded plaster of Paris doves and a pitted silver frame houses a short bio and a yellowy picture of Francesco "Steve" Galvez, a thin man with a mustache, short dark hair and a kind face. Another dead mother's son.

A lovely altar to a man who in 2014 was hit on his bicycle after he purchased bottled water at a nearby store. It was dark and Galvez's bike had its light on. Runover by a cop who was never charged.

Galvez, a sacrificial lamb like Booker. Lives that die around us we hardly notice. Another unnatural death to teach something. Left me in a state of inquiry, how death gives life, and how life is the practice of dying. Galvez was loved, a 49-year-old father and grandfather. First Avenue traffic whizzed by but didn't; the silence Galvez left behind was too great.

Walking home I passed a woman on Stone Avenue moving slowly and singing softly a melody I didn't recognize. It was mournful yet uplifting like a southern hymn. I slowed to make it last. Her tone gentle, prayer-like. It wasn't what I'd ever associate with Tucson but I imagined Galvez and Booker, and my heart broke. I arrived home with that melody stuck in my head, filled with unimaginable melancholia and joy and gratitude, a near-perfect state that no drug or bottle or song or book or film or person or any version of any god could ever provide. Not ever. A long trudge to cap another day, the green more greener, the night more night.

May 19, 2016

GOLD FEVER GENERAL

The General stands outside the trailer. He coughs and points. "That's Killer, he's been the best partner I've ever had." Killer nudges my hand with his nose, just a sweet old thing burdened by a harmless bark and an overfed frame.

"I was layin' here dyin' one day about three years ago," The General continues, "and I hear this moanin'. So I go outside and there he is. I came in and cooked us up a pork steak and he never left. And I don't even know what type of damn dog he is."

The General is thin with an old prospector's face, gray horseshoe mustache and watery blues. He carries himself with strange dignity, part roadside crank, part electable politician – his smoky, cigarette-husk of a voice sustains the air of an old-man sage. Dude's unignorable. For one, he's a walking textbook on the Santa Catalina Mountains, particularly anything related to gold and silver, and mining. Apart from Killer, the 69-year-old's one lasting life relationship is to gold and precious ore. He talks, rants and raves it, like one might after his wife of 40 years had run out on him.

He's flat broke. Been that way for years, lives in a double-wide that belongs to a "generous friend." (Earlier today he bummed a Jackson off one-armed Lefty, an old pal he picks up mornings for coffee and sunrise gazing.) The General's held hundreds of mining claims in the Catalinas; gold, silver and so on. Just as he knows paths up the nearby mountain to countless claims, he knows routes to the bottom. He quit booze nearly a decade ago, for example. Doctor's orders.

The General, as he's called, is William T. "Flint" Carter,

a "seasoned prospector." He's also a jewelry maker, artist and author, among other things.

Killer follows The General into the doublewide. The living room is sizable and tidy and smells of cigarettes, spliff and pine needles. There's a single made bed in front of the TV, tuned to the History Channel, volume down. The TV is always tuned to the History Channel.

His own art and jewelry is arranged neatly on walls and counter space. It's made from serpentine and marble and other materials he mined himself on Mount Lemmon – including his "Codystone," a medicine ball-sized chunk of gold and silver in quartz, named in tribute to his hero "Buffalo Bill" Cody. He points to it. "See that? It's worth a quarter of a million dollars."

Why doesn't he sell it?

"Because nobody believes me. Because no one is into mining anymore."

Like his hero Buffalo Bill, The General has long straddled a line between reality and legend, lived a life of mythic proportions. He talks tons and rarely bores, often cramming two, three and five ideas into sparkly run-ons. One five-minute conversation contained the following: He once saw Lana Turner mow her lawn at a Tucson house she owned at Limberlost and First. ("No one knew she lived here, and no one in the neighborhood knew who the hell she was.") Over the years he was swindled out of millions in gold and minerals and produces various difficult-to-decipher documentations and financial statements to back such claims. ("I once sent two men to jail for fraud.") Buffalo Bill in the late 1800s owned a hotel near Oracle, Ariz., its history and ownership was hijacked. The hotel is still there. The Lost City in the nearby Cañada

Del Oro valley even contained a whorehouse.

His just-released *The Canyon of Gold, Buffalo Bill Cody & The Legendary Iron Door Ming Treasure* is a sprightly little tome. In it, as the "old prospector with a story to tell," he documents his own decades-long gold fever story and mythologies. Calls it historical fiction. (The General also contributed to the recent *Treasure of the Santa Catalina Mountains* by Tucson author Robert E. Zucker. And he was featured in *Beyond the Legend*, a 2010 doc on Buffalo Bill.)

Then there's The Iron Door Mine, supposedly in Cañada del Oro valley below Mount Lemmon. A decades-old news article from the *Tucson Citizen* says The General "hints that he has found the Iron Door Mine." The piece quotes experts calling the mine "folklore," a fiction created in the 1923 novel *The Mine With the Iron Door* by Harold Bell Wright (which, incidentally, became a Sol Lesser-produced silent film shot around Southern Arizona. The film still exists). The General says he knows something they don't. One theory involves Jesuit priests who lived in the area in the 1700s, hid their gold in the mine behind an iron door, and returned to Spain. They never came back. He says the treasure connects to the 100 tons of gold buried at New Mexico's Victorio Peak.

Does it matter if his tales are true or false? His vague documentation proves they're true. Other documents, some by geologists, one in an eight-page spread in a 2015 issue of *Outside Magazine*, seriously questioned his claims after testing his mine samples. (The General says the geologist, Jason Price, was wrong.) The General has lived as a legend in his mind so long that maybe the world has bent to fit his narrative.

His obsession with gold and Southern Arizona began in the early 70s when he purchased an acre of land on the man-made lake Golder Dam (now gone, breeched in '80). He turned a property chicken coop into a solar-powered house, and his plan was to grow food and survive off the grid.

Before that he'd married and had a son. Got drafted (Vietnam) and served in Panama as a military policeman. He returned, divorced and wound up living in Frank Zappa's old apartment in L.A. This was post-Charlie Manson, peace and love was done, but not all the way, and The General talks free love. "I'd go up to San Francisco and Lake Tahoe and we'd pick up every hitchhiker..." The General cuts himself off and smiles. The 500 hits of acid he dropped in '69.

He converted a mail truck into a love machine, interior outfitted with pink and purple shag carpeting. It featured a swinging bamboo chair that allowed passengers to "swing out the door as we were going down the highway."

That machine crashed into the greater Tucson area, en route to the Mardi Gras. "We let this little motherfucker drive ... and he flipped it over," The General says. "We was asleep in the back of it. We slid 385 feet on its side... I expected at any second to hear a falling off the cliff, but we stayed on the highway. We had all this dope, and the cops were there. And when that guy wrecked the truck, he said 'Hey, my family's rich!'... Yeah, they sent us fifty-fucking-dollars."

So The General stayed in town and fell in with an aging Hollywood starlet living here. Hung with Taj Mahal at The Too High Club on Stone Avenue. Says he met Rose Kennedy then too, and lots of bikers. "That's one thing, I knew all these guys but I didn't get into it for the money. I didn't want to end up in jail. Being a cop that's one place you don't want to go."

His bud was Joseph Melville See Jr., "the Princeton hippie," a brilliant geologist. There's a picture of the two of them together at his cabin near Mount Lemmon. See Jr. was Linda's first husband before she married Paul. "I said 'Was you really JoJo from the Beatles' song 'Get Back'? He says, 'I don't want to talk about that shit.'" Paul raised See's daughter, Heather, "and that broke his heart. He died a year after Linda did." (See Jr.'s death was ruled suicide but many suspect murder).

The General's afraid he's running out of time, faster than the rest of us, and bucks autumn-year ennui by holding on to any kind of future that's worth living. Not easy because he doubles over in pain often, smokes weed to alleviate it. Says it's PCB poisoning, which he "contracted from General Electric. My dad used to haul waste from the factory and all the kids would play in it." He swears he has five testicles, like his dad, from the PCB. Mom, dad and half-brother all died from cancer. (PCBs are found in old fluorescent lighting and electrical appliances among other things. PCB manufacturing stopped in '77).

Whether he realizes or not, he's leaving a legacy in donations. Antiquated pieces, such as bolo ties and pendants, have gone to museums and historical societies, like Nebraska's Fort Cody Trading Post, the Oklahoma Historical Society and Tucson's Saguaro Rotary Club. He saves letters of thanks from all of them. He has a little mineral workshop next to the trailer too, and off the driveway there's an outdoor shed filled with books and artifacts from the Oracle area, the Catalinas and old mines, circa 1800s – chunks of metals, pottery, an old confederate bullet belt, pieces of a stage coach, and all manner of rusted things. His vast collection of ore and remnants of mining gear from bygone eras are on display at the Oracle Inn in Oracle, Arizona. He annually hosts Buffalo Bill Cody Oracle Days, a celebration of Buffalo Bill's birthday. He's keen to open a museum, an educational center for future generations, where his gold and minerals and artifacts can be displayed. He needs $200,000 to make it happen.

The General talks about being a man out of time, and his little lonely world, where he's dying. His voice trails off... and he picks up again, talking of painter Ted DeGrazia, who died in early '82. DeGrazia was a friend who lectured him on gold fever. "DeGrazia said to me, 'Boy, you're reaching for that brass ring on the merry-go-round and you're going to find out it's in the nose of a bull...'"

February 9, 2017

SACRED-HEARTED HE-BEASTS

Dawn Brandt pushes her fists together so her finger tats spell out "HIT HARD," and a tiny anvil on her left forefinger serves as a space divider between the words. Pretty much says everything. The hands themselves are sandpapery and burn-marked with strong, powerful fingers and misshapen knuckles, results of oddly healed fractures from a recent crash on her Harley Roadster in Northern California. (Her helmet saved her life.)

She lifts her leg to reveal the silver dragonheads decorating the tips of her russet cowboy boots. They'd inflict real pain if put into action. She wears a tight, sleeveless Harley Davidson T, copper-buckled leather belt and weathered jeans. A curled-brim raffia cowboy tops shoulder-length blonde locks. Brandt's lithely built with colorful tats and obvious upper-body strength. A turquoise choker completes the ensemble. The overall effect is Sturgis biker meets classic Southern rock, naturally fitted.

A five-minute conversation rabbits subject to subject, from Trump misogyny to high-school stoner parties, from her on-again, off-again boyfriend to the art of knife making. She talks iron forging and the seductive rhythms related to heavy pounding and the weight of the tool, and how that rhythm is her meditation, sometimes a connection to a universe bigger than her own. How it soothes her ADD. How "Everybody's rhythm sounds different."

Brandt sits at the industrial-strength table in the kitchen of her airy warehouse work-living space, in an industrial area east of downtown Tucson. It's an inviting balance of clean lines, negative space, found objects and art. Beyond the kitchen, the space (which once housed a grocery store, and, later, a paint store) is arranged with workbenches and a variety of anvils and heavy tools, gas welding gear, and pieces of her art and blacksmithing. There's a bedroom off the side, bathroom in back. It's remarkably kept.

Her work and tastes show a proclivity for the masculine: Brass knuckles and x-rays of busted bones, metallic nods to Hell's Angels founder Sonny Barger and antiquated objects that rolled off assembly lines when the American industrial revolution was humming right along.

Brandt too is famous among old Tucson drunks and bikers, bar owners and aging scenesters. She slung drinks for more than two decades in area taverns and clubs – from the old Dooley's and Tucson Gardens to Club Congress and the Rialto. "You're a girl, you got boobs, you're cute," Brandt says. "You can use that stuff that's on the outside to make a living. I did that but it wasn't who I was."

She managed to purchase a house from the bartending. Married and divorced, too, which left her jaded. ("Marriage is just an excuse for someone to treat you like shit.") One day nearly four years ago she told herself she'd survive on things she created with her own two hands. So that's what happened. It's a now-classic American entrepreneurial story.

That leap of inner-confidence shows in Brandt's Celtic warrior sculpture that greets visitors to her warehouse. He's bruising and tall, communicates poise and self-assuredness. It's a three-dimensional head fabricated from hubcaps and steel mesh, and it's melted, knocked and twisted into being, a rusted pole and heavy steel base for balance. Sculptor John Chamberlain would've loved to have created him. And like

Brandt's work, it's hardly feminine, and exists far away from any barstool.

★ ★ ★

Sometimes her work features simple utilitarian craftsmanship with a devious or wily twist: A piece from a green automobile made in Greta Garbo's day – complete with a copper seat, lighted headlights and blinkers – makes for an industrial-strength chair. A stainless-steel waterfall, richly adorned with angry-eyed fish and underwater flora, stands six-feet tall, lit up in muted colors. A nine-foot iron jellyfish with a shield and many curled tentacles (suggests swordfights with drunks guzzling from goblets). There's heavy mirrors fabricated from horse yokes, living room tables of Ford Model T or Harley parts.

Her shapes and blends of severe iron and mild steel create odd geometries. But as far-off as some of her hammered-in themes may be (from bikers to sorcery to water), her eye for color gives the work a sense of place. From rusted hues to deep blues, the translucent crystals and rocks, her colors are very southwest, day or night. (And there's no shortage of sacred hearts.) Her work could never hail from, say, Tennessee, or even Colorado. She finds emotional responses in her labors too. Sometimes it's Zen: "When you've tried things out in the universe you can actually see how things can be hand forged." Sometimes she "dreams something and wakes up to create it," because she has no choice. It's the work or nothing.

Yeah, she's nervous talking about herself and seems embarrassed at the exposure of her work. Her laugh is untamed. Her sentences expressive. She can talk into tangents, but rarely, if ever, do her words drag. A line of truth like, "I'm lucky enough to know this is who I am," will pass when she's going on about the many workable glories she finds while garbage picking.

This is a woman who learned to self-identify with a torch and hammer, using found objects and steel sheets. She forged a living creating objects that had no preexisting commercial demands. She'd have done it sooner had she had the confidence. One gallery showing and a single Tucson Gem Show appearance was enough for her, just not worth the trouble. Her metalwork is celebrated through word-of-mouth, here and in pockets around the country.

★ ★ ★

Brandt's work is a reaction against her uneventful and normal childhood. It was too damn uneventful and normal: "When I grew up girls didn't weld and they didn't ride motorcycles, they weren't allowed to be one of the guys. I'm still rebelling against having to be a cute girl, I guess."

She grew up on Tucson's working-class eastside with an insurance salesman dad and homemaker mom. (She clarifies: "my mother is still awesome. She handles everything, there was never *a guy* handling things.") As a girl, she'd take things apart to learn how they worked, from the family telephone to her Stretch Armstrong action figure. "I was one of the boys. I hated it when my boobs came in."

Misplaced energy fluttered. By junior high Brandt was making pipe bombs from a recipe involving lawn chairs, strike-anywhere matches and makeshift fuses, and blowing shit up. Such creativity charmed her Sahuaro High School

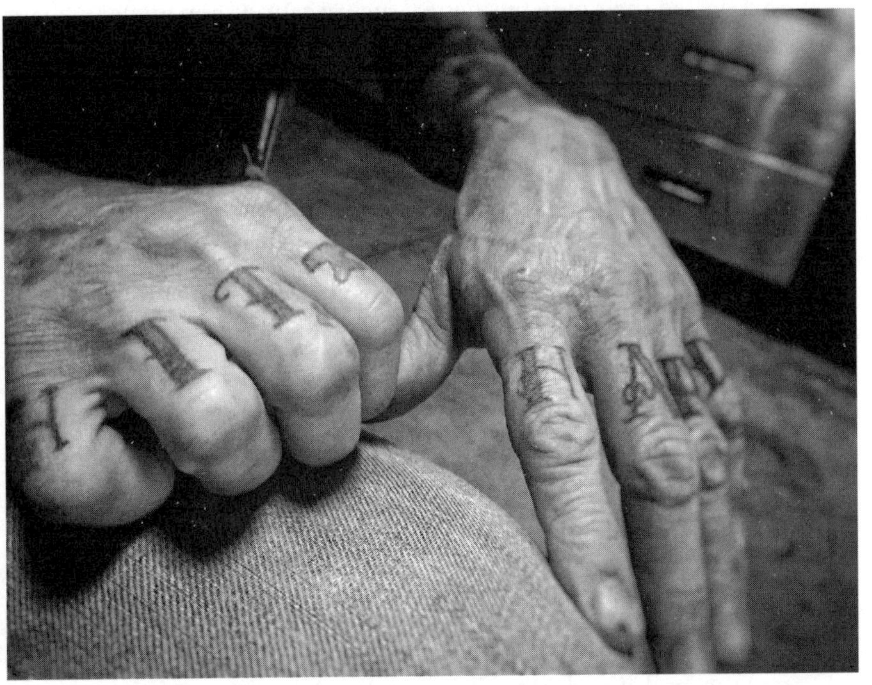

arts teacher, a big influence on Brandt's future in metals and art. "She was cool. She let me be her teacher's assistant. There were real tools there too, a drill press and saws." Her blonde hair and fake ID got her work in bars as a teen. She did some college after high school but chose "the school of hard knocks instead." Her drive outpaced her reach and whatever opportunities available for a Tucson tomboy born in the 1960s. So she self-medicated. "If you're chasing a high when you're younger you're hungry for something."

A decade ago she began little projects – a wrought-iron handrail here, a small-yard fence there, a mural inside a rock club. She got better at it, learned nuances, and began getting the right tools. Other Tucson women inspired her, those who'd started their own businesses, such as tattoo shop owner Donna Mellow and Ali Shulman Edwards who runs CEDR HR solutions.

"They're mighty in what they do," Brandt says. "Women need to support women."

Other inspirations include Hieronymus Bosch, sculptor Andy Goldsworthy, and glass artist Dale Chihuly, as well as those down at Tucson Metal Arts Village. Old biker culture too; its take-no-shit philosophies. Many of her best buds ride. "I like bikers," she says. "You screw them over, they screw you over harder – but they're honest."

Aren't motorcycle brotherhoods all bro culture? Where women are considered second-class?

"Not me," she says. "I always had their respect."

★ ★ ★

Later that week I'm driving Brandt around Tucson to see her work in the field. A Kapala skull with wings above a Grant Road tattoo shop, stainless steel front awnings at two Sacred Art Tattoo locations (she's horrified to see damage to one), decorative wrought-iron pieces in front of homes near Tucson High. There are many.

We arrive at a sprawling ranch-style house in the rural area near Grant and Swan Road. The fence surrounding the house is the largest project Brandt's done, and it's remarkable. It's about 350 feet in length, made up of 10-foot sections. It's a blend of mild and stainless steel, featuring mandala symbols on three entrance gates and bottoms adorned with pre-Columbian designs. The gates are held up by large stone-filled square pylons made from steel and spiked into concrete slabs.

There's low-voltage lighting and an in-set mailbox. Like ocotillo and mesquite, it's both edged and relaxed in that very Tucson way. Nothing like it anywhere.

It took three months for Brandt to survey, cut and erect the fence. She had assistance, the physical labor would've been otherwise impossible. An insane job that made her buff. "It was interesting to watch my body change," she laughs.

It's a fence around a house, yes. But it shows how this woman perhaps unconsciously applies principles to her work, beyond her own perceptions – how she sees a world bashed from steel and iron, hard edges into curves, masculine into feminine, feminine into masculine. How everyone's rhythm is different.

November 17, 2016

TRAILER-COURT SPARKLE

A speeding Oldsmobile swings onto Lee Street off of Columbus Boulevard and nearly mows down a woman pulling two cheilitis-lipped children in a red plastic wagon. She pretty much ignores the car but stops walking anyway. The singlewide glittering in the sun caught her attention. She pulls the wagon around and centers it on the edge of the street so that the trailer frames the fidgety kids. She steps back, lifts her phone and snaps a pic. She clutches the wagon handle and continues towing the kids down the center of Lee Street.

It's no wonder the woman stopped. The singlewide illuminates – no, completely raises hell on – the otherwise dirt-toned, faintly creepy milieu at the Casa Dulce trailer court.

To glance at it. Hundreds and hundreds of compact discs are glued in seamless vector to the outer surface of the mobile home, data side out. In the daylight, when the sun refracts just right, it could be the bottom of an enormous wishing fountain filled with gilded coins, and when headlights hit the trailer at night it becomes a hazy cluster of crescent moons flaming in orange and gold.

The trailer sits on a double lot, which butts up to Lee Street. A flipside to Bosch's earthly delights: Among a few trees, bushes, and a prickly pear, sit a gimcrackery of stuffed bears and monkeys, cracked ceramic lambs and pigs, and dollar-store angels atop pipe fixtures. There's a sun-bleached San Marcos wolf blanket decorating the gate, and next to that hangs a blue bedspread showing a heraldic sun and a half moon. Coal-black tennis balls form scrums on the dirt, and plant stands uphold fake flowers. There's sun-blackened wreathes, hidden rosaries, fabricated metal frogs, and dozens of neatly arranged hubcaps. And so on.

It's chimerical and absurd, but there's whatever-works ingenuity, and some artful nuance. It's shaped by a lack of cash, a lack of modern technology, and so it's a show of resourcefulness, and patience. It's a proletariat proclamation that says the owner of this trailer, Gustavo Orozco, could be an absolute madman. Or it could be that he's grateful to have made it to retirement age alive, and he's simply revelling in the win.

When asked the inspiration behind such decorative flourish, Orozco says he "just did it." He thinks a moment. Adds, "the CDs reflect the heat, and that's why I started putting them up. Soon people were just leaving CDs for me outside."

The word "Abella" is spelled out in large ornate script in two places on the trailer. Tossed-away storefront signs from a local business.

"Abella is an Italian word for beauty," Orozco says, "and I do my best to make this beautiful."

★ ★ ★

It's a sunny day, the birds are chirping and Orozco's giving me a tour of his mini compound. He's wearing cop shades, an NRA cap, a cowboy bandana, a vest and Levi's. Trailer glam. His horseshoe mustache and dyed-on muttonchops enhance a storied face Walker Evans would've loved to snap.

A black cat slinks the ankles. "That's Cyrus," Orozco says, cigarette angling off his lips. "He came around and I started feeding him. He lives here now."

Orozco flips the latch on the heavy wooden gate that opens to a tiny path that leads into the secured Arizona room of his trailer. He hobble-walks through it. Reaching a hand around he rubs his lower back and winces. "I fractured my spine once," he says, "cutting marble. A giant pile of it fell on top of me. I landed my back on sharp piece of marble." Two wheelchair years and "doctors said I'd probably never walk again. What do they know?"

Then one day he spied a guy breaking into a next-door trailer. The prowler slammed Orozco's lower back with an iron bar. "Oh, *man*. I wound up in the hospital again. But I've had about six of my bikes stolen. My tools. I'm not going to let it slow me down."

He pulls up his shirtsleeve and with detectable pride points to a shoulder scar about a half-inch in diameter. "That's one," he says. His forefinger traces down to other places on his body – his chest, lower hip and leg. He slowly counts aloud, considering each: "Two. Three. Four. Five. Six." He nods, pleased. Says, "I've been shot six times."

With his fingers he massages his upper chest, hunting a bullet fragment lodged between his shoulder and rib cage. It continues to create health problems. He laughs. "Doctors thought it was cancer, but it was just a piece of bullet."

Born in San Juan, Texas 65 years ago to migrant workers, Orozco was the youngest of 12. With few, if any, advantages, it's no stretch to understand the family burdens were comprehensive, white bloodlines, education and money rewarded. He's worked odd jobs. Spent much of his life in Gilroy, California, but he has picked potatoes in Idaho, garlic in California, cotton in Arizona. He's worked in a cannery, cut tile, and is an expert landscaper. He dealt drugs too, hence the bullets.

He says he took a rap for drug-dealing buddies and did time in California prisons like San Quentin. "I wouldn't want to be a snitch," he says.

He moved to Tucson to "settle down," but arrest records show his numerous busts here, smaller infractions including disturbing the peace and traffic violations. "When they put the handcuffs on me, I don't know what happens. I can't be put into a cage. I turn into an animal; I'm not going to deny it.

"I did all my time," he adds. "I just want people to leave me alone."

He's never married but he has two adult daughters in California ("I talk to them as often as I can; I miss them so much it hurts"), and a grown son he doesn't communicate with, saying he's in a Salvation Army adult rehab "getting help," but Orozco won't elaborate.

He shows me around the trailer's added-on Arizona room, which he partly assembled from a vintage wrought iron bed (a gift from the owner of a neighborhood bar), slats from baby cribs hauled from street curbs ("you'd be surprised how many people throw away cribs"), and a wall-sized chunk of metal siding from an outdoor patio a nearby bar and grill discarded. All secured with wires and chains and heavy canvas drop cloths.

Several fetching street-rod bikes abound – even a three-wheeler – which he painstakingly built from parts he'd find in junk piles and refurbish, sometimes ordering pieces from a nearby bike shop. His prize pony is painted San Francisco 49er red and gold, after his favorite team. A matching trailer goes with it. No car means he peddles everywhere, the Laundromat, the store, the bar.

★ ★ ★

It's murky and dark inside Orozco's trailer, filled with eerie silence. Smells of baby powder, fried eggs and bug spray. Dusty slices of sun cut through gaps in covered windows. One holds a little AC unit. The interior is a darker version of the exterior – clown figurines, zebra-print blankets, tiger faces and countless toy guns (despite the NRA cap, he says he "doesn't mess around with real ones") surround every inch. A big-screen in a lounge-y area. One could die here and no one would notice.

A kitchen TV monitor shows the outside, the front of his place and main entrance to the trailer park, the comings and goings, the lost and the lizards and dogs. Orozco's been broken into so many times.

He spends $100 a month fighting cockroaches. "The whole park is infected," he says, "and I've only seen one in my place. This place was filthy when I got it. It took three months to clean before I could move in."

Spending a monthly Benjamin on insecticide is a lot, considering Orozco's fixed income of social security and disability totals, he says, $800, plus food stamps. It's $275 just to keep the trailer at Case Dulce. He collects aluminum cans with his friend, Albert Lomeli, who's here hanging back in the shadows. Looks about 30. Lomeli won't reveal much about himself except that he's unemployed, and once lived in the trailer across the way. He stays with Orozco now, helps him with his bikes, collecting cans, working on the place.

"It's always work," Orozco says, "and I can't really lift anything anymore. So I haven't done much to the place lately."

Strolling back into the sun, he says, "But I do hope people will drop off more CDs. We need to put more up. What's that saying? 'One man's trash is another man's treasure.'"

Trash, treasure, whatever, even the display on the rooftop swamp cooler is telling of its owner. It's shielded front and back by heavy acrylic sheets plastered with evenly placed CD-Rs. Precariously bungee-corded to the cooler is a toy horse with stuffed monkey perched in its saddle. The monkey, which Orozco named Caesar, wields a pair of toy machine guns, a faded American flag, and he's posed as leading a charge.

February 25, 2016

STUCK IN THE MIDDLE

We commandeered a big, stupid Budget rental truck from Detroit, Michigan to Tucson, Arizona with all my stuff, slicing a 2,000-mile path straight through this big, beautiful, ugly, joyful, fading country.

The trip was a loud, clammy road song like most, marked by gristmills, soy fields and free-range cattle, the briny taste of its soil on our tongues, and crack-head motels in dry, bible-thumper counties. The corporate hegemony fueled carsickness and one passenger's attendant hangover, but we found indelible beauty in huge skies and chipped-up towns whose boom had long since passed, except for the Walmart.

Also found no shortage of women-loathing race-baiters. They were seemingly lovely working-class folk until queried about the upcoming presidential election. Then long-festering resentments rose and intolerance was suddenly and creepily bracketed by chortles, and diluted by yearnings for "how things used to be." They acted like they had unwavering knowledge of something that I didn't. The Trump fans.

Talked to a couple of empathetic people too.

This highly unscientific American temperature gauge was conducted like this: I approached working-class folks in different states in rural America and asked them questions. Some wouldn't talk. One young Canadian woman in a Missouri coffeehouse giggled aloud at the very idea of the upcoming American elections.

The goal here wasn't to engage like-minded morons such as artists, writers or musicians, or blubbery white dudes in truck stops wearing T-shirts that said things like "VEGUN – One Who Only Shoots Organic." Too easy. I tried to avoid

anyone obviously voting either left or right, except that trio of hard-working Latinos in New Mexico, whom I'd pegged as hardcore Hillary supporters, and whose ill-informed inertia shocked: Angry-faced Marty Salas told me that he "didn't like either one. So I'm not voting." His young Mexican wife with a child in tow was much gentler, and said she was undecided about for whom to vote, but Trump was probably her choice. She couldn't say why Trump mattered to her.

Pissed-off indifference was everywhere. One bewildered

Asian-American liquor store owner in Sapulpa, Oklahoma, who looked about 40, nearly frothed at the mouth about how health insurance costs were killing him, his business. He didn't give a shit anymore, he told me, and wasn't voting for anyone.

The overriding narrative against Hillary was the Republican one, and it came down to two things: She's a liar. And as Secretary of State she was responsible for the deaths of our own, especially those killed in Benghazi, Libya. Trump's incompetence didn't exactly weigh into their decisions.

Most Trump supporters wouldn't give their last names and some wouldn't allow their photo taken, while others waved me off with a dismissive backhand. I attempted to cover a wide range of ages and ethnicities.

This purely empirical observation predicted that Trump could very well become president of the United States. Yessir.

Name: Javin Whitlow
Age: 30
Lives in: Taylor, Michigan
Occupation: Car rentals and student at Wayne County Community College
Voter Preference: Hillary Clinton

Why: I go to church and we talk about different things. It's not a Democratic or Republican thing, it's a right and wrong thing. In past elections it did feel like my vote mattered, but in this election, I don't really know if my vote really matters.

Don't you think a vote against Trump is better for America?

I definitely do. That's why I'm more toward Hillary because it's the less of two evils. That's what we say at home. Now Trump turns me off. He's an asshole. Some of the stuff is just ridiculous. That stuff about make America great again? The past wasn't so great for everybody. It wasn't so great for my ancestors.

Name: Patty B.
Age: 68
Lives in: Cloverdale, Indiana
Occupation: Front desk at an Econolodge
Voter preference: Donald Trump
Why: Trump can make it the way it used to be back in my days. You know? Where government did what the government should. It protected us. It didn't tell every little whoop-stitch to do. Just like Obamacare is a farce. There's a girl here that's a maid, you know how much maids make. She's on Obamacare and the best she could do was a $3,000 deductible.

I think he will make our economy better. I think he will build up our military, protect us better. I think Hillary Clinton is a liar and as far as I'm concerned she murdered those people in Benghazi. My son and my daughter are voting for Trump, too. My son's in the military and he's not too fond of stuff Clinton did, he said, "you never leave your people behind."

I'm still a registered Democrat. I just know that if you don't take care of this great country here, nobody else is. Everybody out there wants to get us. We're the only great country going, and they want to change us, make us socialists where the government takes care of everything. That's not the way it's supposed to be.

Is Donald Trump fit to run the country?

Absolutely. I think he's got some things wrong with him; he's never been in politics and he says some really off-the-wall stuff (laughs)... But compared to Hillary Clinton? She's 100 million times worse at taking care of the country than he would ever be. I'm up to here with the Clintons. They do bad stuff. I'd be first to admit Trump is no saint, but I know he hasn't killed anybody. They talk about bodies buried everywhere from the Clintons. I'm talking even in their private life...

As a woman, do you have a problem supporting Trump?

He's just the way men used to be in my day! It's not offensive to me. You weren't offended by that. I don't get that. Now if they treat you bad, that's a different story, if they knock you around.

Name: Ralph S.
Age: 76
Lives in: Rural Indiana
Occupation: Retired, worked for a pharmaceutical company
Voter preference: Trump. Says all his friends are voting Trump

Why: I don't like any of them. But I'll vote for Trump. Hillary is a liar. And I don't think a woman should be president. Too much PMS (slight laugh).

Is Trump fit to be president?

That's questionable. He's got advisors. There's nothing he's going to do without them. I don't think they would advise him to do the wrong thing. Hillary would lie about anything to get in there. She says she doesn't want to change the Second Amendment, and keep guns out of the hands of people who shouldn't have them. She's saying that now, but let her get in there and she'll change her mind. That's one thing I'm afraid of. She didn't do anything for those who died in Benghazi. I think she tried to lie her way out of it. It was an open and shut case. She's not going to stop lying just because she's president, Madame President, or whatever you want to call her.

Name: Jordan
Age: 29
Lives in: Tulsa, Oklahoma
Occupation: Server at Ruby Tuesday
Voter preference: Trump

Why: He's the Republican Party, man. He's who you gotta go with. We need people to get off food stamps, get jobs, quit living off the government. You know, support their families, not have the government support their families. Quit printing off money and blowing money on stupid shit.

Like what stupid shit?

We spend, I think, like a billion a year on food stamps. I think we can cut that down somewhat. Federal aid, this free housing shit. People are just lazy, man (laughs).

Name: Julia Salas
Age: 27
City: Socorro, New Mexico
Occupation: Homemaker/Mother
Voter preference: Undecided, leaning to Trump

Why: I don't like everything Donald Trump is saying or trying to do. Can't agree with all of it, but agree with some. I come from a family of politicians. I'd rather avoid it (laughs). My dad is a commissioner, my grandpa is a county assessor. So I avoid politics. It takes over everything. But I am going to vote. Probably for Trump.

August 15, 2016

SONG REMAINS THE SAME

Insane greed frightens. Unchecked power armed with an appalling ignorance of the world – its history and people – frightens. Indifference to human rights frightens too. To watch Donald Trump speak about anything is to watch a stroke victim half-aware; he's masking with bluster what little command he has of his words and their meanings. It's almost funny how the fear piles up.

If only he was just one more depressing celebrity douchebag.

Any generalized comfort we felt before Donald Trump's arrival in office has been converted into painful awareness of everything around us. It's as if we have surrendered to every detail of his intolerance and emotional turmoil and are suffocating in his endless feedback loops of narcissism, desperation and pathological deceit. I'm even scared sitting in my benign little Tucson neighborhood, and it's pure working-class. Feels more like home than any home ever could, filled as it is with front-porch La-Z-Boys and low expectations. Shouldn't be scared here.

So where are the protest songs?

Pop music, once ripe for social change, is now about "content generation and branding" – backed by corporate cooze for survival. As soon as Nike kyped the Beatles' "Revolution" in 1989 to sell sneakers, and then secretly settled out of court, the long, slow death of the protest song was set in motion. Suckling tit for coin is nothing new and there's long been dubious support in place to sustain artists in their work. Renaissance-era churches subsidized painters, wealthy benefactors in

19th century French parlors dangled the promise of patronage before street artists and musicians, gay sugar-daddies in post-Warhol Manhattan backed rising artists, and these days there's no shortage of journalism nonprofits on bended knee begging handouts from billionaires.

Pop stars no longer wait a generation to collect paychecks from Pepsi and Apple and myriad others. It's livelihood because, basically, albums and singles no longer sell. Stars don't want to piss anyone off, so corporate tones color modern pop.

John Fogerty was 24 when he penned "Fortunate Son," Sam Cooke had Martin Luther King to inspire "A Change is Gonna Come," and Marvin Gaye had Detroit for "What's Going On?" Record companies, however reluctantly, still backed them. That was then.

While this playlist is by no means some compilation of best-ever protest songs, these are ones on my brain lately, some childhood leftovers, some from before that, some recent. They've each developed in my head an anti-Trump feel, and may bring catharsis if not reassurance that revolution is still possible. But that's unlikely.

Parliament – "The Silent Boatman"

This relative obscuro closed off Parliament's overlooked '69 debut album. *Osmium* is a sonic anomaly among the mostly funked-up R&B sides, an aching epistle to tolerance driven by acoustic guitars, a folk-pop melody and droning bagpipes (playing the Scottish folk standard "Skye Boat Song"). Even with the frighteningly taut Funkadelic rhythm section, it's more Laurel Canyon or Fairport Convention than post-riot Woodward Avenue. Its anti-racist theme hums beneath a journey-to-death metaphor, featuring poetic turns like "When you reach Jordan's bank/There's no money, power or fame/ No third or second class/The fare is all the same." It's so gentle, so stirringly tender. No wonder it was penned by English folkster Beth Copeland, who'd been working with Parliament (and Funkadelic) in Detroit. It's also featured on her own, entirely ignored 1970 debut album.

The Skids – "Working for the Yankee Dollar"

Pre-Big Country guitarist Stuart Adamson and big-lunged singer Richard Jobson advance notions of how Yankee war bucks fatten the super-rich, and how the same lucre can hold Europeans down... or something. This indomitable mix of beauty and muscle rises on sad-punk anthem guitar, dance-y tommy-gun drums and strains of the Celtic folk the band grew up on. Jobson's vowel-swallowing diction assured words were mostly indecipherable (he may have also fancied himself a teenaged James Joyce) but when the sentiments were on, there was no escape. This Bill Nelson-produced boot-stomper might be the only rock 'n' roll song ever in which the doomed protagonist fights in WWII *and* Vietnam. Really, it's the sound of Scottish kids mocking American obsessions with war-mongering and world domination. And it's *danceable*. The ditty hit the UK Top 20 in November '79. The Eagles' "Heartache Tonight" topped the American chart that same week. There you go.

Rickie Lee Jones – "Ugly Man"

This brass-stoked piano-tinkler from '03 is a George W. jab. But it's downright mesmeric if you think of it in Trump time. Inside four minutes of jazz-hep beauty, simple lines land suckerpunches: "He's an ugly man/He always was an ugly man... Revolution, now it's finally going to come... Now we take the country back." Rickie Lee Jones is going down in history as one of the most overlooked of the great singer-songwriters.

Kap G – "(Fuck) La Policia"

Kap G gets under the skin, and this 2014 tune is truth for the borderlands and beyond. Between the slurs and unfortunate Auto-Tune croons, Kap sports an almost indecipherable, strangely laidback, bilingual robotic flow. What wins is the humor, which goes lengths to make his too-often corny gangsta persona likeable (it'd work better as parody), but at the same time Kap shows how rap continues to be a potent pop force, parody or no. Here he's just "rolling with (his) Miggers" when he gets pulled over for too-dark window tint. The rest of the tune's a killer callout on racial profiling and works in the grim reality of Trump's anti-Mexican sentiment: "And I know what you're thinkin' – I ain't got my green card."

Weirdos – "We Got the Neutron Bomb"

Pretty much as potent at anything by the Sex Pistols, yet it rose from So. Cal! This tongue-in-cheek power chorder sounds like it could've jumpstarted the apocalypse, a band festering to implosion, like a proper punk-rock song. Its right-wing slant is sarcasm, a negative as a positive, because if you listen close, the lyric sports a real anti-bomb, anti-war message – a total damnation of nuclear weapons – yet it's as far away from any hippies as you could get at the corner of Western and Hollywood Blvd. in 1978, despite whatever impulse to destruction is suggested in the gnarled Dangerhouse grooves.

YG and Nipsey Hussle – "FDT (Fuck Donald Trump)"

Over a sweaty hypnotic beat featuring lazy bass and occasional Al Green horn samples, this 2016 side (released before Trump actually won the election) is an unsubtle street brawler that'd do any true patriot proud. The chorus is a bangin' graffiti splash: "Fuck Donald Trump!" One soundbite features Trump announcing he'll build a "great great wall" on the Mexican border, and make Mexicans pay for it. The ensuing verse: "Hold up, Nip, tell the world how you fuck with Mexicans/It wouldn't be the USA without Mexicans/And if it's time to team up, shit let's begin/Black love brown pride... White people feel the same as my next of kin/If we let this nigga win/God bless the kids." A remix features Trump's racist blather about banning Muslims too.

Staples Singers – "We The People"

If ever there's a tune everybody should hear weekly, like some aural manifesto, it's this 1972 Booker T-penned sleeper from The Staples Singers' biggest-selling album, *Be Altitude: Respect Yourself* (released nearly seven years after their civil rights barnburner *Freedom Highway*). This brass-and-organ groover (The Memphis horns!) lifts on pure gospel soul-pop and Sly Stone slink. Mavis Staples is an absolute force, equal parts graceful and sassy as she guides us through a we-gotta-come-together anthem that's deviously meticulous on tight harmonies and singsong lines like, "We the people/Got to make the world go around." It's protest through positivism that didn't, in its day, appeal to any specific black, white or brown upheaval or umbrage. Still doesn't. It almost feels manipulative, but there's *waaaaay* too much emotional heft and swagger for that.

Randy Newman – "I'm Dreaming"

This sardonic monster relies on a character who's "dreaming of a white president/Just like the ones we've always had," (yes, it's purposely "White Christmas" sideways) someone who knows "where we're coming from." Written when Obama was in, the song's really a deceptively literate tribute to the man. But just like right-wing idiots misinterpreted Bruce's "Born in the USA," so it is that this gentle workout – with Newman's now cool-y aged vocals – was hilariously misread by old rich white guys. Newman was even mocking himself. Now this 2012 single mocks Trump: "Whiter than this?" Newman sings repeatedly over the piano ostinato in the song's finale. It's one of those songs whose power and humor can't be muted with overplay.

The Byrds – "Deportee (Plane Wreck at Los Gatos)"

An overlooked *Ballad of Easy Rider* gem of the often-covered Woody Guthrie song (you should also hunt down the Dylan/Joan Baez version on Youtube). This version's remarkable as it was recorded with a loose, country-rock grace and a vulnerable Roger McGuinn vocal, in 1969, precisely when (literally the same month) the hippie utopian peace-and-love dreams were killed off by Charlie Manson (album producer Terry Melcher was, it was widely speculated, Manson's target at the Tate house murders). Its waltz-time jangle and pedal steel upholds the hair-raising sadness in the lyrics, which were inspired by the tragic 1948 plane crash that killed 28 undocumented immigrants on a flight from California to Mexico: "Who are all these friends scattered like dried leaves/The radio said they were just 'deportees.'" The tune might be more relevant in 2017 than it was the year Guthrie penned the lyrics, and the year this version came out. The Byrds helped solidify this song in the American musical canon.

Junior Murvin – "Police and Thieves"

It's a toss-up which is better, this or the beautiful genre-crossing turn by The Clash. This stunning Lee Scratch Perry-produced original (with Sly Dunbar on drums) probably has more heart. Junior Murvin's vocal betrays real ache and warmth, and features a kind of sexual groove that might've stopped Marvin Gaye in his tracks. It's deceptively tender, despite the unflappable Jamaican soul conceit built upon the idea of social unrest, and fear, in the politically charged, near-riot zone that was Kingston, Jamaica in the mid-70s. Its relevance never wanes; it's about police in the streets and the corporate thieves in charge. The song transcends suffocating confines of pop – it's reggae evergreen; a sort of call for peace that will forever resonate as long as rich, white and bloated Trumpster mooks roam this Earth.

August 10, 2017

RADIO HEAD

When Frank Luna returned the call last week I had no idea who was on the line. That voice, a percussive, bass-heavy thing, woke me from deep sleep.

He said, "Yes! Hello? Is this you? Yes?"

"Hey," I said.

"This is me... *hello*." Sounded like a Latino Stewie Griffin, but deeper, heavier. It scared the hell out of me. Had to be a joke.

Later that day I'm standing in Luna's dark, slightly foreboding one-bedroom apartment. It's in a cool 50s complex, sun-faded into melancholy brown. I hear his other voices too, 11 at last count. They're in Spanish (his first language) and English and Spanglish, in the parlance of old Hanna-Barbera or Beetlejuice or pirate, or a kind of old-school radioman freakout, there's even a Katherine Hepburn (hoarse and all) in there, each wickeder than the last.

When he plays it straight I swear I know that voice from late nights in the borderlands, in Sonora or Southern Arizona, buzzing out from dad's dashboard dial, long before AM began to soundtrack its own decline, as if broadcast from some half boarded-up small town. Yes, his percussive soothing syntax sounds like the end of some golden age. A voice slicing through crackles of high-school football scores from distant lights in the rearview. One chattering of UFO sightings, and introductions to blooming Mexican waltzes, and, dear God, The Open Road, where your heart could still break suddenly for one you'll never ever find.

Listen now and you can hear the sound of America shifting so quickly none of us has the time to hear and see and feel what's happening. Luna's voice lulls like narcotics when it softens, and it does for several reasons, not just affect. I might as well be the last person on Earth tuned into it.

His sole companion, a black Chihuahua, stiffens his back and dances around our ankles on the carpet and yaps at his master's commanding and hilarious patois. Luna regards the dog. Says, "that's Oona, which in Gaelic means 'one with the Earth,' or, in Spanish, 'Uno con la Tierra.'"

★ ★ ★

His face alone puts one at ease. It's Fred Flintstone friendly with salt-and-pepper hair, gray mustache, a Breathe-Right nasal strip centered perfectly over the dorsum of his nose. In day-hang clothes – old swag T (Hot 98 radio), baggy shorts, Nike flip-flops – Luna does comedy with arm flailing and voices to make any gaggle of third-graders howl, or, really, any group of adult beer-swills too.

Though still in his mid-50s, Luna uses a walker. (A back injury suffered in his early 80s Air Force stint in Guam.) One hardly notices because he's so animated. "I worked with many people who had disabilities," he says. "At KHYT one guy had no arms, he'd flip records with his feet, and it was like he had arms. But we loved radio, broadcasting and music."

His love of older cartoons matches a kid-like passion for anime (especially the Tucson fest Con Nichiwa), and radio, and broadcasting. He'll rattle off old pop-culture facts, names of old-cartoon voiceover artists. For example, Ted Knight from the *Mary Tyler Moore Show*: "I recognized his voice, and Vic Perrin's, who did the scary *Outer Limits* narration, from *Super Friends*!"

He lives and breathes this stuff, and because of it he's built recording studios and got entire radio stations up and running. If you grew up in Tucson in the 80s and 90s you've likely heard Luna's voice, on AM or FM. He's the last of a dying breed of radio journeymen, having DJ'd on about every damn radio frequency on the Southern Arizona dial. He was working at KIKX radio the day it went off the air for good in 1981 ("a sad day for radio"). But later, his "El Chavalo Loco" persona ruled on R&B/hip-hop giant KOHT-FM (Hot 98) where listeners were treated daily to his between-song shenanigans and voices. In all he has voiced roughly two dozen radio stations – from all-Spanish talk, all news, rock music, and jazz and new age to country music, hip-hop and R&B. Such places as Tucson's Tejano 1600 and KTUC and KNDE, and KKHG "The Hog." There was KAVV in Benson, K101 in Sierra Vista, and one or two in Nogales. He even worked Skyview Traffic. It's remarkable the details of things he hasn't forgotten, nuances of each station, their indie or corporate owners, and the exact start and end dates. You could say this guy is a piece of Tucson's soul, so deep runs his broadcasting history.

Then one day in 1999, while working at KXCW and KTZR, he tired of greedy bean-counters poking him to soften edges. Corporate interference had sucked all joy from his on-air work, so he switched to the other side of the mic. On-air he was an entertainer, comedian and impersonator, a newsman and music curator. He wraps this job description into a succinct little phrase: "When you're able to make pictures with sound, the sky's the limit."

His fascination for radio and audio festered in childhood. At 10 he got the crap "beaten out of him" for overhauling his old man's hi-fi, an antiquated Packard-Bell with a turntable and AM-FM. "But," he adds, "I got it sounding better!" A teacher sparked his electronics curiosity at Sunnyside Junior High. "Good teachers were few," Luna says, "but one, Pete Kozachik – brother of Tucson councilman Steve Kozachik – took a real interest." Kozachik went on to become an Oscar-nominated visual effects expert. A short time later, at Tucson's old Rodeo drive-in, Luna pounded on the projectionist's door to complain the picture quality was scratchy. "So the guy broke the rules and let me in the booth because I was so inquisitive and young," Luna says. "I saw the blinding carbon arcs on the projector, and he taught me the cue marks and the countdown to change reels." In high school, teachers called him "golden throat." Luna did the morning announcements through the main school PA system, all four years of high school.

By 15 Luna was a KOPO radio intern where he cleaned tape heads. A morning DJ heard his voice, and soon the station made him an on-air personality. Kid fascination becomes career.

★ ★ ★

Inside Luna's living room there's a stereo and turntable with lots of radio-ready outboard gear, from sonic maximizers to hard drives, where he assembles broadcast quality edits of shows and music. The wall above it shows art and framed photos of, or done by, Luna's daughter, Katrina. It's a pedestal, decorated with green things: a Gumby, hanging leis, a lamp throwing green light – green was Katrina's favorite color. The 24-year-old, one of Luna's two children, from his only marriage, which lasted from 1983 to '96, died of an accidental overdose in 2013. He changes; banalities, humor gone. His defenses. He looks down between his hands on the walker, and says, "When you lose a kid, this is where the adult comes in, you have to move. You have to continue. You have to.

"That's when the friends come in. That's when the shrinks come in. That's when family comes in." He pauses. "When it starts to get the better of me now, that's when I bury myself in my work."

Luna was born in the middle of five. The youngest and oldest of his siblings died well before their years from health-related issues. His own father, a Nogales-born Korean war vet, committed suicide in 1977.

Maybe the mirth and voices and comedy are a series of gestures designed to blur pain. Like Frida Kahlo's idea of painting her own reality, other options don't work. Luna eschews alcohol, for example, its depressive kills. Suicide runs in his family and in response he's super self-aware. His world is fueled by joy-filled mannerisms and self-created radio voices because it's his way of channeling those he lost. He says as much.

"I get to live lives for those I loved, those who died before their time."

★ ★ ★

Luna never considered a career outside broadcasting, though his throat would've earned him lucrative voiceover work in Los Angeles. He stayed in Tucson out of provincial loyalty, though admits he'd go to the grave happier if his voice got used in a cartoon. Since 2000 he's been employed at Sahuarita-based KEVT-AM radio (Power Talk 1210), one of four AM stations in Southern Arizona broadcasting at 10,000 watts or more during the day. Luna's lived through numerous format changes there – from Spanish religion to all-talk news. The station is one of the last of the mom and pops. Luna likens the job to a good university tenure. "I've earned my tenure." There are caveats: AM-radio station budgets these days are as thin as those in journalism, such that Luna does "the job of eight people. If I were to quit there would be no station."

Power Talk's local on-air lynchpin is boom-voiced Tucson news legend John C. Scott. There's a roundelay of syndicated progressive stars too, including Stephanie Miller. Aside from various station IDs – at KEVT, as well as a few others around the country to which Luna's freelanced his voice – you won't hear him on the airwaves.

This afternoon Luna's busy in his apartment, transferring audio files of recently aired Scott shows for airtime because the host is out. He regales with yarns from his decades in radio. He reaches into a closet and produces CDs and 8X10 glossies signed to him by Eminem, Will.i.am, and even Wilson Phillips, mementos of a career rooted partially in fandom. He began record collecting at nine years old, and thousands line walls in his apartment. Including LP rarities by Hawaiian-born crooner Ernie Menehune, a Tucsonan who ultimately altered Luna's life. Menehune was famous for his big-band-fortified Polynesian revue and lounge act, which raged from the late-50s through the 70s. Menehune was a huge club and lounge draw in the Western states, played Caesar's Palace, and released seven now-highly collectable albums. He performed up to his 2015 death. He became a bone fide Tucson music legend.

Luna was 8 years old when he first met Menehune. It was in 1968 at Tucson's long-storied Spanish Trail club, where the crooner had a residency. "I was coming out of the pool and made my way into the lounge where my dad was at the bar having a drink," Luna says. "Ernie had just finished his set. Here he is in his Hawaiian shirt and the whole thing... I was like a bobbysoxer meeting Dean Martin or Frank Sinatra for the first time."

Cut to 2010, and Ernie's 87 years old and hosting a Hawaiian luau. Luna drives out to Menehune Ranch, the singer's sprawling Hawaiian-themed Tucson spread to purchase tickets directly from the singer. Luna hadn't seen Menehune since that day in 1968. But he never forgot him. Menehune doesn't remember Luna the boy but after that ticket-buying day the two became close friends, bonding over the fact they'd each lost a child.

Menehune trusted Luna enough to give him control of the master tapes for his albums. Luna promised Menehune he'd get all of his music reissued. When Menehune died, Luna had already begun the reissue project, painstakingly transferring the master tapes to digital, with help from longtime Tucson studio men Lee Furr and Jim Brady. When the two-track masters were too damaged, where audio restoration would interfere with the integrity of the songs and recordings, Luna had them remixed from the original multi-tracks tapes to sound like the original. Remixing is tricky because it alters history, the sonic context of the time of creation. Luna has taken his time to get it right. The limited-release CD reissues on Luna's own imprint (Luna Recorded Archives) so far sound amazing; warm and analog-y, judiciously mastered, direct from the master reels. "I'm a very big stickler when it comes to sound," Luna says. You can find the discs at Zia Records locations.

The third Menehune album – *Showtime: Live at The Spanish Trail Supper Club* – will likely be out this summer.

"Getting Ernie's music out is a project of the heart," Luna says. "There's no money, whatever it earns has gone back into the project. Getting the music heard, and getting new sets of younger ears to pay attention isn't so easy."

Others in radio help, and he singles out KXCI radio – Tucson iconoclast Al Perry in particular – for keeping the spirit of Menehune alive by playing the music. "Before Menehune had died he was tickled his music was back on local airwaves, and now, because of Perry, people are picking up on his music."

★ ★ ★

Luna grew up certain of what he wanted from the world, and in large measure he has attained it. Who can say that? This radio – this broadcasting, fading as it is from the golden age of American culture – has defined him, and will continue to support him into the foreseeable future. "AM radio is dying," he says, "but it will never just die."

Does Luna get lonely?

Without blinking, he says, "I have Oona."

He laughs.

"I'm probably going to be buried in a big transmitter box with my headphones and maybe a bottle of good tequila. And if I was to die tomorrow I would die happy, a simple human being who loved what he did for a living."

Before I leave, Luna cues up on his stereo a 2014 recording that he made of Menehune, a year before he died, recorded here in Luna's little living room. A single mic captured live in one take Menehune gently singing Martin Denny's "Tiny Bubbles." In Menehune's hands, in his aged croon, the song is fragile, filled with resplendent sorrow, a love epistle far more melancholic than Don Ho's radio hit from years ago. As it floats on the line, "With a feeling that I'm gonna love you/Till the end of time," Luna's body shudders, and he breaks down, and weeps. And then he apologizes. Says, "It's an honor to be able to keep Ernie's music alive."

April 17, 2017

'XANADU' AT THE MINT

Maybe it says something that when Bryan L. starts talking about five holes drilled into his head I can't stop listening to him even though "Moonlight Mile" is playing. The song's a tune-everything-out heart-stopper that freezes me in my tracks, in my very being, no matter where I am, every single time. The greatest Stones song there is.

Then he looks down at the table where we are seated so I can see the top of his head and he parts sections of his thin blond hair to show me just where those five holes were drilled. He describes in clinical detail how he felt the pressure of the drill as it bored into his skull.

Over the rare Jagger melancholy, I learn that Bryan was never prone to headaches or hangovers before the real headache kicked in and when he visited a doctor they discovered the three tumors rooted on his brain. "I should've been dead a year and a half ago," he says.

So he's legally blind in one eye, the radiation medicine made some teeth fall out and the cancer is in "medical remission." And he about died before that, too. He'd suffered childhood leukemia and onetime nearly had his head knocked off inside an army tank. Then they cut melanoma from his face, and just in time.

Now Bryan's handsome and eloquent in a Truman Capote sort of way though people other than me tell him he looks like Philip Seymour Hoffman. Nevertheless he's unsatisfied with his reflection in the smudged mirror behind the bar, between the obscure silhouettes, and so he hates having his picture taken, unless he's doing karaoke. It's Sunday karaoke tonight but it's dead so the jukebox is on instead.

One night several months back I watched in awe as Bryan donned a red feather boa, a too-small fedora and employed a chair as a dance partner to perform a slinky-sweet karaoke take of "All That Jazz," channeling both Catherine Zeta-Jones and Liza Minnelli, if you can picture that. Right here at the glorious Mint, this scuzzy-resplendent den that sits on that stretch of proletarian blue near Alvernon Way on Grant Road, as it has for decades. (The Mint's newly updated interior of blousy curtains and western motifs probably didn't come cheap, relatively speaking, yet it still somehow adds to the bar's scuzzy resplendence.)

Bryan drinks quality liquor and has one of those bitter-happy smiles that says many things but mostly that he's defiantly jolly, celebrating life in the moment with woots and toasts and songs and karaoke, sometimes shouting things with arms spread, exclamations that begin with words like "I'm alive." He's a droll storyteller, and is immediately kind, and can be sort of bitchy with his lifelong friend Roberta Dawn who's sitting right here with us. They've known each other for decades, since they each lived in the Asarco mining company town of Silver Bell, near the older Silverbell ghost town in the desert west of Avra Valley. Their town is gone now – forever shuttered around '84, houses moved or mostly leveled.

"It might've been in the middle of fucking nowhere in the desert but it was green and beautiful, there was a park and a post office, fire hydrants and we had corrals for horses." Bryan says. "My parents were there since the 1950s and it was a great place to grow up. If I can find the cattle guard I know where I am."

Roberta, or "Bert," as she's called around here, is 52 years old but looks 33. She hosts the Mint's karaoke three nights a week and DJs its weekend burlesque shows. The heavyset woman tells me she adores the work but it's barely a living. Lady's got some pipes on her too, and it's obvious when sometimes during karaoke she sings silly macho hair-metal with an alluringly feminine spin.

You could say Bert and Bryan are best friends – I'd say that based solely on tonight's observations – and there's sibling-like love between them. They "were Bobbsey Twins" at Marana High School back in the 1980s.

They tell each other's stories and tragedies, like how Bryan lost a few real siblings. A sister to whom he was close overdosed on methadone and an alcoholic brother died too young of a heart attack as he was "just driving down the road." Bert has three children from a deceased ex-husband, and her own parents died separately before she was a teen. She'd left Arizona years ago but returned to Tucson from Washington because she says something told her Bryan needed her help, right around the time of his headaches. They hadn't seen each other in 30 years. Their reminiscence-heavy yarns involve troubled family histories and their Silver Bell years and a particular "mean-ass mule-packing grandmother." Stories captivate and lift beyond the heightened narrow assessments overheard rising from another nearby conversation.

When it's not crowded inside a bar, other conversations seem louder, and I overhear one later being exchanged between the pretty bartender and a trio of bearded beer drinkers sitting at the bar. Each would obviously love to get into her tiny shorts so they're forcing flatteries on her involving her abilities as a pourer and even about the bar itself, but there's not much competition between them for her attention because each guy knows, deep down, that they don't have a ghost of a chance with her. They soon split.

Bryan lifts my forefinger and drags it over his left brow. There's a small deep crater under his skin. He spent a decade in the army and served during the Gulf War and he came out of it with near-death experiences, prove-it scars and no evidence of bumper-sticker braggadocio.

This scar shows how he got smashed by "a huge piece of steel" while showing a trainee how to fire a cannon inside a tank. She pulled the trigger with no warning and the casing recoiled, smashing Bryan in the face. He basically died, was revived by his war buddies with emergency blood, duct tape and a needle, and then medevaced to safety. "I was out for three weeks," Bryan says.

Bryan was also married and has a daughter in another state with whom he is close.

"I was actually married to a woman? Ha-ha. Does that surprise you?"

Not so much. But I wonder if it was difficult? Army, marriage?

He lifts his shoulders and lets them drop.

The karaoke resumes for a few songs and Bryan strolls onto the little stage to no fanfare backlit by hazy reds and greens and some stringed lights and offers up Billy Joel to four or five in the house including the bartender, and only I watch. This is where karaoke can be incredible. Bryan's got that intangible look in his eye, that there's-nowhere-else-I'd-rather-be glint. I swear 100 indie bands touring the country in dumb vans right now could learn something from that look in Bryan's eye.

A middle-aged man named David comes over to me while Bryan sings. There's something about David that'll break your heart. We talk. I wind up asking about his life. He tells me about the accidental death of his 10-year-old son. He says, "I'm just a normal Joe who lost his son."

After a long moment, he says, "It's beyond comprehension."

His eyes well with tears and he sways to and fro and I want to hold on to him to keep him from toppling over and hurting himself further, to keep him steady, to keep him. Sometimes I wonder if there's any pain greater than what's felt by a parent down a son or daughter. Makes me grateful I didn't die on my parents, and weirdly grateful that I have no children of my own.

Then David is gone. Just like that.

On a night like this The Mint feels like what I imagine a bar on the main strip in some insignificant blip like Safford, Arizona might've felt like in the 70s, sad places disguised as happy places where people would go just to keep from falling off the Earth. When you can't afford much else, the safety of gravitational force and the pitchers of beer come cheap. Where folks come alive after having been numb all day and I remember that feeling of coming alive and it makes me want to get drunk, hard, especially after being dead all day, most every day.

Sitting here not drinking but thinking that some of my darkest family shames happened between these Mint walls, back when I was as tall as a barstool. My head fills with filmy scenes that bloom into melancholies so rich I swear I hear my own mother say, "There's a lot of ugliness out there. That's why I come in here, to find the pretty."

Wait. That isn't my mother talking. It's Bryan, next to me talking truths over Bonnie Tyler, pulling me from dead places.

That's why I adore The Mint, and all the places like it that are vanishing, because my nostalgia might not be my own but it's weighty enough in here to feel like mine. It's more profound than the sentimentality and self-pity.

When I stand to head home, Bryan is huddled in front of the juke, eyes closed and mouthing words to Olivia Newton-John's "Xanadu." The karaoke is shut down for the night and there's no irony here. He doesn't hear anything else and it's like he's suspended off the ground like that, and rocking back and forth slowly, and Olivia's singing right into his ear and the sonics and words and vocal inflections float directly into his bloodstream straight into his heart. I see now how he's grateful to be here at all.

October 6, 2016

THE FIGHTER

The two boys, about five years apart, had lots in common. Their mother, Mercedes Perez, adored and cherished them. And she worked hard, mostly long days at the Tucson Mall, and had moved to the small town of Catalina outside Tucson to get a fresh start away from the town's southside drugs and gangs, and family squabbles. Her onetime partner, the father to her eldest son Andrew Perez, was a too-tough, womanizing pro boxer who'd been sent to jail, serving a 20-year stint for dealing mad amounts of drugs. One of her sisters, Patricia Perez, was murdered by her own husband in front of their 10-year-old son.

Young Andrew had always felt like he was living two lives, his American side, out in Catalina, and his Mexican side, on Tucson's south side with his many cousins, and nine other half-brothers and sisters (on his dad's side). Though he has learning difficulties, he never stopped speaking Spanish at Grandma's house, across the street from the Tucson Rodeo Grounds. But Andrew was glad to live outside of town, in a tiny neighborhood area folks call "Little Mexico," which sits inside a white enclave.

He immersed himself into the new culture of Catalina. Hearing stories about his dad being a fighter, he became a huge fan of WWF wrestling, which, at a tender age, he thought was real. He gravitated to wrestling young and, in his teens, mixed martial arts. (Diego Sanchez was his teen-years idol.) At school wrestling matches, he was "envious of the kids whose dads got to watch them." That's what he wanted. He grew up going to church, mostly Catholic. Communion, confirmation. In some of his high school years, he was a group leader in church, and a counselor at the YMCA.

Andrew and his little brother, Adrian, were molested too, by a female babysitter. She'd force them to touch each other and touch her. When Andrew talks about it now, it's obvious whatever bitter traumas in the recesses of his character had been buried under agonizing shame, because no way was he ever going to tell anyone what happened. Andrew's cousins, whom he looked up to, preached "toughness," and to be a man.

By 2004, 15-year-old Andrew was a special ed student with a slight stutter, and a good high-school wrestler. He still had severe difficulty reading and writing – and he'd have trouble in class. He'd find himself ineligible to wrestle when he couldn't get his grades up. But like any sport, motivation to wrestle is often a reaction against something else entirely. And he rarely had much confidence in himself. Says he "started hanging out with the wrong crowd."

Then the first accident happened.

Mom had been teaching him to drive, a stick, and he was getting good at it. One day, she allowed him to take the car one mile to the Burger King on Oracle Road. As he pulled from the house his brother was goofing around and hopped on the hood. Then he slipped off and the car rolled on top of him.

"I just remember him getting up and falling into my arms," Andrew says. "He was just screaming for my mom."

The dark, hushed interior of that same Catalina house where the accident happened is a home his mom worked hard to make livable and cozy. Framed photos on walls, stuffed leather couch, flatscreen, Easter-colored flowers atop corner book shelves populated with little antique clocks and tea-light candles, angels and Japanese figurines. Andrew is seated at the kitchen table. He's old-school good-looking – bushy eyebrows, forever 5 o'clock shadow, resembles a young Robert Blake, *In Cold Blood*-era. A self-designed tat ornaments his upper chest, a rosary and the words "Stay Strong." We can hear Andrew's girlfriend and daughter in the back bedroom, watching TV and laughing.

Andrew continues.

"When I saw him – Adrian Daniel Perez, that was his name – in the hospital, he was bloated and swollen."

Andrew begins crying softly. "I went to him and said 'Adrian, it was an accident, I didn't mean to do this. Please. I need a sign that you know this was an accident. And he moved his hand. And then he moved his foot. And I said, 'don't joke with me, please do it again.' And he did."

A few days later, doctors pulled Adrian off life support and little bro was gone.

"I just remember knowing I was going to be OK – because my brother knows it was just an accident. Though everyone knew I killed my brother. I had to live with that too. Sometimes I'd say to myself, 'I did it. I killed my brother.'"

When he did, he'd act out, get violent, post-traumatic stress. He'd punch walls, doors. His mom didn't repair the holes to remind Andrew of the wreckage he was leaving behind. Those holes are still there.

"Sometimes, my mom would get a little drunk and blame me," Andrew says. "I expected that. But how is a 15-year-old who just ran over his brother supposed to control something? I know how emotions go, and I understand that now. But I still sometimes blame myself for things to this day."

Time moved on. Andrew attended counseling sessions, mostly through church and what his mother could afford. His mom trusted Andrew again too – the anger issues – though he kept "things bottled up." Mom promised she'd do anything for him if he stayed free of smoke, drugs and alcohol until he was 21.

He promised and steered clear. He was her angel, Mom told him. Her new man helped too.

"So the best thing was when my stepdad came into my life. He was younger than my mom, maybe 25. Not that much older than me then. He was changing me, and I didn't even know it. He moved in and had me change my work ethics. You know, 'If you want something, you've gotta work for it.' So, I'm actually passing my classes and doing my homework.

My junior year, he never missed a wrestling match. He got me to graduate high school. He's still my dad.

"But there's times when I exploded with my mom," Andrew adds. His solicitude could almost be the cower of a defeated person. "Because I didn't know how to control my anger."

At 19, he dove headlong into mixed martial arts (MMA), and worked at it, hard. He made his amateur debut in 2009, a cage fight at Tucson Convention Center. Around 35 people showed up just to see him – cousins, brothers, sisters, stepdad, mother. Andrew won. Then he aced his next seven fights. He won eight straight as an amateur.

"All these stories I heard of my dad being a fighter," he says. "And I was like 'I could actually do this.'"

Some fights were better than others. "I remember fighting in Globe, Arizona, in back of a Fry's grocery store. A parking lot where they set up the cage... where maybe 400 people showed up."

Like any hard-won career, in the arts, in sports – or anything in this world – to be truly great, everything else in life suffers. It's how one transcends the conventional, the ordinary, the tragic.

"I got a lot of support from my family and others," he adds. "My cousins knew I was going to be something. And I've grinded. I've done so many sacrifices."

Andrew talks a lot about how he pulls strength from those who've been father figures or family figures: his neighbors, his grandma (who died in November), one particular neighborhood family who brought him to and from school and practices. His coach. It recalls passages from a new, go-to PTSD tome called *The Body Keeps the Score* in which Dr. Bessel Van

Dee Kolk writes how "deep down many traumatized people are even more haunted by the shame they feel about what they themselves did or did not do under the circumstances. They despise themselves."

★ ★ ★

Mixed martial arts (MMA) is a brutal, full-contact hybrid of martial arts, wrestling and boxing. It's punk-rock fast and prize-fight grueling, and at first resembles street brawling, except that it's heavily refereed, ruled and coached.

Good fighters are serious, well-trained athletes, no joke. Hints of masculine grace transcend cage-fight viciousness and unintentional homoeroticism. Basically, two fighters duke it out inside a chain-linked, octagon-shaped cage while employing (enduring) three basic tactics – striking, grappling, and controlling. Submission, a knockout or a referee decides match winners in many bouts.

MMA's popularity has risen drastically since it's '93 inception. A 2016 *Washington Post* sports poll said 25 percent of Americans count themselves fans of mixed martial arts, a percentage that rivals boxing. MMA's premier organization is the Ultimate Fighting Championship (UFC), and any local fighter worth his or her salt is keen on it. But you have to be good, and storied.

Today we're at Tucson's Apex Mixed Martial Arts gym in Northwest Tucson. This state-of-the art facility is hardly *Rocky*'s Mighty Mick's Gym; it's upscale, airy, well-lit. Even smells clean. There's a boxing ring, an octagon-shaped ring wrapped in chainlink, a sprawling floor mat, workout machines. MMA championship belts hang near the entrance.

A trio of MMA fighters, Andrew, Joel Champion (his real name) and Jeff Anderson, are in the boxing ring completing the first phase of before-noon weekday training. Downdressed in sweatpants and tees, the sweat-sheened bros bounce and punch like pantomimes trapped inside bubbles. Kanye and Keith Urban pump the in-house stereo.

During a break, Andrew says of his training partners, "These guys are my brothers, my Ninja Turtles."

Andrew is mastering MMA's multiple skill sets. He's been christened "Golden Boy" since turning pro in 2011, mainly because it's being said that nothing can stop him – no death, no drug addiction and, now, no opponent. It's telling how his body looks almost humble compared to other fighters; it's not overly gym-sculpted, and it radiates a humanness that's doesn't seem at all mean-spirited – but in action it's absolute force.

As his coach says, "There's something there that you can't see."

Andrew's only professional losses came (he's chalked up four total, against seven wins) when he was, his coach points out, "self-defeating."

His coach, New Jersey-born Joey "Boom Boom" Rivera, is a chiseled, semi-retired fighter and owner (and much-decorated black belt champion) of the Apex gym, where Andrew trains nearly every day. He's got piercing blue eyes, thick pony-tailed hair and a firm command of platitudes ("Everybody, in some way, is a fighter. That's what I believe"). He's a father and husband whose long-winning track record and low body fat go lengths to explain his confidence. His fighters all listen to his commands with the high-stakes focus of war planners in a military room. In MMA worlds, Rivera's a badass.

In 2009, Rivera took the troubled fighter under his wing,

his heady work ethic a rebuke to Andrew's inner traumas.

Andrew, who turned pro in 2011, says he'd be nowhere without Rivera. Rivera says "Andrew made his career. I only helped with some decisions." Either way, Rivera is big-bro/father figure to Andrew. He doesn't suffer horseshit, from Andrew or any of his fighters. Andrew's always been straight-up with Rivera.

"Andy comes from a bad place; it just happens that he was a right student," Rivera says. "And when he got here he was an absolute savage, undefeated as an amateur."

Good MMA fighters like Andrew work grueling hours in daily training sessions, pay physical and emotional dues and damages. And they hustle. MMA fighters gleaned much from the hip-hop school of self-promotion; like street rappers, fighters brand and merchandise themselves gratuitously, obtain sponsors. It's how they survive. Andrew's living relies on sponsors, mostly private ones – families, friends and local business owners – and also his winnings. He has no other job, though most fighters at his level do, even a guy who holds the WFF pro championship belt in the lightweight class. (He defended the title in February this year, against an older fighter, Thom Ortiz, who actually knew his biological father.) Andrew won't reveal how much coin he's pulling down but acknowledges the risk/reward ratio is low. He fights three or four times a year, the most any human can absorb. If he gets hurt, he's screwed.

But his overhead's low. He rides the bus from Catalina everywhere because he can't drive. (Part of his training includes a run to the bus stop.) He fights in the Arizona-based World Fighting Foundation (WFF). The theater-sized regional fights, held mostly at casinos, are well-attended. The thing is, Andrew is closing in on his goal of getting into the UFC. Even if he does, the median salary for a UFC fighter rivals the median salary for a U.S. worker, about $44,000 a year. Not exactly retire-for-life dough.

Though Andrew has left his coach a couple times, Rivera says Andrew has always had a home at Apex. "Look," he says, "we all need to feel wanted. We're all the same. So there was never a time when I turned my back on him." He pauses. "The hardest part of the fight is with ourselves."

★ ★ ★

At 22 years old, Andrew was believing his own hype, thinking he "was better than I actually was." So, he stopped training and developed a taste for opiates, Percocet specifically. And their magic in erasing excruciating memories, "those images of my brother."

Soon enough he couldn't control it.

Exactly five years ago, Andrew hopped in his Ford pickup to go "score another pill" and headed south down two-lane rural North Twin Lakes Drive. It was nighttime on an unlighted road. Says he saw a coyote or dog in the road, swerved, hit a pot hole, lost control, went into "a fence or a tree."

But news reports said Andrew had crossed lanes onto the opposite dirt shoulder where a "victim was struck... then ran into some smaller trees and brush before returning back onto the roadway."

Andrew swears he didn't know he hit anybody. His mom, family and court agreed. He got charged with leaving the scene of an accident involving death. The fighter got probation. The parents of Jacob Lee Wyckoff started a Facebook page called Parents Against Vehicular Homicide.

"When I came home, the only thing I was thinking was my mom was going to whoop my ass because I messed up the truck," Andrew says, back in the kitchen of his house. "I remember getting a call from my dealer, 'Hey, they got the road blocked off where you crashed.'"

Andrew returned to the scene and turned himself in before he knew there was a body there. "His name was Jacob," Andrew says. "He was 22. I'm still sorry. And I know people are gonna read this and be like 'Aw, he deserves much more.' Some made it seem like I did my brother on purpose too. You know a lot of them say 'this is his second death. He's ran over two people.' But I'm telling you right now it was an accident. I never met the kid. If anything, maybe I saw him once because it's a small town. But that's it."

Did he ever speak to Jacob's parents? "No," he says, pricks of sadness returning to his eyes. "Jacob's parents hate me. Of course. I don't blame them. I'd hate me too."

Andrew and his family are still recovering from the debt; the lawyer alone demanded a $40,000 retainer. "The lawyer is who got me this plea," Andrew says, "and I remember when I violated parole even the judge was telling me, 'Your lawyer did amazing work.' He wasn't even happy with the plea I got."

Andrew didn't want to live after the accident. The opiates got him. He dropped dirty urine, violated probation and went straight to the big house. Did a year and a half at Florence and Yuma state prisons.

When he got out, he was ready to fight, like there was nothing else for him. That's when he won the WFF championship in '16.

Because of the fighting, local kids look up to him at the gym. He's a hammer-knuckled cautionary tale not hiding anything, who acknowledges his story, and sobriety.

"When I was doing the drugs, I didn't know how many people looked up to me, and I let them down," he says. "I knew I was gonna overcome it."

Before Andrew's fighting career ends, coach Rivera's "100 percent convinced" Andrew will open and operate an MMA gym and coach a corps of young fighters. It's Andrew's dream too. "To open a gym in Catalina, or maybe Mexico, where it could help kids."

Then he stops. He's got the felony rap on his record, and Jacob haunting him.

After a long silence, he adds, "In the beginning, I would just wish more that Jacob's mom knew it was an accident. I didn't do it maliciously. I didn't know him. Because she did lose her son. I know how it is."

April 5, 2018

MUSLIM COWBOY HEADSHOP

It's almost midnight and Cowboy rolls up on his fourth-hand Gary Fisher mountain bike, slides to a stop, hops off, leans the machine against the storefront window, and steps into the severely lit shop. He triggers the too-loud entrance beep, steps past the trio of Marilyn Monroe wall hangings, and is greeted like a trusted old pal.

"*Cowboy.*"

We're in the newly opened, astutely titled Rock Smoke Shop, open 24 hours, seven days a week. The store launched a month ago, and its owner, Mohammed Kitama, and his corpulent sidekick Nael Polus, are an odd couple, a Kuwaiti-born Muslim and a Christian refugee from Iraq who met each other in Tucson a year and a half ago. They eschew Arabic in politeness to this monolingual, though Polus' English is negligible. The radio plays classic rock and the place is scented of freshly burned hookah tobacco, faintly exotic.

"I forgot his real name," Kitama says to me, "I now know him only as Cowboy."

Cowboy looks around in the center of the shop, its clean new walls and display cases lined with smoking paraphernalia, legal stimulants, flavored cigars (the sweet blunts), hand-blown glass pipes and glimmering water bongs. His person is militarily organized: a holstered hatchet dangles from his backpack, and a portable CD player hangs around his neck, earbuds attached. A miniature stuffed Santa clings to a front loop of his black trousers whose belt buckle secures a fixed-blade knife with a pretty burnished handle. A white cowboy hat and black fingerless gloves complete the sartorial excellence. His teeth are perfect. His face and hat recall Bill Paxton, Dinky Winks in *Spy Kids 2* and *3*.

Cowboy hustled up coin earlier in the night but he's not in Rock land to procure anything to enrich some smoking experience; rather, he purchases a packet of Brix (Quality Fragrances for Men), and in doing so relates a story of a woman who said he smelled wonderful the last time he wore it. He grins. "Maybe I can get lucky."

Now Cowboy has been homeless 19 years, and, yet, by miraculous fluke – evidenced by his teeth and shaven face – his world maybe isn't strictly defined by uncontrollable pursuits of the negative. He's made it livable, to a degree, yet it's obvious he's seized by some enemy within.

Kitama treats Cowboy with respect, and he's known him long enough to learn others treat him like dirt. Kitama gives Cowboy work, though there's not much to give – fixing a toilet in back, helping with the sign out front, watching the store when a break for food is needed, that sort of thing. Tonight they converse about an electrical problem in the shop, Cowboy offers up theories and Kitama listens, and then it's figured out.

Before Cowboy arrived, the two gents were seated on folding chairs behind the cash register, facing each other across a short table and playing cards. Time long, patrons few. The previous customer was a weed-scented Latino whose unsteady focus was impressively held by Katima's persuasive sales pitches, which included hefty discounts on an array of smoking apparatus. But the kid only walked out with a couple bucks worth of Banana Smash cigarillos, after much internal deliberation and at least one trip out to his car to talk with his girlfriend.

Kitama and Polus are banking on the Rock Smoke Shop to succeed. It's just the two of them, 24/7. They work a lot.

"My friend," Kitama laughs, pointing to Polus, "is single. He has nothing else to do. So he works here." Later in the night, in a more serious tone, he says, "This man is my brother. He is Christian, I am Muslim. No matter. I trust him, in health, in money. I pick him to do business together."

There's a glut of Tucson smoke shops, and dubious, fly-by-night concerns, but this one, with its bare customer essentials, is one of pure entrepreneurial spirit, minus the 'tude common among newly minted, albeit somewhat myopic Tucson residents who relocate here calling the town "a blank slate," a place only to be improved upon. These particular gentlemen, who have no personal history here, are fascinated by the city's frayed charm, accept its troubled economics.

Customers are beginning to trickle in too, enough to perhaps give Kitama hope. Kitama reckons the store needs to net, at the minimum, between $5,000 and $6,000 a month to get by.

The desolate late-night offering sits on Grant's north side, near Treat, between Tucson Boulevard and Country Club Road. The white-washed edifice shares walls with the graffiti-logoed Classic's Barber Shop ("Shaves and Fades"), and is garishly lighted in and out, with colorful pennant string flags and handmade black-on-red placards that read, "We Open 24/7" and "For Med Night Press Bell," and red, white and blue block letters on the façade, "Rock 24/7 Smoke Shop."

Barriers drop, the suspicions, and the Kuwaiti-born Kitama "opens his heart," as he puts it, to explain the route from a comfortable career in Kuwait to a Grant Road headshop. Speaking family his melancholy green eyes lighten. He has

three children (two sons and a daughter, the oldest is 11), and a wife to support, and they live in an $850-a-month apartment on the northwest side, chosen for the good public school and low-crime neighborhood.

His mother, dead now, taught English in Kuwait and Kitama's fairly articulate in it – there's a less-is-more edge that accents his strident observations of American life, and how he's a fan of business logic. He's educated, and had built a life in Kuwait and Jordan, worked as an area manager (his territory covered the Middle East) for an oil wholesaler. He cashed it all in for, he says, the Arabic dream of living in America. "My boss said just take a vacation here, maybe three months. I was making $12,000 a month, had three cars and a boat. A boat is an extravagance you don't see there."

He arrived stateside with his life's savings ($235,000), and in three years it's gone. Startups failed: A grocery store, a restaurant, a headshop. He says the failures had much to do with a feud that erupted after a partner (a relative) cheated him. So his 80-year-old Jordanian father loaned him the Rock Shop startup cash, with the caveat to stay away from said relative. The 43-year-old has his pride, isn't exactly proud to involve his father.

Kitama can talk world politics, and does, stopping at Donald Trump. He shakes his head. In terms of leaders, Trump's just another trigger-happy narcissist in a long line of tyrants Kitama and, especially, Polus have seen, or endured, in epic war and tragedy, in the Middle East. Kitama isn't afraid of getting rounded up and shipped off from here. He can't help Islam extremists, or Yankee illiterates who make Muslim a dirty word. (He's been on the receiving end of ugly racism, the name calling, the shouts "to go back home," etc.) He shrugs his shoulders; he's already lost so much. But not his children. They're gaining wisdom of a foreign life, of cultures, Mexican and American. And Tucson's public schooling, compared to Jordan, is attractive. Because war-traumatized Assyrian refugees have poured into Jordan (whose population has nearly doubled to 9.5 million in the last 15 years) real estate is prime and entropy has set into the public-school system, and private schooling is priced out of reach. It's become too expensive to even survive, Kitama says.

His dad has a two-bedroom place in Jordan, and he has two siblings there, and if the Rock goes belly up that's likely where Kitama will end up. But it would be absolutely humiliating for this father and husband.

"To sell everything just for the plane tickets... and then no work there, no guarantees," he says. After a pause, he adds, "It may still be an Arab dream to live in America, but it's cruel. If you lose your money here you're homeless, drunk or doing drugs, or you shoot yourself. There are no homeless in Arab countries.

"I've had two heart attacks since I've been here," he continues, pulling on a smoke. "It's the stress of the American life. I'm always thinking, always." He didn't bother with the hospital after the second heart attack. "Why? They put wires on and watch monitors. They take your blood. They give you results. They ask me questions. I pay almost $10,000 for questions. They tell you to stop smoking. This I know. I only started smoking like this in America, the stress. When I left hospital, it was $380 a month for 16 months to pay off. But I paid them."

Kitama has difficulty understanding certain American fundamentals, differences, and his own observations are exacting on crime, Yankee greed and, in particular, his belief that women should stay virginal to marriage. For example, he'd throw his own daughter out if she got pregnant out of wedlock. It's difficult to grasp, especially when Kitama is brought to tears talking about his young daughter Marwa – named after his mother – who couldn't understand his need to leave for work earlier tonight. How Marwa let his "tears get out."

"Why do you have to work?" Marwa had asked him earlier. "And why are you sad?"

"I call your name," he told her. "You are my everything. And when I call your name I think of my mother too."

America is only for his children. "Kids are a tree, the fruit. So, good education, good life – that is why I work so hard. Your kids are your future, and my kids will put me in my grave." Kitama adds, "I do my best. I am not a cheater. I believe in God. Everything's in God's hands. We trust ourselves and our customers. We are honest." His eyes narrow. "But if Trump touch my children, I make crime. I want my kids to be safe, that is all."

Polus nods along in kind. (Polus, the Marilyn Monroe fan, landed in America in 2007, spent time in San Diego and then Detroit, among other places. He ran a gas station in Tucson that went belly up. He has no children. He doesn't talk much.)

Later, Cowboy is standing outside the shop in the light the Rock throws to the middle of Grant. He talks of his living area – squatter's quarters a few miles away, a lucky predicament that allows him a certain amount of control in his life, which has brightened his world considerably. Better, he may be able to move into a space behind the Rock – there's an apartment back there that Polus rents – but it's questionable. No one knows if the Rock will be here in three months.

Cowboy, now smelling a bit sweeter, hops on his bike, earbuds attached, spins around and heads west on Grant Road into the late-night. Rolling toward some unknown place on the land, he disappears over a slight rise at the Grant Road Lumber sign.

April 20, 2017

NOT FADE AWAY

Whenever Johnelle Hunter swings his arms behind his back, shifting his electric clipper from one hand to the other, it's like a well-rehearsed soft-shoe worthy of some 1960s Motown Revue stage, such is the swift, graceful movement of his arms, hands and legs. A knee lifts, and then the other, as he sidesteps over the clipper's power cable, completing a quarter-turn.

He's built like a member of The Temptations too – long-limbed with narrow-shoulders – but you can somehow imagine his powerful yet slender fingers, with those impeccably manicured nails, cupping the top of a human head and lifting it straight up off of a neck. In a pressed uniform of khaki slacks and matching button-down shirt and russet leather shoes, he's as put-together as old David Ruffin, complete with specs and tight graying curls. His is an area of outdated style that never goes out of style. You just can't fake this kind of real.

This gent's on his feet all day. No mean feat considering he hits 80 in December, and that an infection took his right-foot big toe decades ago. The loss not only informs his movements to a degree, but makes it even more challenging to negotiate the 20 or so heads he sees on any given workday.

It's the last day of summer and Hunter is trimming the close-cropped hair of Ryan Clowser, a University of Arizona physics major, and former high school football star from Sierra Vista. Two customers are seated on waiting chairs near the entrance.

Without query, Clowser comments on Hunter's work: "He gives the best haircut I've ever had." Then he says, "It's also really cheap here."

Yes, it's Clowser's second-ever visit to Hunter's, and he's not about to say anything disparaging about the guy holding his head hostage with a straight razor. Still, it's hard to argue with Clowser. Anyway, an "adult" haircut here sets you back all of 10 bucks, and Hunter can't remember when he last raised the price. It's been years.

And that's not surprising. In the context of a world of infinite consumer choices based on vanity, Hunter's small, homespun barbershop could be – or is – from a land time has all but erased. Striped paper graces the south wall above four barber chairs, mirrors and fabulous clusters of haircutter accoutrements, sprays and ephemera. There's a mid-'70s Pepsi vending machine where a soda costs 50 cents (the machine recently sputtered – Hunter's waiting on the repairman), a few placards that emphatically read "No profanity!" and scattered about are magazines that suggest a dude-heavy customer base: *Men's Journal*, *Sports Illustrated*, *Outdoor*, etc.

"Oh, we do get women," Hunter says, tossing out a number that's quickly calculated by the folks in the shop to be about three percent of his total customer base. Notable regulars over the years have included ex pro-football players such as Ron Gardin, and former Tucson Vice Mayor Charles Ford, as well as a colorful assortment of preachers, lawyers, and politicians.

The barber pole that protrudes from the non-descript olive-green façade outside is so hard to spot from the street it's almost secretive, like it might actually represent bloodletting and tooth extraction as it did in the Middle Ages. There's no exterior sign that lets anyone know this place is Hunter's Barber Shop, or that it's called anything at all. But Hunter has all the custumer action he and a couple of barbers (including his son Lamar, a physical education teacher employed here Saturdays) can handle, and the shop thrives on throwback street cred and word-of-mouth (social media? Heaven *forefend*). To him, the internet is some newfangled technology that has little to do with, nor could it ever enhance, the kind of human interaction he trades on in his work.

Though he's been at this North Stone Avenue location near downtown for 26 years (the shop was housed in central Tucson before that), the place feels steeped in a tradition of a million crewcuts belonging to men who only know each other's first names, who wear the same aftershave workday after workday, and who aren't so vain as to calculate to impress others. It's also a tradition that began fading years ago to the kind of moneyed folk who move into neighborhoods like these, displace its inhabitants and overtake damn near everything. But it's a tradition that symbolized Hunter's independence from an even older idea, one that involved taking orders from higher ups.

He talks of his life as he trims, shaves and cuts, and he's so nerve-calmingly spoken, with a hint of a Southern inflection, that one must strain to hear him at times.

He's been cutting hair for more than 60 years, but not always for a living. He grew up in northern Louisiana, experienced ugly southern racism firsthand. He and his six brothers (there were no sisters) attended segregated schools and his granddad was a sharecropper who had 24 sons and daughters from two marriages, and "maybe some others."

"So your grandfather was a stud," chimes in one waiting customer.

"He was, for real," Hunter laughs. He pauses. Shrugs gently, and says, "Those were different times."

Hunter's dad owned an 80-acre farm. "We lived off crops

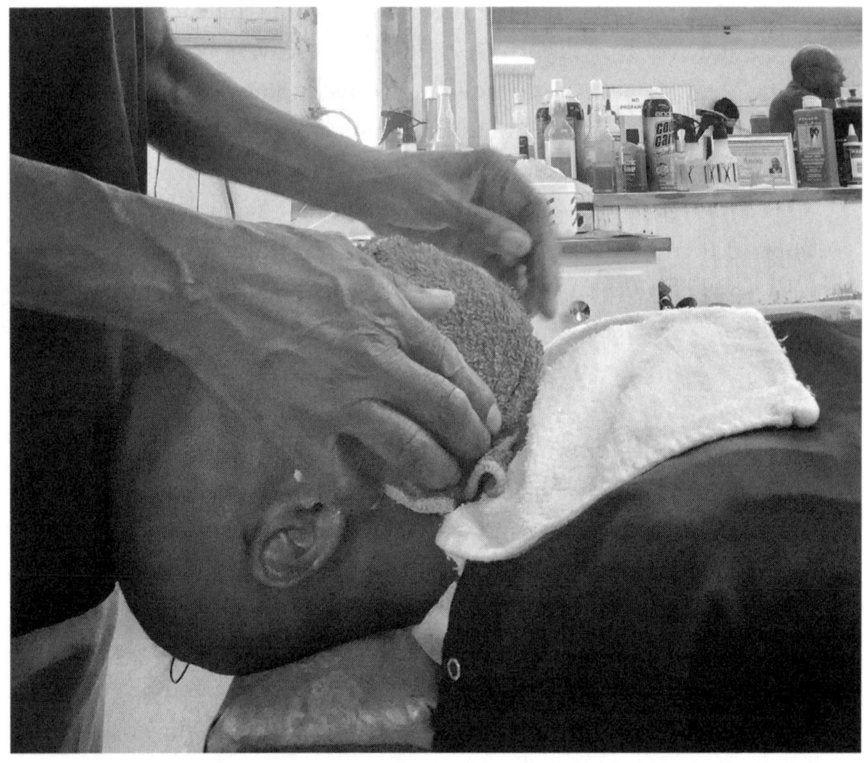

and the animals we raised," he says. "It just wasn't easy to make a living on a farm that small. Dad had to sell the farm but we never went hungry."

The family moved straight to this cowboy hicktown from Louisiana in 1951, after two of his brothers, both military men, had relocated here in the 40s. (Even before that, his tuberculosis-suffering aunt had moved here for her health.)

He and his brothers sang, having grown up immersed in gospel music and spirituals. They formed a vocal gospel group called The Silver Wings when Hunter was still knee high. Old group recordings reveal a persuasive, non-secular sound built on complex harmonies that'd do The Temptations proud. The brothers never released a record but they performed in Tucson churches and schools in the 50s, and later.

Hunter's dad was a minister too and pastored his own church in Nogales, Arizona, and later, the Morning Star Missionary Baptist Church in Tucson (where Hunter is a deacon and sings in the choir.)

Hunter graduated from Tucson High in '55. After a year-long run in the Marine Reserves, he joined the Air Force, staying about four years. (He tells funny stories of setting up a barber shop in a supply room at South Carolina's Shaw Air Force Base in the late 50s.) American Airlines hired him next, as a baggage handler, then ticket agent, and he lasted 28 years (retired in '87). In that time with the airline, he married twice, raised eight children, and opened his Hunter's Barber Shop. He can't remember the exact date, but "sometime in the 1960s." He'd opened a barbeque joint (using old family recipes) alongside the barbershop, but it soon shuttered. Two other jobs proved too much.

Hunter's hands soothe and Clowser's eyelids get heavy. He returns the clipper to its holster, one of a half-dozen neatly arranged and hanging from the counter, and chooses a slightly smaller one. He slips in a fresh blade, fires it up, and ambidextrously alternates hands, going for the sideburns and a trim of the sturdy hairline. Minutes later he reaches for a spray bottle of mystery elixir, and mists Clowser's hair while working his fingers into the scalp. Then he lifts an air hose and blows trimmings from Clowser's head, neck and throat.

Between clients Hunter produces a weathered obituary showing his grandmother's sister died in 1972. She was 127 years old. Yes, 127 years old. Many in Hunter's family lived long: His grandfather died at 112, two of his uncles lived to 108 and 109. His dad made it to 98.

He talks about losing a son. He'd rather not revisit the circumstances but says his boy died in the mid-90s and was 30 years old. He thinks of his son every day.

Hunter peppers sentences with half-invisible truths, turns of hushed insights born of wisdom earned from aging with certain grace, understanding there is no perfunctory order to things. He brackets subjects like "racism" and "loss" and "murder" in terms of acceptance or forgiveness.

"It's the only way the world can work," he says.

Hunter sings and hums as he works to songs streaming through the shop's little stereo speakers. New-country Toby Keith or old soul Bill Withers or a traditional gospel number performed by Hezekiah Walker. Doesn't matter. He knows the words.

How long does Hunter see himself running the shop?

He scrunches his face, surprises with a room-owning guffaw, and responds vaguely with, "Oh... a few more years or so." Or more.

Cameron Purdie, 40-ish, has been a Hunter customer since he was a teen. He settles into the chair and Hunter shakes open the barber cape and fastens it at the back of Purdie's neck. No words are spoken. No need. The barber knows Purdie's needs, and he's soon humming quietly to Al Green while applying white shaving cream to a side of Purdie's buzzed head. The afternoon is coming down, the long melancholy shadows on Stone Avenue, and everything that's important is happening right now, right here inside Hunter's Barber Shop.

October 1, 2015

FLYING UP OLD SPANISH TRAIL

Caution Somemore looks like a kid but says he turns 29 in October. He wears glasses and an unzipped hoodie and has perfect skin and close-cropped hair and he smiles sort of. He doesn't have that shame or foreignness that makes him look away when he talks, which surprises me a little given the circumstances. His sign reads "Homeless" and it twirls side over side and I wonder how he does that because I've seen people in disturbing Statue of Liberty costumes on major thoroughfares at tax time spinning signs the same way and I'd love to run them over despite knowing how cruel and absolutely insane that would be.

This night time scene has that slightly smarmy feel of street schtick so maybe he's dealing shit? Says he isn't selling, and anyway he really is homeless, it turns out.

We're standing on a desert corner at Old Spanish Trail and Camino Seco on Tucson's eastern outskirts, so it's weird to find a guy entreating donations, however gently, from passersby on a little road that bends up out of safe 70s suburbia and into the desert toward the heaven of Saguaro National Park. He waves hello to cars before they hit the intersection like a guy working a carwash because he knows people and understands how to earn coin – he's smart and savvy like that. He has to be. Or he starves. He flies his sign at night because drivers are less judgmental than in the daylight and he won't smoke because that's a donor turnoff. If he flies his sign in the rain folks have more sympathy and he earns more coin. (Holding a sign saying you're homeless or that you'll work for food or whatever is called flying.)

He discovered this corner without having to dispute another flyer for it like he did recently over at Broadway and Camino Seco, that lady who actually has a home but who, Caution says, claims homelessness "so she can earn her daily $60 and order things online."

And beneath this suburban topsoil, under black skies and mostly in silence, but with that dreamy smell of the desert, there's a peculiar underbelly of street hassle: He hears the most racist shit you can imagine, mostly from white kids. It's not lost on him that the yodels and threats have gotten worse lately too, in frequency and in tone, since Trump's rise, and all he can do is be entertained by it all.

In the months Caution's been flying, no one has stopped to take action on their words, and I'd wager he's one gangling black dude who could scrap with the best of them.

"Let 'em try," Caution says, pokerfaced with unblinking eyes. "They have no idea what they'd be dealing with."

His own anger has backed him into corners in life, fueled his paranoia. "I spend a lot of time meditating to quash my anger."

His two kids stay with his mother and he's not allowed to see them because CPS snatched them away, and their mother is down south somewhere. But she's coming back, Caution says, and then he'll get right with her and his kids but in this moment he's not up to talking about his children except to say with a WTF look that he's in lots of pain and missing them hard.

He's worked in kitchens, dishwasher mostly, steakhouses and the like, but then his anger gets in the way and the jobs go away. Over the four days of Memorial weekend, he earned $260 at Broadway and Wilmot, flying between two and six hours each day. A good take but there's hardly a wage worth the humiliation of flying where "even making the sign strips you of your pride."

What looks like a rental car rolls to stop at the intersection and the passenger window comes down. Caution steps over, retrieves a bill, and thanks the man. He steps back and talks paranoia, the kind that keeps him sleepless and walking all night. Sometimes he uses whatever internet access on temporary phones to stay occupied, for hours.

A woman strolls along in the dust. No one strolls out here at night. She's ravaged and gray-haired and moves with that hasty, limp-challenged street gait of anyone who's lived too long without walls. Without breaking stride, she hands Caution an unopened package of fudge cookies and continues into darkness toward 22nd Street. Cars pass her on Camino Seco and she seems a long way from the lives inside of them. Her presence leaves me feeling lonely.

"She lives around here," Caution says, and leaves it at that.

A half hour or so passes and three white dudes appear, moving toward us up Old Spanish Trail. They walked out from the desert dressed in beiges and blues and reds. They look like they're from good homes and maybe stoned or something else and they sort of drip of menace in that bored white suburban way, which is in my experience the worst kind of menace.

First thought: eminent beatdown.

Caution diffuses whatever real or imagined menace by telling them that I'm "from a newspaper" and writing shit down.

The one with short blond hair, Josh, says, "we've been on an adventure since noon." The taller skinny one says he's Caleb and he's all twitchy, scratching his face and arms. The third is walking around the desert, kind of circling.

The 23-year-old Josh can talk. Like anyone who talks too much, there's a part of his cognitive sense that seems to detach and so he becomes his own enthralled audience. He's interested that I'm writing stuff and begins to talk whiskey and Iowa and about a narrative essay he's been writing. I overhear Caleb telling Caution that his head got smashed in by his girlfriend last week. He says some other shit and Caution suddenly packs up his backpack and sign and milk crate and is ready to go to Taco Bell, "*now*."

We split and find Caution's friend C packing up his shopping cart – he's been flying for hours in front of the Taco Bell on Broadway near Camino Seco.

They're an odd couple, Caution and C. Caution digs Insane

Clown Posse and C likes blues, jazz, folk. C's a wrench-puller's son from Indiana and has four siblings. He drove an 18-wheeler for years, coast-to-coast. He looks older than his years, a gray swath of hair wraps the lower region of his bald head, and he mostly gums his food. C has no wife nor is he father to a family. Says one time he walked in on his wife fucking his best friend and that was that. He left.

C was the family outcast, but had dad's work ethic, "where you start something you finish it." He was very close to his mother and when she died, C spread her ashes around Tucson, in her favorite spots, and around where he flies. She'd lived in Tucson. She'd taken what little money she had after her husband died and left Indiana and rented a little apartment here. That's what brought C to Tucson. He was taking care of her.

The bipolar thing runs in his family and he has a bad temper and was told by doctors he should never work. They told him that and yet he can't get on disability here but spent seven years trying. He and Caution sleep in stairwells, behind industrial centers, between bushes, places cops won't hassle them. The two hooked up several months back, and sometimes C talks and Caution's eyes roll: he's heard C's yarns. The two aren't lovers but they watch each other's backs like lovers.

"You have to," C says. "It's dangerous out here by yourself. And I tell you, if you don't have anybody to talk to or socialize with you will go crazy."

"Where do you shower?"

They both laugh.

"Where do you poop?"

C shakes his head, and Caution, looking around the muted orange and chocolate interior of the Taco Bell, says, "places like this." C nods. "You buy food, you use the bathroom."

They get uncomfortable when asked to divulge their proper names. Caution Somemore's the name he uses on his Facebook page. C says that beyond the eat-shit humiliations he deals with daily, all of which add up in his psyche, his anonymity is all he has left, "if you can believe that." He figures that's why so many out here only go by nicknames.

C's been on the street solid for more than three years. Sometimes he writes "will work for food" on his sign and gets work, but only when it's not so hot out. His gift of subtle humor becomes obvious when he describes things that aren't normally funny, like fact-resistant lunacies of holocaust deniers, especially those he'd met over the years who've tried to denounce his uncle's World War II presence after he was one of the first Americans to see horrific insides of concentration camps.

They talk ins and outs of flying signs like anyone would around a crappy job water cooler: "Youth's an asset on the streets and Caution looks young," C says. "He does well, looking 16 or 17," and he laughs, "it makes me sick. But that's not to say that it's not racist out here. People think it's not as racist as it used to be, but in many ways it's worse. Some people ought to be dropped into a time machine and shipped back.

"Homelessness is a disease that's contagious," he continues. "If you let it get too far..."

"... You might never make it back," Caution says, finishing the thought.

"That's right," C adds. "Put in a job application when you're homeless. Right."

"And when people give you food you need to wash it," Caution says. "People spit in it."

"I opened a hamburger someone gave me and it had a used condom in it," C says.

It's hard to explain but Taco Bell's kind of wrenching inside and it doesn't help that some lady, I'd say an old lady, squinches her face into a dirty look at us, and makes a point to walk wide around us as she's heading out. These guys are outside all day everyday and they smell like how people smell when they're outside all day everyday and they look like that too, and this old white lady had to show her absolute disgust.

Ceej works the Taco Bell counter and she has a good eye on things, so she steps over and says to me, "these two are really nice ones. Sometimes the homeless aren't like that here. Be nice to them."

C takes lots of time to eat, and Caution's lost patience and is outside in the parking lot. C stops chewing, and says, randomly, as if airing a private thought, "Mom said I was a miracle baby. I wasn't given more than 48 hours. It's been 48 years."

September 22, 2016

DOG DAYS OF SUMMER

Slate-gray eyes skitter about the avenue like a desert bat obsessed on a streetlight. She's street-tough and trembling, searching out some joy. Then the final, clumsy realization that, between New Mexico, Seattle and now Arizona, from detox wards to university classrooms to the streets, she's seen it all and is living long on borrowed time. Panhandling Fourth Avenue, she begins to weep softly.

Shelly Johnston is without a home, pushing a baby stroller that contains things obsessively dear to her now, including her sleepy dog Moe and a Big Gulp cup filled of water and ice that hasn't yet melted. She's hoping to earn enough coin to eat on before the long trudge to her bleak refuge in the bushes somewhere behind the Tucson House, before cruel urchins ransack it and seize her spot on the Earth. She's not wearing shoes but her filthy feet and ankles look powerful, manly and athletic.

Then Gino appears, a pointy-shouldered street musician with equally flitting eyes and kickass hair, long and straight. He's raw and he hugs me often. He can talk: his stolen tambourine and a broken guitar and how a woman's breast had fallen off and had to be taped back on.

And a homeless black guy called Wildcat, stooped beneath a streetlight, behind blurs of sidewalk passersby. He's frightened, invisible there a little.

The trio form a community around Dorreen Martinez and her hotdog cart, a wheeled and silver-glow kiosk on a well-lit section along Fourth, between Eighth and Ninth Street. She's doling out gifts, including one mesquite-grilled dog with all the fixings that looks like an entire meal in Johnston's shaky

hands. She hooks up Gino too, gratis. They each offer up their love of Martinez before disappearing into the night. Wildcat is no fan of dogs, especially wrapped in bacon, despite the hunger.

He rubs his bloated belly. "I can't eat pork, man, and I'm eating for two." Martinez understands Wildcat's predilections, hands him a bottled water, and asks if he needs anything. He moves up the street shaking his head.

EDM thumps from open car windows, hip-hop blurts from outside speakers at O'Malley's Bar & Grill, and Tucson Streetcar brakes squeal. Another Friday night and Fourth Avenue teems with the well-groomed and floppy-fringed, the thick and the thin, boozy boomers and millennials, the El

Salvadorians, Asians, Jamaicans, Mexicans, Native Americans, and whites and so on. An impossible-to-dissect melting pot of ethnicities of the new Old Pueblo, at least how it's revealed down here on Fourth.

It's Martinez' street parade. Returning customers kick-start the same conversations that didn't end the last time they saw her – last week, last month. She remembers. She works and slaves over dogs too, in piquant, grease-flamed smoke. All sweat, haste and love. The smell of sizzling zeppelins and bacon brats and Polish sausages, the Sonoran-style dogs with beans and green sauce, just as her handmade menu advertises, ranging in price from a buck to $4. She's on her feet, talking, laughing, cooking, preparing. Hours tick by fairly quickly, fatigue slow-builds, and this is obvious.

Martinez is one of those who can't help but remind you of the little wonders of city nights: The straight-backed dignity of a wheelchair-bound woman rolling up the sidewalk among a pack of walkers, world-softening streetlight refracting from smudged windshields and storefronts, the lovely train whistle that forever adds a sense of melancholy to this scene.

A tall bearded guy with a strange toothy grin collects Diet Coke cans from Martinez' trash. She recognizes him. She sets down her tongs, steps from behind the little grill, which throbs of reddening mesquite, to stand beside him on the sidewalk. She points up to the rounded moon, marvels at its color and shape. The can collector nods. He's just collected another, greater, thing.

She returns to the grill, kohl eyes squinting in the heat. She talks petroglyphs, beautiful ones outside Tucson, while serving customers. "Just when you think you know everything there is to know about Tucson," she says, "you see that..."

A motorcyclist slowed by traffic revs his beast hard, punctuating Martinez' comment. A graybeard in line caws, "Get a Harley. Pussy!" Folks cheer.

Minutes later, lubed-up gent Miguel Madrid orders four dogs. He's been a Martinez customer/fan for months. "She's the biggest money-maker down on Fourth at night because everyone gets *druuuunk*. This homegirl takes care of every*one*!"

Her tolerance of drunks is admirable, nothing petty at all.

Madrid continues firing loud hyperbole at Martinez, same thing over and over. ("This homegirl takes care of every*one*!") Catches himself, is outwardly embarrassed, and adds sheepishly, "I had a bottle of Jack, you *know* me."

Then his credit card is declined: "That just fucked me up *for real*!"

She lets him off: "Pay me next time."

Andy Isham, a long-standing employee at nearby Moon Smoke Shop, calls Martinez a Tucson tradition, an entrepreneurial success story. "And you know," he says, "there's not many of them left."

Every night but Mondays, Martinez hitches her food cart to her red Jeep, arrives at the same spot at 10 p.m. and sets up. It's streamlined and she's efficient: She warms buns on a propane-heated steam table filled with hot water, where she keeps accoutrements, beans and grilled dogs hot. Paper plates and things are boxed within her reach, and bottled water and pop fill a camping cooler. A bucket of mesquite wood for the fire sits beneath the condiments table.

After bars close and the street clears she packs it up (and cleans her area of the street). She's usually home by four a.m. Dreadfully slow nights have her home earlier. And it's not always close to effortless.

★ ★ ★

In leather booties, a black skirt and white top, the Tucson-raised Martinez resembles a pretty Tuesday Weld in later roles. She married at 21 and stayed that way 25 years, divorced fairly recently. Says marriage often wasn't even close to the best of times and relates generalized customer comments to simplify: "They would joke and laugh about how grumpy he was."

Martinez and her then-husband purchased this very cart with a tax refund 22 years ago. Taught herself the food-cart ropes and has been stationed on Fourth for those 22 years. "I'm not really crazy about changing," she laughs. "That's not to say it's been so easy. We've had to go to the city council and plead the changes in city ordinances that would've made it extremely difficult to stay in business.

"And the health codes are such that no one should ever think twice about eating off a food cart."

Martinez won't reveal an average nightly take but it's good enough. Her Jeep is paid off, and she can live comfortably in an eastside house. Her personal philosophy: "I'm working as hard as I can, the universe makes sure I have all that I need. If you sit and pay attention in the desert you see so much. There's so much there. Watch a bird, how they get water and sustenance, and you keep watching and you see how the desert takes care of them; they get the fruit of the saguaros and prickly pear... It's magic."

Philosophy of experience honed from observation and motherhood, homeschooling and suffering.

Martinez had four kids in those food-cart years (she worked while pregnant or with one strapped to her body), adding to the couple's total of nine (yes, nine). She raised nine children, worked home care for elderly folk, all while running a food cart and overseeing lots of homeschooling for their children?

Yes. Once the food cart showed financial stability, Martinez retired from elderly folk care. "I learned so much from them but there was so much dying."

Too much death.

★ ★ ★

A knife pierces a heart on Martinez' wrist. There's an angel on her right shoulder. Tattooed salve for the void her oldest daughter left when she died in a 2009 car accident. The emotional encumbrance of Tess' death comes in abstracts, or in stories of her life, or how it impacted her other children. Martinez nearly laughs about how her daughter had to overcome a lot. (Tess studied to become a writer and journalist, and was a contributor to, among other publications, the *Tucson Weekly*.)

A few years ago, another of her children was nearly killed when hit by a car while riding a bike. "I don't think the universe is going to take two of my children," Martinez says. "That's how the world is, that's how my world is." She wraps a dog in a napkin, hands it off. Says, "there's lots of love."

Four sons and one daughter have helped mom with the cart through the years. One son is now an attorney in Indiana. Another is stationed in Korea, military. The other children live in Tucson. She's a grandmother now, too.

It's been decades out here on the avenue. It retains the familiar, an aesthetic (if not emotional) sense of older Tucson. Martinez gazes down the street. Except the one time someone ran off with her tip jar, she's never felt threatened here. "This is the last spot that hasn't changed," she says. And Martinez could be operating a larger food truck. There's been opportunities to open a restaurant. No thank you. She wants to stand next to the person, "ask them how their day was."

★ ★ ★

"Wieners!"

Some guy in a purple striped shirt weaves in place, shouting. Drunk-dude menace, thinks he's funny. He almost is.

"Wieners! How do you want to garnish your wiener?"

He turns to Martinez. Chirps, "Hot dogs! This is just a regular *hotdog stand*!"

She retorts: "No, this is an *irregular* hotdog stand."

He grins, steps back and shouts, "a regular hotdog stand!"

He spots Wildcat, who'd vanished earlier but is now sitting there under the streetlight again. Drunk guy steps over and looks down at him pityingly, tongue lingering slightly out of his mouth. I brace for Trump-inspired hate to burp from the drunk's mouth. But wait.

Wildcat looks at the guy, goes, "You ashamed to talk to me 'cause I'm a Wildcat?"

"You think I'm ashamed to talk with you because you're black?" Drunk guy says.

Wildcat turns away.

"Let's go," the drunk says. "I'm gonna take you somewhere nice so you can sit down and have a proper meal."

Wildcat looks up, shocked. "Me?"

"Let's go to Lindy's," the drunk says. "Best burgers in Tucson."

Wildcat stands and the two disappear into the Friday night humanity, alive on Fourth.

The night winds down. Martinez garnishes and dresses more dogs, exchanging them for cash or plastic. Elle King's "Ex's & Oh's" rises from her portable player perched on the shelf next to the mustard, and she sings along softly, swinging her hips and shoulders. Lighted faces pass, noses to phones. They're missing the present tense, the life and little exaltations revolving all around them. But it's like they have radar, their last-second sidesteps to avoid folks in the hotdog line.

July 28, 2016

COPS AND TWEAKERS

He once watched a guy blow his face and the top of his head off with a large-caliber gun. The gory suicide isn't necessarily what shocked him. It was how the guy survived for a short time afterwards mangled like that, necessary pieces of him gone forever.

So tonight is nothing to Tucson cop David Lewis, this father and husband, college grad and ex-skateboarder. Hell, he nearly died once, on the job, more than a decade ago, dragged 150 feet beneath a car, the left side of his face shredded off, eye out of its socket. He's had to fight for normalcy after that –

still does – and he nearly lost it all.

It's around midnight when we arrive on a usually dark stretch of Campbell Avenue near Ft. Lowell Road lit up by pulsing yellows, oranges and reds. A guy attempted suicide by car. He's pinned beneath a Honda, pants bloody, his legs and boots protrude slightly from underneath. His shirt's snarled around a rear tire. It takes a minute for this particular brutality to come into focus because this could be death, and that kind of shock is always delayed by a few seconds, or minutes, or longer.

The Honda's driver stands on the side of the road shattered and trembly because she ran over this man, and Jesus how will she get to sleep tonight? I squat closer and see behind the car's front tire a distended belly and hairy chest and shredded skin crushed by an engine block. There's not much blood but an awful secretion foams from his mouth, and a pool of vomit has formed under his head and beard. His right arm is stretched out in the form of somebody who's desperately reaching out for something, like a cigarette, or god. The smell of booze mixes with exhaust from idling fire trucks and ambulances and cop cars, and I'm probably 10 feet away from him.

I wonder in that moment, as he groans and slightly squirms in agony, if it's possible that he could only be dreaming, or if he's aware that this world around him has suddenly stopped and all its eyes are on him? I wonder if he has a mother or daughter, a brother or wife, and if they'd ever consoled him? Maybe he thinks the paramedics saying calming things to him are angels?

These florescent-vested paramedics and cops work quickly, employing the kind of orderly precision that would take any of them far in any career of their choosing – this guy could be dying but that's just not going to happen on their damn watch.

Cops find it hard to believe the guy is still breathing, and say he probably wouldn't be if not for the Hispanic kid witness who quickly procured a carjack and raised the Honda enough so that the guy might survive.

As he's placed carefully on a stretcher and lifted into the ambulance, Lewis agrees that if the man were sober he'd likely be dead. (One good thing about getting run over by a car when you're drunk is you bend like a ragdoll.) At first, I think Lewis is mocking the guy's horrific circumstance, but soon I understand that he's making light of something bigger. He's making light of the absurdity of the insanity of having to work every day with so much torment and sadness, the very kind that finds a woman driving innocently down Campbell Avenue suddenly part of another's insane suicide plot.

The tone helps Lewis stay detached, saves him and other cops from becoming crippled by the misery of others. It's how he can still be a dad and a husband, and a guy who can relax enough in his spare time to train dogs and play guitar. Still, even that, he says, is difficult. The work, "wreaks havoc on your family."

We climb into Lewis' tricked-out 2016 Chevrolet Tahoe patrol SUV and follow the ambulance to the University Medical Center, lights flashing. Disturbed's "Down With the Sickness" plays softly in the cab. It's strange to think cops listen to music when they work.

★ ★ ★

The 43-year-old, Tennessee-born Lewis swears his threshold for trauma is high. Got it from his old man, a tough, 41-year John Deere mechanic who died not long ago at 65. Lewis basically grew up in the neighborhood behind his police precinct, around Jacobs Park.

After high school he worked eight years as a prison guard (including death row at the Arizona State Prison in Florence) while attending college. He met his wife Cimmon at UA and they've been married 18 years. She now works as a probation supervisor at Pima County Juvenile Court. ("She understands my work," he says.) Lewis degreed in political science instead of becoming a lawyer. But once he did a ride-along with Cimmon's cop cousin he "got the bug to be a cop." That was that.

The Operations Division West police substation is hardly *NYPD Blue*; it's all mod cons, a big glass and steel structure, spacious – imposing but airy with hard-angles, muscular and patriarchal. Like a modern church in suburban Omaha. It houses around 11 uniformed squads of about 10 officers each, and receives 1,200 to 1,300 calls a day. Tucson's high crime.

Much of Lewis' job is paperwork (85 percent he reckons) and there's even a kind of writing lab inside the station with a number of computers. A cop's reporting needs to be accurate, accountable and detailed, to hold up in court, for one thing. Lewis edits reports of others too because he's an LPO (lead police officer), which is a sort of intermediary between a sergeant and a 10-man squad.

The substation fits Lewis' personal code, a cop's code, a militaristic way of orderliness and conduct and cleanliness – from his perfectly pressed uniform and strict tactical training to officer protocols, and there's a million to memorize. Even this night, a ride-along with him in his cop SUV, he's acutely aware that something's always required of him – from overseeing trainees to quelling bickering addicts. Even simple street observations reveal senses working in overdrive; he's many feet away interviewing a witness yet overhears word-for-word a conversation I have with another officer. Driving through neighborhoods he detects slights in the dark that I don't and points them out – the faintest whiffs of weed, a possible stolen car, a couple arguing deep in the dark. And he knows he terrifies pretty much any driver he's behind, just by his presence. "If they only knew that my mind was doing 10 other things," he laughs. The code offers salvation too: Some of Lewis' patrol work deals in literal filth – the feces – and maggot-riddled existences of folks he comforts or confronts.

He knows cops scare people. I tell Lewis I've had horrible experiences with cops over the years. Mostly entitled white cops in Phoenix using undue force for no reason. I've had my head slammed down on hoods of cop cars, found myself handcuffed and searched more than once after just riding my bike at night from Circle K with my beer in my barrio hood, where I happened to be one of four white people living. Been picked on by cops elsewhere too, in Detroit and Texas and Iowa… Maybe I looked like a drug addict and that made me an easy target for lazy cops. That's nothing compared to what myriad others suffer.

U.S. cops have killed 800 hundred people so far this year. And the clash between the violence-baiting law and oil-pipeline protesters and Native Americans in North Dakota is inhumane.

There's been a spike in murders of cops, too.

Talking police brutality, the articulate Lewis chooses words carefully. Assholes populate every profession, he points out. I say it seems like a bigger group of them come together around guns. He nods. He's been hassled by cops, too. On down time, riding his motorcycle with all his tats, pulled over. He's seen it. He knows. Look, he tells me, if there's anyone around his precinct who's not straight up, "I myself will set him straight. It's just not tolerated here. I started in 2000 and it's always been like that. Who's using force and how much is all tracked now," he adds. "Big brother is all around."

This PR spin horseshit?

"It's not PR horseshit," he says. "We get thanked everyday here for doing our jobs. That hatred toward cops just isn't happening in Tucson."

The night before we meet, one of his own was shot, a bullet grazed his head. But still. Lewis shakes his head. The police in Tucson are taught well, he says, better than in many rural areas and cities. It takes a year and half of training, from the police academy through field training and a probation period, to be a cop here. He trains still, all the time, whatever comes up, "human trafficking, terrorism, narcotics, you name it. People don't realize that you just don't take a test and become a cop."

This cop has never shot anyone with a bullet. He's never killed anyone. He has used less lethal ways of apprehension and self-defense, such as pepper ball shots and blasts of beanbag rounds from a shotgun. He knows what that feels like too; it's part of their training to be shot by such.

But Lewis many times figured he was a goner. Like that time in October 2004 when he joined a miles-long car chase through Tucson. Cops and a police helicopter chased two burglary suspects in a Dodge Dynasty. The Dodge blew through lights hitting 100 miles an hour at 11 p.m. on Tucson streets with their headlights off. Anthony Stringer wasn't stopping for cops and he had guns in his car.

"Back then we didn't have road spikes and we weren't trained to use the pit maneuver, where you actually hit the back of the car," Lewis says. "And the pursuit lasted a total of 55 minutes, went all the way up to West Cortaro and Camino de Cerro, at a trailhead with a parking lot. The helicopter was telling us it was a dead-end and to be prepared."

The Dodge flew into the dead-end, and its passenger leapt out.

"I pull in and stop, put my car in park and as I get out of the car to chase after him I see headlights."

The Dodge was heading straight at him.

Lewis talks mechanics of the accident in startling detail, details only hinted at in court documents. The Dodge driver was trying to kill him and he hit Lewis' car head on, lifting it off the ground. The Dodge "hooked my foot and dragged me 150 feet on pavement." At one point the Dodge slammed into a pole as Lewis was still attached, but behind the car.

"He was trying to put it in reverse to run me over," Lewis says. "I got up and pulled my gun and screamed at him to get out of the car. He did. I handcuffed him."

Another pursuit car arrived. The cop looked at Lewis' bloody face and knew something was horribly wrong. His eyeball had popped out and his nose was filleted into his sinus cavity. Pieces of his skull were gone. He had brain trauma. Airlifted to University Medical Center, Lewis stayed bedridden for weeks.

Photos of his face from over several years, progress of surgeries, frighten. It's a painful, recurring nightmare. He says the entire left side of his head is "basically prosthetic," fitted with 15 titanium pieces. He's still plagued by headaches.

So far he's endured 18 reconstructive surgeries, nearly losing his left eye numerous times in the processes. He can't blink so that eye tears up, which means it's prone to problem-causing bacteria. Some surgeries failed because skin grafts died. (Skin grafts are necessary to maintain his eyelid and areas around his eye, and because scar tissue tightens and shrinks, he undergoes operations at least once a year. He will for life.)

"I had surgeries in Tucson that did not go well," Lewis says. It took a world-renowned specialist based in Scottsdale, Ariz. to save his eye. "Because of him I'm back at work."

Doctors lifted skin or cartilage from Lewis' neck and arm, and from his ears. His hearing suffers because his ears are now pinned back, slightly misshapen and smaller.

His family suffered too. The worst part, Lewis says, came after. He was out a year as a patrol officer, seeing only light duty between surgeries. Long recovery stretches fueled depression, frustrations and anger. His marriage about ended. He got hooked on painkillers like Percocet. He began self-medicating with booze to blot out the disfigurement, the physical and emotional pain, the life. His dad was an alcoholic and his only sibling has struggled with addiction for years so Lewis was aware he was on slippery ground. Then his job tried to push him into retirement.

Why didn't he retire?

He laughs.

"Everybody asks me that. I worked my butt off to get this job, I was two years in. I wound up fighting to keep my job."

The Tucson Police Department awarded Lewis the Medal of Valor and the Scarlet Shield Medal for still taking down the bad guy after suffering so. He received a commendation for his actual court testimony. Support letters arrived from around the world.

★ ★ ★

We drive around the Grant Road and Oracle area, neighborhoods filled with low houses and trailer courts, bare-bulb lit porches, roaming dogs. Folks scatter as the Tahoe moves through, or wave with clinched teeth, forced smiles. The mix of classes and people living here, the college students, the refugees, the meth and heroin. Lewis patrols it old-school, talks of serving its people and a greater good. If he's seen-it-all jaded, he keeps it hidden.

In a moment we're stopped. A couple brawling on Stone Avenue, in darkness between Speedway and Drachman. They look lost and broken and feral. Lewis steps between them, nearly takes a few punches. According to the mounted laptop inside the Tahoe, the man's lengthy arrest record reads like a character's background in a modern tragedy, from car theft to meth sales. Lewis convinces the guy to head home. He drives the woman, who's been crying, to a safe place nearby.

Minutes later he's in front of a Circle K dealing down a shirtless dude in shin-length sweats and a menacing face and his pole-thin underage girlfriend. A beer heist gone south. The K clerk is there too. Soon they're all laughing, late-night surreal under fluorescent lights, and beer banner blues. In less than 30 minutes, Lewis defuses two ugly scenarios.

He hops back into the Tahoe and talks at length about his teenage kids, a straight-A student daughter and a son who's looking toward a possible career in computer engineering, "if he can get his grades up." He talks therapy too, not the physical but the emotional. How it helped him navigate the surgeries, the marital problems and the near-death experience.

★ ★ ★

We're waiting for life or death word from Sharon the charge nurse.

Doctors, med students and nurses move quickly, attaching tubes and medical apparatus to the guy who attempted suicide, and they're talking with him, too. His name is Wayne and he's laid out on the bed inside the brightly lit University Medical Center emergency area. He's conscious sort of and breathing, still smelling of booze. His voice sounds like a busted fan and he's scared. A chaplain hangs around.

Lewis paces the area waiting to hear whether Wayne will live or die. The cops have closed off that section of Campbell, because should Wayne die a criminal investigation will ensue and the street will stay closed. Should he live, Lewis will radio the news and the street will clear.

A long while passes. The doctors and students finished testing Wayne and have moved on to other patients, other bodies. You can hear Wayne breathing. That dark part of Campbell near Ft. Lowell remains closed.

"I'm not thinking that Wayne is somebody's dad or son," Lewis says. "I'm processing in my head all these things that have to be done for me to do my job. But, man, I'm just like anybody else."

Nurse Sharon steps over. "Yeah," she says. "You can't let it get to you." She shrugs. "But it does. Usually when I'm home drinking a beer in the shower."

She looks over at Wayne on that bed connected to all those tubes and things. "He'll have to try suicide another day," she says flatly.

Lewis phones his sergeant and Campbell Avenue clears.

Pulling out from the hospital parking lot, Pearl Jam's "Daughter," a song from the POV of a girl who's molested, plays in the cab. Lewis says, "You can't say that I've seen it all, or that any cop has seen it all, because the very next day something will top it."

November 3, 2016

FEAST OF SNAKE

There's this guy standing in line at Circle K with a live snake around his neck. The last time I saw a guy wearing a snake around his neck I was scoring meth off him at an L-shaped, weekly-rates motel in west Phoenix, where dogs barked and babies cried, where the only cheer was the year-round Christmas lights that dropped between a nail in the roof's fascia to a nail driven into a sad palm tree.

Another lifetime ago.

Now I occasionally run into gentlemen in Tucson (well, twice since summer) sporting fangs-bared snakes creeping up their necks. Both times walking 22nd Street near Walmart. Each guy glowered, drunk on menace, hustle and too much sun. But those snakes were only tats, and I'm no expert on tattoo iconography, but I'm pretty sure they figured the etchings biblical. Evil, sin...

They had had nothing on this guy at Circle K, off Glenn on Tucson Boulevard. If you're really a badass, wrap a fence-post thick scaly reptile around your neck, one that stretches out to six feet. A snake whose head bobs in unpredictable, soundless ways, shows fangs. A snake who just as easily could strangle you. Like this guy's.

And who strolls into a K with a snake wrapped 'round his throat?

This gangling gent with a Yosemite Sam mustache is no hustler and he's not trying to scare anyone. Claims no faith-healer proficiencies. He's Sherman Ramsey, a dude struggling to get by like the rest of us. He developed a fondness for reptiles young, perhaps as a way to tolerate a brutal childhood. The snake, christened Satan's Little Helper, works a visual metaphor too, one might say.

A few days later I'm in his apartment, a well-organized two-bedroom duplex off Glenn, a short walk from the Circle K. It's sparsely decorated, the essentials of anyone enduring burdens of modern economics. The living room walls: a signed Insane Clown Posse promo pic, a mirrored Becks beer sign, and framed Doors album covers greased with fingerprints with snaps of his four children slipped into the frame. A TV connects to a PlayStation, and there's a couch. He smokes cigarettes outside.

The snake's a non-venomous Dumeril's boa. In its living-room aquarium, Satan's alive in transverse bands and mushroom patterns of brown and gray. Ramsey feeds Satan rats. There's an empty aquarium to house his other snake, no longer here. Ramsey had to sell him off, $40 bucks. He paid $140.

In a Guinness Beer T-shirt and Levi's, and sitting on his sofa, Ramsey looks younger than his 38 years, but his steely dark eyes show lived-in days, bloodshot; equal parts desperation and kindness. He's guarded – secrecy suffused with an inherent suspicion of others – so his personal narrative takes time to unfurl.

After graduating from Tucson's Cholla high school, Ramsey apprenticed to become an electrician. When the economy nosedived, his days of sweet take-home pay – a steady job of seven years – ended. Put him on another collision course with life, which included a pair of DUIs.

Life's rarely in step with your heart but Ramsey's on fairly solid footing for now. ("I stopped doing all the crazy stuff.") He scrapes by on unemployment and help from his dad and uncles. It's harder and harder in his trade to find work. He lost his last job in October.

He's hopeful; there's his electrician's job interview tomorrow. Hopeful for his kids, his life, his loneliness. Treading water can eat a man alive.

He has four children by two mothers, all with their mothers and grandparents, for now.

It's never easy to erase brutal tender years, the ingrained stuff that defines. Ramsey knows. He stares at the carpeted floor at his feet and sighs in a mild way. His own childhood is stuff of terror and loss and displacement and homelessness. Says, "you'd be surprised what a kid can pick up on."

"I tasted weed for the first time when I was five. I could

show you how to cook up heroin when I was six because I'd seen it so much."

Phoenix-born, Ramsey never knew his real dad. Mom traded sex for drugs. "She was a biker whore to feed her habit," he says. "I saw a lot of guys coming and going." Grandma abused him too, bad, out in San Bernardino.

One night his mother and her boyfriend were arguing. The pissed-off boyfriend, likely "high on something," walked the 5-year-old Ramsey out to the railroad tracks near their place in Phoenix.

(As Ramsey relates the story, Sophie, his strangely beautiful pit bull-Chihuahua mix, antagonizes Junior, a larger dog confined to the patio, the other side of a sliding glass door.)

The two waited at the tracks. As the roaring train approached, the boyfriend went and put himself on the rails. The trusting little boy watched the man get decapitated. A suicide barely reported in the news.

Mom couldn't care for her boy. So she dumped him with friends in Tucson. When he showed up at school with a black eye, the cops intervened and placed the 6-year-old in Casa de los Niños, a local home for abused kids, which jettisoned him into the foster care system.

"I guess I came from a hard background," he says. "I block most of it out of my mind." He laughs. "My mom taught me well, I could steal a loaf of bread and a gallon of milk without anybody noticing me."

Change brought some gratitude, Ramsey says. His foster parent, Robert Ramsey, a now-retired schoolteacher and pianist at a local Baptist church, adopted the boy after one year, sparing him a life in and out of foster-home hell.

And Ramsey's not holding his childhood against himself

or anyone. "I never did heroin or any of that because I saw what it did to my mother. I could be fucked up on some sort of drugs." He shakes his head. "If you're going to have kids, don't be drug-addicted."

He turned 21 and reunited with his mom. The tear-filled reunion inspired his move back to Phoenix. He wanted to be with her.

"I hadn't seen her since I was six," Ramsey says. "I wondered about her every night. And for a long time I blamed her for everything. But by the time I saw her again I didn't hold any resentment. I thanked her. Who knows where I would've been, or if I would've been here at all if she hadn't given me up?"

But Ramsey didn't jive with mom's current boyfriend and left. He returned to Tucson, back to electrician's work. His mother died several years ago under bizarre circumstances involving a head injury. The boyfriend vanished, and Ramsey and his uncles are calling it murder. No charges were filed.

★ ★ ★

Ramsey lifts Satan's Little Helper out of its tank and drapes him tenderly around his neck. As Satan snugs into place, Ramsey says, "He's got the death grip. I could overpower him if he ever tried to strangle me."

His talking voice is softer now, but higher in pitch because Satan's got his throat. He strolls outside and down the block to the Circle K. Everyone stares, the two kids on bikes, faces in cars. Ramsey seems unaware how he can frighten passersby, and insists he's not trying to. Satan goes where he goes, like a personal history. He's his companion. "I took him on the bus once and the driver got all mad," he says. "He made me get off."

A corpulent dude inside the Circle K sports a "Trump that Bitch" button on his T-shirt and too-small plastic mirror shades. He's not pleased at the sight of Ramsey and Satan, so he huffs with righteous indignation as he pays the cashier for his smokes and twelver. He exhales extra loud, pushing hard out through the glass doors, into the evening.

Debbie's a regular here, her long gray hair, her little Chihuahua on a leash. Satan's incongruity, his shimmer under fluorescent lights, stops her. She marvels at his beauty, quizzes Ramsey about him. Her dog wears a sweater, speeds in circles at her feet, and growls.

Ramsey, his voice still pitched higher from Satan's grip, politely answers Debbie's questions. She reaches out a finger, connects timidly with Satan's head. "Just so beautiful," she says.

March 10, 2016

KEEP THE MOTOR RUNNING

Wednesday Night

It's nearly 10 p.m. at Tucson's Independent Distillery, off Arizona Avenue, an alley that not so long ago smelled of piss and filthy Dumpsters. It's clean now, and lighted and alive with soused university students and flawlessly trimmed beards. Al Foul is inside perched on a stool, performing his one-man-band – right foot commanding a kickdrum, the left thumping a homemade percussion box, his sapphire Silvertone guitar raging through a little Fender amp – to an audience of two. One of the two is a grinning French tourist here to see Foul, and he's shocked to discover an empty house.

A noisy gaggle with pricy haircuts and colorful cocktails fills a nearby table. They ignore Foul.

A big old drunk wielding a half pint of something dark, who looks straight out of downtown Tucson circa '79, and who'd be tossed out of this place if he'd set foot in it, leans in the chain-locked backdoor and slurs to Foul between songs: "Play some Dylan!"

Foul glances over his shoulder at the grizzled dude swaying to and fro, and, without skipping a beat, turns to the two fans paying attention, and grins, "Man, I keep this guy on my left shoulder everywhere I go."

Then he sucks from a double whiskey and Coke, reminds folks of his tip jar, and to tip the bartender, and articulately orates an introduction to the next song with all the seasoned hutzpah of a stand-up comic who's logged in north of 50,000 on-stage hours, as if this sleek cavernous saloon was packed to the gills:

"This song, ladies and gentlemen," he goes, "is a song about being in love with a peepshow girl. Yes, I was 19 years old, ladies and gentleman, and it was a long time ago. I fell in love with her at the peepshow up on Oracle Road. This song is a beautiful little love song called "Dropping Quarters for Jane.""

He launches the tune with gusto and verve, and you'd never guess he's played it a million times live. (The overlooked Texas Trash and the Trainwrecks covered it on their 2014 album *Gimme a Hand*.) The kickdrum oomphs and the percussion box clangs and an inescapable three-chord riff upholds Foul's heady treatise on loneliness, which is brilliantly juxtaposed inside a singsong country-punk context, echoing foot-tappers by nearly forgotten greats in song like Roger Miller and Hasil Adkins: "My search for love has turned into quite a pain/My lack of social skills it makes me so ashamed..."

There's a sadness that hums beneath the wit and hat-tip to another era, an inescapable kind of personal truth that resonates, and lasts. What shocks is that Foul isn't more popular.

Thursday

The following day Foul's dressed in the same thing he wore the night before: indigo shirt, black trousers, Indian head belt buckle and beat-up boots. Even at 44, Foul looks exactly like the guy I first wrote about back in 2000. The omnipresent grin, broken front teeth and forever slicked-back hair still suggest a hopelessly backdated 50s blue-collar man straight from a David Goodis novel.

"The men in my family looked exactly like me," he explains. "My dad, my grandfather..."

Tips
Thank

Foul's motoring up Interstate 10 toward Phoenix, behind the wheel of his silver and red RV, which he refinished himself. The beast, called a "Dolphin," which Toyota made for two years in the mid-80s, sports a four-cylinder motor that guarantees a top speed of about 55 MPH, on the flat. Colorful Mexican serapes cover windows, and Foul used wooden planks to handsomely reconstruct the camper door. Pots and things rattle about in the back. There's a tiny bathroom, and because Foul doesn't pay rent anywhere, he sleeps in the little loft above the cab. This is his world. Where he resides.

"I love my life," he says, lighting up another American Spirit. "I don't have the responsibilities of other men; I don't have parents getting sick with Alzheimer's, I don't have kids. I consider myself lucky."

He lives and breathes and drinks and eats the music. He's averaging three in-state gigs a week, and he lives on the profits, as he's done for years. Between the tip jar, merch/music sales and venue guarantees, he's not getting rich. In fact, he needs to save money to put new tires on the RV.

The man has proven to be a gifted songwriter and entertainer on albums such as *Keep the Motor Running*, *Spank That Ass* and *The One, The Only*, which have earned him followings in various places around the States and especially in France, where he's been touring annually for years. (His new, as-yet-untitled album drops later this year.) Tunes reveal a sort of autodidactic, street-ripened philosopher, just like old Goodis (the French called him "the poet of the losers"), and a master of deceptively simple, yet funny, song narratives that offer little redemption, filled with busted-luck yarns of four-time losers, jailhouse bikers, day drunks, speed freaks, souring marriages – all things, folks and follies he's discovered on his travels, imagined or true, or bestowed upon him by his father, or wreckage he's crawled from.

Foul (born Alan Lewis Curtis) comes from a long line of blue-collar men, the kind who fought in wars, who drank hard and lived hard. His old man worked the steel mills, and when they closed up he worked as a machinist and then took care of Foul's mother, a schoolteacher stricken with multiple sclerosis at 21.

"She went from a cane to a walker to a chair to a bed to the grave in 15 years," Foul says. "Man, I had a real fear of getting MS. They say it's not hereditary but my mother's mother had it too."

A fear of heart attacks to boot. They run in the family on his dad's side. His pop had his first one at 40, and the last one killed him at 63. ("Dad had a big gut; he ate Spam all the time.") A heart attack took his grandfather at 38.

Foul grew up in a hard, mostly Irish and Italian section in south Boston called Hyde Park. Racism rampant. His dad grew up a hard-ass "greaser" and a "rocker" who fought in the streets, "a true juvenile delinquent of the 50s, and an absolute terror when he was young because he didn't have a father. But a lot of kids didn't have fathers in the neighborhood; they lost them in the war."

The men on his dad's side of the family, old-school New England Protestants, disowned Foul's dad because he married a Polish woman.

Foul learned exactly how to react and not react by watching his father, and rebelling. Says dad was mean and brutal but had a big heart, a man disquieted by contradiction, feeling trapped and overwhelmed with a sick wife and three children.

"There was not a door or wall in the house that wasn't

kicked through," Foul says. "Inside the house was a cacophony of noise and arguments. My dad could verbally abuse his family like nobody. If you pissed him off he'd hit you with a belt. All the neighbors would sit outside drinking beer and laughing their asses off."

His "Archie Bunker type" dad happened to be a self-educated Malcolm X fan who read "a book a day." A gun collector too. They were "broke as church mouses" but dad always had money for new guns. His addiction.

"We never sat at a dinner table once," Foul adds. "Never once. Partly because my mother was sick. If you were tall enough to fix your food you did."

Christmas ended for good when Foul was 8 years old. "Dad scolded us, yelling 'you ungrateful pieces of shit, no more Christmases for you!' And he kept his word."

Yet Foul was close to his dad, describes long walks they'd take when he was a kid. And he credits the old man's record collection – which included Link Wray, Charlie Rich, Johnny Cash and others – for inspiring him. He learned from dad how to surmount crushing hopelessness by simply barreling through it.

"Before he died he respected me for getting out of Hyde Park and that I didn't become a local bum slinging coke at a local bar. When I finally did get out he missed me. We were close. We wrote letters to each other all the time. I'd write him and tell him things were shitty and I couldn't pay the rent and he'd write back and say 'You can always come home.' He'd give me advice, like, 'Al, whatever you do, don't you ever get married.'

"In a weird way," Foul continues, "I'm living the life that my father should've lived: I was going to be a rocker. I wasn't going to stay in the same place. I wasn't going to work a shit job."

Foul got his first guitar at 11, and later made his band debut with the Foul Mouthed Elves (a named coined by his dad), which is where he got his surname. "I'd like to go back to my real name. It's probably a little late for that now."

Early 80s punk, like the Dead Kennedys and Black Flag got him young, and by '85 he was hitting shows. At 15 he began staying away from home and left for good three years later. He'd sleep on benches in Manhattan or "sometimes I would go and sleep by the Charles River. It was the only one that didn't have fleas."

He met Tucson punks Texas Trash and Lenny Mental before he lived here, drifting around the northeast. In 1989 Foul and his then-girlfriend hitchhiked from Minneapolis, headed for San Francisco but instead landed in Tucson. By '91 he was playing music here and washing dishes at a Sizzler. ("I was employee of the month four times even though I was shitfaced off my ass every day.") He also learned to repair antique furniture and began making his own pieces. Did that for 10 years before playing music fulltime.

Thursday Night

Foul arrives at Rips Ales and Cocktails in central Phoenix as the sun drops. Bellies up to the bar for tallboy PBRs. Then he loads gear in, sets up, soundchecks, finishes a burrito and begins his set around 9:30.

"Ladies and gentlemen," he says on the mic. "I didn't have the pleasure of writing this next number. No, ladies and gentlemen, this was a big hit for Dave Dudley way back in 1963.

I think it'll be a big hit for me here tonight..." He kicks into "Six Days on the Road."

There's 25 Foul fans here tonight, and they're happy. On stage Foul's a brothel priest delivering a whorehouse sermon in song. Some know the words and mouth along. Fans send him shots of whiskey, one after the other, add bills to his tip jar. It's a pretty good night.

Foul completes the first of two sets and leaps from stage and lands on the dancefloor with legs and arms spread wide in victory stance. He holds like that. Then he pulls a comb from a rear pocket and pulls it through his hair. The crowd howls.

When the show ends he climbs into his RV, which stays parked in the Rips lot, and watches several WWII documentaries on his laptop, using the Wi-Fi from the club, before going to sleep.

Friday

Foul concedes a hangover on the return drive to Tucson. You'd never know. His conversation ranges World War II, spaghetti westerns, Link Wray, and his favorite NPR shows. He talks Trump douchbaggery, and derides anyone who thinks 1950s America – particularly the McCarthy era – was a great place to live.

"It was a horrible time in America. That's when my dad grew up."

He talks up Mammoth, Ariz., where he lived until a painful split with his longtime girlfriend more than a year ago. He still co-owns an old bar there he fixed up, and some property. He talks old neighbors: "They've had Harley Davidsons since they were teenagers, but they've never been anywhere.

Not even Flagstaff, Prescott or Bisbee. I'm not kidding. Just untraveled and ignorant motherfuckers. Their idea of travel is getting on their bikes and heading to Curves [strip bar] in Tucson.

"My whole attitude changed since I started going to Europe," Foul continues. "The travel changed me. I became more polite, for one thing. Now, the culture shock is more about coming back to America..."

He assumes a hillfolk drawl to show the thickness of one Yankee he met at Charles De Gaulle airport in Paris: "You got a ree-aal good sheriffff down there in Arizona."

His theories about why women are our teachers reveals his humanist thinking. How to live and eat right. How to see things. He figures he'd likely be dead if not for things he learned from women in his life.

Saturday night

There's no shortage of polka dot blouses or hairclip flowers or muttonchops and wallet chains. A sprawling crib up a winding driveway, like some cartel's Arizona hideaway. It's clean, sleek and high-ceilinged, with red velvet curtains, Buddha statuary, calavaras imagery, free booze and well-mannered dogs. Not an old alleyway in sight, and lights of Tucson sparkle in the distance. The stage, with its amp backline, colored lights and P.A., is in perpetual setup mode, thanks to homeowner/party-thrower Chris Stamos.

Tonight Foul's backed by guys who've played with him on and off for years: Lucas Moseley on snare drum, Naim Amor on guitar, Eric Eulogy on stand-up bass. The quartet pumps out a peerless hillbilly wallop of country rhythms and rockabilly slams, surf beats and monomaniacal freakouts. They defy the room's principles of velocity. (The nearest house is down the hill.)

Foul's face expands and contorts as he sings, his mouth and cheeks elastic wonders, and his head juts forward duck-like to accent croons and throat-shredder howls. He owns the songs, the millionaire's living room and the 30 crammed into it. It's that voice, which owes as much to yesteryear country star Marvin Rainwater and Scottish folkster Lonnie Donegan as it does to Jamaican crooner Ken Boothe. The life that Foul leads, his personal history, makes him compelling, draws others to him.

Later Foul's drunk, stoned, hilarious. And tireless, always tireless. The guy who says he "ain't in it for fame" but "he'd love to one day be a legend" could be the hardest working near-legend in the western states. I've never met another like him. Because Foul won't man the RV when he's drunk or stoned or both, I drop him off down on Fourth Avenue in Tucson to find a woman he's seeing. As he hops out I swear I can see that grizzled drunk, the Danny Trejo doppelganger who Foul joked about keeping on his shoulder. The drunk's walking up Fourth, swaying but determined, right at Foul.

April 7, 2016

LAST EXIT TO TUCSON

In the cold dark drizzle it's hard to tell the jagged edges between Earth and sky. Rain fills potholes. Yellowy light from the Triple T refracts across an acre of wet carless pavement over by the freeway. Out here lurking for menacing worlds or roadside cons or desert derelicts, but it's dead. Eerie windy black.

Out back, dozens of 18-wheelers with trailers holding 30,000 pounds or more are parked at right angles, lined in three quarter-mile length rows. Could be hulking tombstones but some just hum in idle. Warm cubed cabins with hearts beating inside, screens glowing on unshowered bodies stretched out on beds.

You'd think New Year's Eve, a night forever filled with primal sexual urges would be in full tilt, filled with false joys and grim buoyancies, truckers going out of their skin, hurting for comfort. Not a lot lizard in sight. Not a single distant howl.

Beyond these trucks to the south sits the independently owned trucker landmark, Triple T (Tucson Truck Terminal), on I-10 at South Craycroft on Tucson's far southeastern side. There's a Circle K and some chain-linked yards east of the trucks.

Inside Triple T is Omar's Hi-Way Chef Restaurant, a 24-hour heaven that tonight closes at 1 a.m., given the holiday. Its interior coffee-shop is a lovely anachronism of American nights. Trimmed in cerise and pinks and greens, it features a fetching horseshoe-shaped counter and an elaborate menu.

It too is dead. Almost.

A woman relates a story of how her friend dropped weight by only eating pizza ("can you believe that, and pepperoni *too*"). He sits across from her at this table, their food long eaten, listening hard.

There's another guy, late 60s, old Reno lounge handsome in a dark blue shirt and a killer gray pompadour. A true silver fox, aged in white Cadillacs. I peg him as a trucker blessed with a natural sartorial flare, but he has a woman in tow, and she doesn't appear too roadworthy, her hair is even more perfect, and she carries a purse. On his way out, he pays Kelley the cashier, works his lower teeth with a toothpick and carefully examines pie slices displayed behind glass – pies so good that this diner has received attention on national TV shows.

There's no hurry in their steps. The rare rain outside.

Kelley counts money, alone behind the cash register near the entrance where a million travelers have passed. She seems happy in the company of co-workers. I think maybe it's because her own children are grown and gone, or there's deeper or unspeakable sadness she's learned to dull with neighborly civility. Could be she's just damn happy.

When an employee whose shift ended departs saying "I'll see you next year!" it's sad in that beautiful way old diners are sad, full of stories and reminiscences, virtues of dead generations. Can't be replicated in new diners modeled on fake nostalgia. But it's exhilarating because it's easy to fall in love with strangers who don't look alike, who aren't trying to be anything.

Kelley's register opens and she swoops change from the drawer, counts it and drops it back in. The pair of older waitresses in matching green shirts chat softly with a bespectacled gentleman server wearing white kitchen overalls, and a dishwasher they call José, who moves in and out. Its ambience is a song much better than "Auld Lang Syne," or anything a media-anointed star or show could ever create at 11 p.m. on New Year's Eve.

Darin Jones orders takeout for himself and his wife, who's back sleeping in their truck. The 45-year-old is friendly and lucid despite the road-weary eyes. He's hauling onions from Lancaster, California to Miami in a flatbed, and the persistent rain presents challenges; the tarp that protects the produce from moisture requires constant adjustment.

This guy has been a pro driver for 16 years but is only recently independent – he doesn't haul for a specific company – so he doesn't exactly know what happens if he delivers a sour load, it's never happened. He owns his truck outright, has another back in Ohio. He's got some kids. It's never easy.

His loads come through brokers, who take a piece of his action – upwards of 30 percent – and he's responsible for his own insurance, truck upkeep, gas, tags, the whole bit. He's hoping once he and his wife drop the Miami load in two days, a broker will have arranged a new load to Ohio, otherwise they'll lose good money heading home.

But, he adds, they had a load to Oregon from Ohio and that took them to see a relative. "Sometimes it just works out that way."

I remind him it's nearly midnight on New Year's Eve. It doesn't register much. He collects his takeout, pays and heads out in the drizzle to his wife.

Big Bob and Irene Myers shuffle into Omar's and he announces to no one if his "belly don't fit, I ain't gonna sit." Not sure if that's self-awareness or bitchiness. Fleshy belly protrudes from under a blue Titan T-shirt, the breast pocket holds pens. He wears leather suspenders joined with Buffalo nickel heads, custom made.

Bob and his wife Irene drive for Titan Transfer. They're hauling a load back from California toward Tennessee, and they'll be there in a day and a half. They've put nearly 120,000 miles on their company truck in six months. They've been married going on 22 years.

They each squeeze into the spacious booth, and, as if sick of the sight of one another, bicker. Irene reads the menu out loud... "Sounds better than meatloaf!"

But they're not sick of the sight of one another. They live and drive and breathe each other, day in day out, in a truck, and at home in Silver City, Tennessee. They relate to each other in redundant rudeness only they understand, a lover's lingo. Yes, they finish each other's sentences – they finish each other's histories. Their thick dialect is rural Tennessee.

When asked if one would survive without the other they look straight into each other's eyes and laugh.

Gail the waitress with the gray braid down her back, walks the couple through the menu, like she remembers them.

She might; the couple have driven through here many times before.

"I'll have a root beer, too," Bob says. "Only beer I can drink."

Irene and Bob met on the road, sort of. She's a security guard, he's a truck driver. She explains Bob suffers arthritis from a horrible motorcycle accident years ago. "It was in the 80s, I went head-on into the back of a pickup stopped at a traffic light, going 60." He'll retire from trucking in September 2017. "I'm done with it."

They'll only work for a trucking company like Titan now. Owning your own truck, he says, is risky as hell and "it ain't worth it. You're responsible for everything." Now, if his truck breaks down, Titan fixes it. "You don't worry about insurance, tags, fuel. None of it."

Gail soon returns with the over-portioned meals, and the couple dig in. Bob has no teeth and gums his food. No need for dentures. Irene says the toothless thing is easy: "He can even eat *steak*!" Bob nods like he's blessed. "My mouth was all full of poisons and she made sure I got my teeth pulled." Sometimes a noodle drops from his mouth onto his shirt. Irene won't let the moment pass without derision. He's a good sport.

The clock hits midnight – it's 2017 – and Irene produces pictures of her Boston Terrier on her phone and launches into family histories. They're equally tragic and sad. How her sister died two years ago from cancer – her husband was bringing asbestos in daily from his worksites – and how she takes care of her 74-year-old mother and 28-year-old nephew because no one else in her family will, and she obviously loves them. She had a hysterectomy and the cancer is gone. Three and a half years ago she and Bob came off the road to find their doublewide home burned to cinders, everything they owned stolen or torched. The sheriff investigating the fire died mysteriously soon after.

"They got some places up there where a person might never be found," Bob says. Irene produces phone photos of the burned-down property and they shudder and chuckle, because that's all there is to do.

So they bought a house nearby and its neighboring property for $35k, and it'll be paid off with one final payment when they return home. They've been working every day except four days a month to earn the money to pay off the place. They can earn 2K in a good week. She produces a picture of a pretty little modular house with aluminum siding on acreage filled with forest. Hard to believe they got it so cheap.

"It's because it's Tennessee. Nobody can afford nothin' there," Bob says. He blames his county's economic disenfranchisement on Obama. He listens to Fox News when he drives. Gail, a server for the ages, overhears. She steps in and talks of her dogs. She has six. Her eyeshadow matches her watch and shirt.

It's nearly 2 a.m. and we're out in the lot. Everything is oversized, the trucks, the sky, the roads, the diner sign, the rainswept parking lot, the people. Bob gives a tour of the Myers' truck. It's a formidable 2017 Freightliner 18-wheeler, able to roll at high speeds a max gross load of 80,000 pounds. The driver's area is like an airline cockpit, with up-to-the-moment enhancements and systems to help prevent inelegant driving. Bob says it "ain't what it looks. It's pretty easy to drive." The back sleeper cab sports a double bed, a microwave and other such homey additions.

The Myers have a tough schedule, so he drives nights, Irene days. They kiss and she climbs into the sleeper to crash. And soon the 500-horsepower motor fires up and rumbles, and the monster rolls out and exits this remote desert lot, where rain always feels like an ambush. Bob and Irene turn and head east on the freeway, toward all those corporate truck stops that are nothing at all like the Triple T.

January 12, 2017

THE BIKE WHISPERER

Came to with a blurry finger in my eye. It lifted away, was attached to a hand that was attached to an arm that belonged to a guy with a big forehead wearing a white laboratory smock. Next to him was a chubby nurse with pretty bangs. She was holding two little paper cups, one contained water and the other pills, which she handed to me, and said, "Swallow." I sat up. My head thundered. One side of my body flared in pain like it'd been dragged over a giant cheese grater.

"You have a concussion, son," the man said. "We've cleaned and bandaged the abrasions on your body. You're banged up but you'll be fine."

I swallowed the pills and water and rested my head back down on the pillow. The previous hours returned:

My handmade, emerald-colored Gilmour hummed beneath me as we tore up a hilly road near the red cliffs outside of St. George, Utah. Sundry details included the stinging in my chest and legs, the crusting snot on a shoulder of my long-sleeved team jersey, the smell of pines and horse manure. I was in a breakaway group with older bike racers, well-trained, lithesome gents like future Olympic gold medalist Alexi Grewal, and the race winner on this particular day, surfer-blond national team guy Larry Shields. We motored turns in a "pace line," creating a slipstream, backs low and straight, aerodynamic. We had probably 30 seconds on the field and our lead was increasing. We crested a hill and began to sweep down a descent. My teenaged legs, powerful little pistons informed on thousands of training miles, controlled by my bursting heart, and an inner agony that controlled my nervous system,

told me that my body had its own mind and no way would it slow down. We were less than 5 miles from the finish of the race, which started 50 miles ago.

I was a boy among men in this sport of suffering, bicycle racing my religion, my bone marrow and blood. Figured I'd be a top Euro pro, so did Andy Gilmour, the guy who built my expensive road bike and gave it to me for free. His circumstantial generosity and sponsorship helped me to afford things like travel and to enter races hundreds or thousands of miles away from home.

Then the gaping pothole. Plowed right into it and the bike fishtailed every which way and yet – Holy Christ! – I managed to keep the thing upright and careen forward. But

I could no longer steer. Something in the bike had snapped. I couldn't fucking *turn*. Didn't stop because I was arrogant, figured I'd still win. I thought that if the road stayed straight I'd make it to the finish line.

Insane. Thinking.

I sailed off the pavement, airborne into an arroyo at 30 miles an hour.

Then the finger in my eye.

A steering column is the part on a bike that connects the handlebars to the front fork. Gilmour had drilled holes in it to lighten the bike even more. Maybe not the smartest move. I should've quit the race. But I was 15 years old.

Cut to late December 2015. I haven't seen Andy Gilmour since the 1980s. We're standing in his Gilmour Bicycles showroom, whose walls are lined with bikes – dozens of his custom frames as well as other vintage machines in for restoration. The showroom's attached to a spacious and somewhat organized workshop, where Gilmour creates and repairs bikes and frames. It smells like a Jiffy Lube, and is outfitted with milling machines, high-pressure welding cylinders, frame straighteners, industrial-sized ovens for paint and welding purposes, myriad tools, and creased bike-racing memorabilia.

This appointment-only shop sits in a little industrial area near Tucson and Broadway boulevards. Gilmour's dressed in blue; blue sweatshirt, blue cardigan, blue jeans, and he's a little heavier now, his hair's gone gray. He's got an impish grin. His impossible laugh comes fast and furious:

"You were my crash-test dummy! *Ha-ha-ha-ha-ha-ha*."

Indeed.

Gilmour always had a priestly passion for his work. So it's no wonder he's still building custom-made bicycles for a living, having survived big shifts in bike technology. He's churned out more than 5,000 frames since beginning in '74. Not mass-produced bikes in uniform sizes and shapes; no, his specialty is hand-made racing – or heavy touring – machines designed specifically for the purchaser's body specifications. They're not cheap. Gilmour takes in limb lengths and even hip placement on the bike to determine the most efficient pedal strokes, as well as tube angles and frame stiffness, all details that have a cumulative effect on how a bike rides and handles.

Some want just the frame and others want the full bike – the wheels, handlebars, derailleurs, etc. There's also aesthetics to think about, the paint and colors. And when you get to know the person who's building your frame from a pile of tubes, it gives the bike a kind of soul, some personality, corny as it sounds.

Gilmour is punctiliously eloquent when detailing the frame-building process, from tube cutting to jig fitting to painting. Especially the brazing and TIG welding part: "Everything in air is a pollutant to a weld, oxygen, nitrogen, hydrogen. When you excite the molecules of the metal..." Then he talks with boyish enthusiasm of "kicked out fron-tends" or "shallow steering" or the surface "strengths of glue versus brazing."

At one point he settles into gracious and bittersweet stories about his younger brother Robin, who owned a successful construction company in San Diego, and who died suddenly in November of a heart attack. Today, Gilmour's wearing that company's trucker hat. I knew Robin too.

Gilmour has the look of an accomplished and self-made master craftsman. He's been with the same woman for 20 years, which is the same amount of time his shop has been at this location. It's mostly a one-man show around here these days, but years ago, between 1982 and '92 when cycling was a Tucson boom sport, Gilmour's shop was on Speedway Boulevard, and it featured a full retail side. He had 10 employees and he cranked out the frames (up to 300 a year; no mean feat) in a small factory in the back. Gilmour Bicycles sponsored racing teams and riders, including the Tucson Wheelmen. (In the late 90s, Gilmour was actually coaching a Tucson-based women's cycling team). After relocating his shop, walk-in traffic faded and so did the business' retail side. Doesn't matter. The 61-year-old says he'd never have "become a bike builder if money was a driving force."

This Scottish-born son of a geologist father was a star swimmer at Tucson High ("I'd train for five to six hours a day"), and that's when he was hired on at a local bike shop, which stirred his interest in bike building and racing. In the early 70s, Gilmour began modifying old steel Schwinns into mountain bikes. He began racing too, so he was there in the ragged beauty of the early Arizona bike-racing pelotons, when cyclists traveled like hippies from race to race, eating health food from baggies and living off nickels and dimes. That's when super-humans like John Timbers and Tim Wilson – now folk heroes in these parts – ruled the roadways. (The third bike Gilmour ever built was for Wilson.) Gilmour retired from actual racing (including a few triathlons) years ago, but that first-hand experience informs his work.

His craftsmanship has earned global success over the years. Professional cyclist Andy Bishop rode a Gilmour in the highly prestigious 1990 Tour of Italy while on the Motorola team, and Ecuadorian track cyclist Mario Ponds won a 1999 world championship in Manchester, England on one, and there have been multiple Canadian national championships won on his bikes, and so on.

We tour Gilmour's workshop and he points to a bike-in-progress fit for a giant. "The customer is 6-foot 7-inches tall," he says. "So tall he had to have his bike custom made."

"I once built a bike for Brian Williams," he continues, "who had changed his name to Bison Dele, a real hot basketball player who went on to play for the Chicago Bulls and the Detroit Pistons. He walked away from his basketball career and died mysteriously in the South Seas. Anyway, he was a real nice guy... He didn't stand up very straight so as not to look so intimidating. I shook his hand and I felt like a little kid – this fucker could palm a beach ball."

In the early aughts, bicycle frames changed forever when carbon fiber became the material of choice for pro racing bikes. Carbon fiber frames are particularly light, expensive, and difficult to repair. Gilmour, who's one of around 100 custom bike-frame builders in the country, builds mostly from aluminum or steel, which renders him old-school.

"Most of the carbon fiber bikes now are done in what's called monocoque, and they're done in molds," he says. "Molds are very expensive, so little companies can't even do it." He says a kid coming up doesn't need that much money to race bikes; you can still get a raceable, non-carbon fiber bike "for $2,000."

Did the rise in carbon fiber popularity decimate the specialty frame-builder market in the United States?

"Yeah, but a lot of guys cleverly got into niches like building fancy city bikes and commuter bikes."

Which direction did you go?

"Well, I stayed with my racing bikes," he laughs.

But you're still surviving...

"Yeah."

There's an artisan revival for the classic steel road bike, similar to music's vinyl resurgence. Good thing for Gilmour. Also, moneyed folks from around the country send Gilmour their classic bikes from the 70s and 80s for restoration, a new Gilmour specialty. He still builds around 25 custom frames a year.

January 14, 2016

MAGIC JOHNNY APPLESEED

A little girl wearing a striped overshirt and floral skirt steps up to the Magic Shop booth, flicking back her flat shoulder-length hair. An oversized purple and white chiffon hair bow seals the deal. Her voice a schoolyard taunt: "Show me. Magic!"

There's a flurry of voices and passersby behind her – leisurely strolling lovers, candy-amped toddlers, fatigued moms, tubby dads, teen girls in urban swag – but this girl's presence commands, her big brown eyes tuned to the magician's graceful hands and manicured nails. Her face a study in wonder and puzzlement, just like the countless who've watched him before.

She ignores the sweet reek of camel manure, frying onions and popcorn, and the bright yellows, reds and greens on the fairground midway, Mom and dad flank her, half-skeptical but hardly bored. Little brother's too short for the action but tries to pull himself up to the counter anyway.

"Let me show you the most popular trick ever sold in the magic shop," he says to the girl, his headset mic booming through mounted speakers. His hands visible on matching TV monitors for all to see. "That would be this deck of cards. It's a very special deck. Do you have a finger you're not using?"

The girl nods. Follows his instructions to choose a card.

"I won't look; I've seen the trick before," he says.

He nods at mom, says to the girl, "Make sure your sister sees it back there."

She inserts the card into the deck.

"Now that card has taken a liking to you. It's going to start

LOVE

following you around the fair here for the rest of the night. Kind of like a stalker, but it's not a bad thing, OK?"

She nods.

"How old are you?"

"Eleven. But I'm little for my age."

"Eleven? That's how old I was when I was your age."

He counts cards, and the 11th card is the one the girl chose.

She's stunned, as are the 15 who've gathered around.

"It pops up when you least expect it. Kind of like an old boyfriend," he says, nodding at the mother. "You know the one I'm talking about, right?"

Mom laughs.

Next, the deck returns to a single suit. The girl cries, "They're all the same!"

The graceful hands return the deck to normal, diamond and hearts, spade and clubs.

"See, the deck isn't so special at all," he says.

The kids fall in love. The card deck is for sale here, with lots of other gags and tricks. The magician's skills are pitch-perfect. They have to be.

Grayed Ken-doll hair and bespectacled, the married, 64-year-old magician looks more like a tent preacher crossed with an insurance salesman than a third-generation magic man steadfastly adhering to the old-school illusionist's codes and oaths. There are no masks or wands or hats here, and he won't reveal any trick secret. This is the magician's work-a-day, all night long. The coffee mug and home-packed food behind the curtain of his impressive and elaborate self-built booth. (Said booth folds into a trailer and attaches to his GMC van. Four months each year he's on a fair circuit through the Midwest and South, bringing magic to kids. Saves a grand a week sleeping in the one-seater van – it's tricked out: a comfy queen-sized bed, refrigerator, TV, internet etc.)

He's self-contained for the modern magic world. That same world reflected in the magician's telling tagline, which he just uttered to the hair-bow girl, "Do you want fries with that?" The line is a joke, yeah, but a total self-own. Emory Williams Jr. knows where he stands.

Tonight, he stands between Dippin' Dots ice cream and Mary Kaye cosmetics inside Thurber Hall at the Pima County Fair. The booth boasts a "Magic Shop" banner and a hanging picture of his magician dad and mom. Decks of cards and other magic trinkets and gags for sale, neatly displayed on his wide, clean, felt-topped counter. He runs the prices down again, third time this hour. The repetition must be brutal.

"But you can buy everything in a package at a discount, $35... It also gets you a DVD that teaches everything, exactly the way I do it. I know because it's me on the DVD. It's kinda scary, it means I go home with you."

Soon he sells a single ball and vase trick, a few bucks. "And when you open it you'll know exactly how it works," he tells the teen customer. "It's that easy, OK?"

Some tricks here are old as the hills, he'll point out – the ball and vase illusion, for example, has likely been around since ancient Egypt.

★ ★ ★

Close-up magic is difficult as hell. Requires dexterity, uncommon grace. The trick sciences are well-known. But the presentation and performance, the art of it, is what sustains magic. Illusion is presentation; it's the handling, the patter, the charisma.

Hardly matters Emory looks like any boomer with good hair. No need for costuming or style consultants. Emory maintains entertainer intangibles to back up mad skillsets, even when it amounts to selling tricks for kids. It's easy to spot the sensation, the inspiration, a look in his eyes, in his mannerisms, that there's a bigger purpose here for him. This sharply intelligent manboy sees lots, knows lots but reveals little – his head for precise detail, and of Illusionists and illusions that came before him, is a magician essential.

There's also the honed acumen of a pitchman able to read the body language of kids and parents. Emory entertains the kids, and they hit the parents up for the trick sets. It's the kids who sell the shop's wares. (Yep, and maybe there's a sucker every minute: Up close, nearly a dozen times, I've watched Emory turn a $1 bill into a $100 bill – no crumpling, and he's wearing short sleeves – and each time I'm flummoxed.)

Some call Emory the Johnny Appleseed of magic.

"I'm out here planting magic seeds all over the country for all the little kids to get into. Problem is, most of them won't follow through. It's a point-of-sale, an impulse purchase. They buy and then they go to YouTube and prank their friend and never go in the magic shop again. But every now and then you get one."

If he's in the mood, he'll blow minds. And why not? It's in his blood. He's been at it for decades. Been a member of the prestigious Academy of Magical Arts, the international magician's guild housed in Hollywood's Magic Castle. Emory has performed there many times since joining in '75.

So he fits into the pantheon of old garter-sleeved magicians in the post-Criss Angel world. (Angel's sort of the Mötley Crüe of magic – almost single-handedly finished off the fraternal order of magicians. The predictable, showy money-grabs and calculated outrage for sell-outs under the guise of art.) A good magician is egoless. It's heretical to make it about themselves. Teller of Penn and Teller doesn't speak. Conversely, The Masked Magician, the onetime Vegas-y sensation, gave away countless trade secrets on a tedious Fox TV show.

At five years old, Emory was learning magic from his dad, Emory Williams Sr. Now dad grew up in Missouri farmlands, 1930s, the youngest of 12 children. He'd apprenticed with magicians in the 1940s, married his childhood sweetheart (still married) and pursued magic for life.

The parents settled outside of Tucson, a planned retirement, but instead opened a magic shop on 22nd near Wilmot street in '89, which became a clubhouse of sorts for local magicians. The place expanded, several times.

The younger Emory went on to study theology in England. But he became a hunter of truth in Southern California – an insurance investigator, worked as a litigator too, a non-attorney hearing representative who negotiated million-dollar settlements. ("It helps if you watch a lot of court TV shows," he laughs.) He's done other things, too, including video game design. Like his dad, performing magic was a constant. He and his wife moved to Arizona in '96, joined up with his folks at the Williams Magic Shop, for fulltime magic. Emory soon stopped performing publicly to market the business.

The tradition of magic had been shifting, and when the economy tanked in '08, the 22nd Street shop, with its thousands of square feet, shuttered. Williams Magic opened a store in Vail, Arizona, which now operates a small storefront, seven nights a week, in Tucson's Trail Dust Town. It's run by Emory, his wife and his parents.

The family also created a mind-bogglingly customized 42-foot RV to contain an entire store inventory of illusions and magic, thousands of items. Their intent was to take the Williams Magic Shop (and teachings) to customers around the country, which they also do. Thirty-seven states and counting.

Emory offers a road analogy as umbrella explanation: "Route 66 had all the little cities and stops and shops along the way. When the interstate came in, they bypassed the little towns and all the little shops started to close and the towns started to dry up. That's what happened to the magic industry. It used to be if you had an interest in magic you had to go to a magic shop, or you may have done it through mail order – if they were in another city. The internet came in and it's bypassed all the magic shops. Now, kids can just get on their phone and can find the same thing made in China for a third the price and buy and have it delivered. They don't have to walk into a magic shop, which means they're not getting face-to-face contact. They're not being coached on how to entertain and to present and interact and how to become a magician. They're buying pranks. So magic shops dried up. When the shops dried up there's no one to cultivate the next generation."

Yeah, you can't mess with change and progress, and the guy who made horse-buggy whips had to quit too, etc. But this isn't forward movement, not when technology so ruthlessly speeds us into murky futures we don't realize so much beauty has vanished. It's that way in the arts, in music – and magic too. Pranks and gags, The Masked Magician and short attention spans. The antithesis of the art. The arguments are the same – the kids no longer pay attention to anything, the internet has ruined magic, long-held secrets revealed.

But really, magic is storytelling. Magic is humanity, passed down generations. There's apprenticeship, study and long-hour suffering – the 10,000-hour rule, at least. Like any art, one must understand what came before to begin to master it, to ensure evolvement, to even be any damn good, worthy of attention. It's about devotion. It's like writing books or painting canvases or recording good records or practicing medicine. Without total effort it's a cheap trick.

★ ★ ★

Michael DeSchalit, a compact guy with close-cropped hair, the gestalt of a reality TV star, he of hypnozone.com, appears at the fair's magic shop booth with his wife and daughter. This longtime magician, who's performed everywhere – from the Four Seasons in Vegas to the Magic Castle in Hollywood – has known Emory for nigh 30 years. He has just sold his Tucson home and is leaving the illusion trade to focus more on his hypnosis business and shows. He's big in the certified hypnosis game, as a lecturer, performer, etc. There's little money in magic and illusion anymore he says. He's moving to Vegas.

He's talking magician's toil. How guys like Emory and his family can survive on the little sales and magic sets, keeping the spirit of illusion alive.

He shrugs. "He does well enough. Selling the stuff. It's the $1.50 movie principle. Fill all the seats or charge $10 and see."

If Emory's tired of shtick, there's no telling. Not with an audience of doe-eyed kids with candy-smeared lips giving off adrenaline, energy. He feels that too, man.

A 15-year-old girl stands all wide-eyed at the booth, her show-me attitude fades to a drifty grin and concentration. She almost invests in some magic but instead chooses a bottle of invisible ink. Emory produces a tiny bottle. "That's $2."

She digs out the bills and hands it over.

His knowing nod. "Would you like fries with that?"

May 3, 2018

THE LEGEND OF BAMBI

We'd drive by The Bambi in the family car, and I thought it a bar where moms disrobed. The boxy façade, the curtained glass adult-shop doors, the sign's fetching logo and mule deer caricature. An ominous sanctum in which nothing good could happen, but somehow everything great. I knew it wasn't *H.R. Pufnstuf*. When I was a boy.

The Bambi's been here since this end of Speedway (5050 East) was dirt. "Old Man" Guy is the bar's 90-year-old proprietor. He lives nearby, appears nightly just before closing to count the till, restock the bar and feed the feral cats who prowl outback in the smoking area and gravel lot. He hangs until morning and serves coffee to other folks heading to work. Like the place never closes. Again, Guy is 90.

It's a bar forever ensconced in Tucson lore. (Think of "Hoss," a one-time regular who died more than 30 years ago while conversing inside the bar's phone booth. A skeleton's propped there to honor him. People swear Hoss haunts the place.)

Dale Roche didn't know Hoss, knows of him. It's assumed knowledge. Roche occupies a stool on the impressive, squared-horseshoe bar, and works a draft beer, one of maybe 12 other drinkers. A corner flatscreen barks baseball updates, ESPN.

Roche, who looks like Mickey Rooney at 70, nods to a section of wall photos. Aged pale and dappled, faces frozen happy. "That's the wall of death," he says. Laughs, "I might be here one day."

Roche graduated from Rincon High in '66 when Tucson's population was still south of 250,000, and "gas was 15 cents a gallon." When Dan Gates and Frank Kalil ruled KTKT-99 radio and pushed Tucson's Dearly Beloved to No. 1 with "Peep Peep Pop Pop." When serial killer Charles Schmid Jr. ("The Pied Piper of Tucson") had the entire town horrified. Roche remembers the Pied Piper; his friend dated Gretchen Fritz, one of the three teen girl victims.

"Yeah it freaked me out," he says. "We had sock hops on Saturday, and I used to see The Pied Piper at the Sunset Rollerama. Everybody knew he was strange; he was like a freak – his hair was all done up all the time, wore long coats. Beer cans in his boots to make himself taller. Make-up. But back then there was a lot of rebellion. People stood out, but who'd have thought this guy would be a crazy motherfucker?"

Roche survived Vietnam, as did his two brothers. His Navy-vet uncle didn't. He later worked blue collar in California. Returned to Tucson ("I still live in the same house we had in 1962, 20th Street and Craycroft"), became a Bambi regular, lately "about every day." His ex-Marine older brother, Eddy Roach, a former disc jockey and onetime Bambi regular, died in February. Dale had been taking care of him for five years. The Bambi hosted an "all out" memorial for Eddy.

Dozens of black-and-white caricatures of bar regulars create multiple wall displays. The artist would stare at customers, go home and sketch from memory. Roche is proud to be included. Linda Ray's there too, a beloved regular Roche dated years ago. She died.

So, yes, The Bambi's a cornerstone of local humanity. A lonely-hearts gang partial to friends in real time, guffawing, polluting livers. The living-room luxury and the warmth, its holy workingclassness.

Barroom novelties abound: a still-warm hotdog buffet. An 80s pic of regulars seated around a giant monsoon puddle in The Bambi parking lot, pretend fishing. A backlit beer clock whose hands aren't dead, its yellowed, dusty face reads "BAMBI" where it should "Hamm's."

There isn't a soul here not saddened that Tucson dens like The Bambi recede while cold micro-brews and ersatz speakeasies rise. Moneyed places serving fruity cocktails and coffee'd whatevers to over-paying "urban pioneers" who use the adjective "creative" as a self-referencing noun.

Good thing this lounge sits miles from downtown Tucson and anything called a bistro or brewery. "I hear it's nice," Bartender Susie Williams says unironically of downtown. "I haven't been there in years."

Susie's like that cool mom who'd let you and your friends drink beer in the backyard because she knew you'd drink the 10th grade summer away anyway. Converses with cheerful, fitful amusement, busy yet outwardly curious about people. It's like she forgets she's a bartender and settles into the person she is. It's easy to feel worthy in her purview.

Susie was 11 when her homemaker mom died. At 16 she arrived alone in Tucson after scamming a Greyhound ticket back home in Indiana. Had four bucks in her pocket. Nothing against her old man, a plumber, and her siblings, but a boy had captured her heart. He stole a car, broke probation and avoided jail by moving to his mother's Tucson home. "Honey, I didn't know my ass from a hole in the ground," Susie says. "But on the way out here, I should've gotten my period and I didn't. I was in love. Also, he was kind of a rebel."

A teen wedding ensued. The hard-partying hubby died at 42. Their child, Serena, is now 42. "It was terrible," Susie says. "Lived fast, lived hard, died young. What do you do with people like that?"

Hired eight years ago here, Susie logged in 12 years prior at The Mint lounge on Grant Road. Daughter Serena worked The Mint before mom did. Incredibly, Serena's own daughter is 22, which is one year older than Susie's youngest son. Susie and her daughter raised their children together.

Susie explains: "I was a grandmother at 37, and then my youngest son was born when I was 38. So, I have a granddaughter a year older than my youngest son. They grew up like cousins."

Susie has slung drinks in Tucson for 30 years. Her second husband owned JW's Lounge at First and Fort Lowell, where she honed her skills. They had a son, now 32. "My second husband was 20 years older than me." She pauses. "Both of my husbands are dead, and I'm still goin'. I wasn't together with him or the first one when they died."

On marriage: "I'm not doing that shit any more. I'm together with the father of my third child. We're as married as anybody. Life goes on."

Elsewhere in Bambi, a pole-thin black gent with a severe limp and cane, and a starched white button-down shirt, mutters softly. He has no interest in talking or having his photo snapped. Susie's seen him in here once or twice.

He fascinates – it's his uncommon Sunday-sermon grace. A whorehouse priest. Granite cheekbones, tattered formality. Like slow motion he wraps long fingers around glass, lifts from bar to lips, sips. He lowers glass gently to the bar. Counts his money, carefully places crisper bills on top, a neat pile. Arranges the napkin alongside, symmetrical. Lulled, glassy dark eyes fixed straight ahead. So alone. The last place on Earth – tonight, at least. He's tuned to the same frequency as the others here. Conversations roll one end into another. There are no secrets. He listens.

Dale Kiernan listens too.

His shape on the barstool next to me: curved back, heavy knuckles, healthy paunch. His Y&T T-shirt a love-nod to the metal of his Wyoming youth. Nods and laughs whenever he says a disparaging thing about himself, which is often. He's a chef at Tucson's Senae Thai, but I'd never mistake him for a guy floating on executive chef bravado, that certainty he can do what he wants. Nothing dull or tedious about him.

Working a vodka and ginger ale, he talks freely of his heroin addiction, rip-off rehabs, alcoholism and culinary delights. Speaks of geohydrology, working oil fields and his anthropology degree from University of Wyoming. How he switched to kitchens after culinary school in Oregon. ("It's not like you get out of culinary school and land a sexy job. I went to work on a Greek food truck.")

He spent months preparing food on a fair circuit and "a religious deal in Boise." He's worked kitchens in California, Colorado, Utah, Wyoming too – landed at Tucson's only five-diamond restaurant, the ill-fated Ventana Room.

Like any chef I've ever known, his capacity for toxins is impressive. He wound up strung out on heroin with Jennifer, a junkie prostitute, and was kitchen-manager at Ten's, the gentlemen's club a spitting distance from here. ("That was during my fall," he says. "But the food was great when I was there.")

He landed in rehab. Jennifer's in jail.

Susie wanders over, pours Kiernan a fresh vodka, wipes the bar, listens. Adds, "You dive into a bottle of anything you're going down fast. I have nothing against drinking – I love my whiskey. But it doesn't agree with some people. I have a son who's just like his father. It takes all kinds to make this world. No better do you learn that than in the bar business."

Kiernan agrees. "I've been a coke snorter for 30 years. I taught myself how to cook crack. But smoking heroin is what took me down. My mom was out-of-pocket $17K to send me to rehab in 2015."

I ask how Kiernan can still drink.

"Control," he says.

"Amazing."

Moments, maybe minutes, pass. Then Kiernan says, "Luckily I moved close to The Bambi. Other than The Bambi, I had no desire to stay in Tucson."

Jesse Salazar works a cigarette at a table in The Bambi's outside smoking lounge. A good talker. His English rings with Spanish and hip-hop burrs in a musical patois. A regional dialect I've only ever heard in the Southwest. He grew up on hip-hop and its magazines *The Source* and *XXL*, moving back and forth between Nogales, Arizona, and Tucson. He played guitar (but, he insists, nowhere near as a good as his brother) in makeshift Nogales jam outfits that'd set up regularly in their front yard, blasting till the cops showed. He's 34 but looks 20.

He pedestalizes his mother, for good reason; herculean efforts raised Jesse and his four sibs. Mom was pregnant with her last child while the family lived in a Nogales homeless shelter. She went back to school with five kids and no money and became a paralegal. His PTSD-suffering Nam-vet dad, who Jesse has only met "a couple of times," was a family no-show. Jesse recently learned dad had a stroke. He knows that much. And mom suffered a massive heart attack several years ago, and she's weak now. He drops his head; "I'm not shit compared to her."

He calls himself an underachiever who knows the streets. He's a "floor technician" at Santa Rosa, a nursing care center. He may not realize the work seems life affirming. "I can dress the title up anyway I want to," the floor tech says. "But I buff floors."

He talks of one patient there named Jeffrey. A guy dying in a wheelchair with a colostomy bag. "Not that old," Jesse says, "Like 50."

But this guy Jeffrey could move two fingers. "So he'd put his paintbrush between his thumb and forefinger, and he would paint. And I supported him in his thing. He watched Bob Ross videos and things like that. You know, 'happy little trees.' It was heartbreaking, man 'cause I would see him every day, and he told me real stories about how his wife got into crack. He had a cool New York accent. Eventually, he ended up calling me his kid brother."

One day Jesse was mopping up the hallway at the Santa Rosa, "'cause, you know, I'm a floor *technician*. Jeffrey told me to close my eyes. So I followed him into his room, and he displayed a picture he painted for me, a landscape of a beach, with shrubbery and mountains off to the sides. Done with just his index finger and his thumb."

There was no gesture anyone could've done or said for Jesse and Jeffrey that would've said more than that painting. Soon Jeffery died, and the picture now hangs in Jesse's apartment. Jesse was the only non-nurse who'd visit Jeffrey.

"Even if he was an asshole, don't you think someone would show up to visit him? It would really fuck with me if I got to know these people and then watch them pass away. It's happened so many times. Jeffrey stands out though, 'cause he called me his kid brother. And then when he died – it's like I would love to beautifully describe this – but all I can say is fuck."

Jesse has a friend here tonight who steps out back to the smoking area, wonders if Jesse is still into playing pool. Jesse stands to join him inside. He stops, turns back and says, "Sometimes you see people, and you're the only person they see – they're daughters of daughters of daughters. I've seen body bags wheeled off after some die, and it's so sad." He puts his cigarette out. "I bet if Jeffery was still alive, he'd want to go out. It makes me want to go out and live life."

April 19, 2018

TENACIOUS C

In early December 1992, 16-year-old Corinne Schram and two girlfriends headed to see the Grateful Dead at the Compton Terrace Amphitheater near Phoenix, driving up I-10 in Schram's Daihatsu Charade hatchback. Schram was headlong into teen rebellion then, the parties, the drinking, the drugs. All of her friends and boyfriends were older, a concerned mom's nightmare. But people her own age bored her. She attended public school, mostly in the advanced GATE (Gifted and Talented Education) program, and was to graduate high school a year early. She hated it, so she quit.

Schram was in the front passenger seat, and they were somewhere near Casa Grande. The girl driving turned to say something to the girl in the back, got distracted, and the little Daihatsu jerked out of its lane and swerved off road into the median. She over-corrected, the weight and momentum of the turn was too much and the car flipped.

But they were lucky, because no other cars were involved. They were lucky because investigators determined that the accident wasn't alcohol-related. They were lucky because the driver miraculously emerged from the crash unscathed. They were lucky because the windows of the Daihatsu were large enough to accommodate the girl in the backseat, so she hurtled through it into the cold air and only suffered a broken collarbone and dislocated shoulder.

Schram wasn't lucky. Or maybe she was, if you consider the number of corpses that freeway has given up. She was found alive and broken, hanging from the wrecked car. Her head and face had slammed so hard against the freeway that it

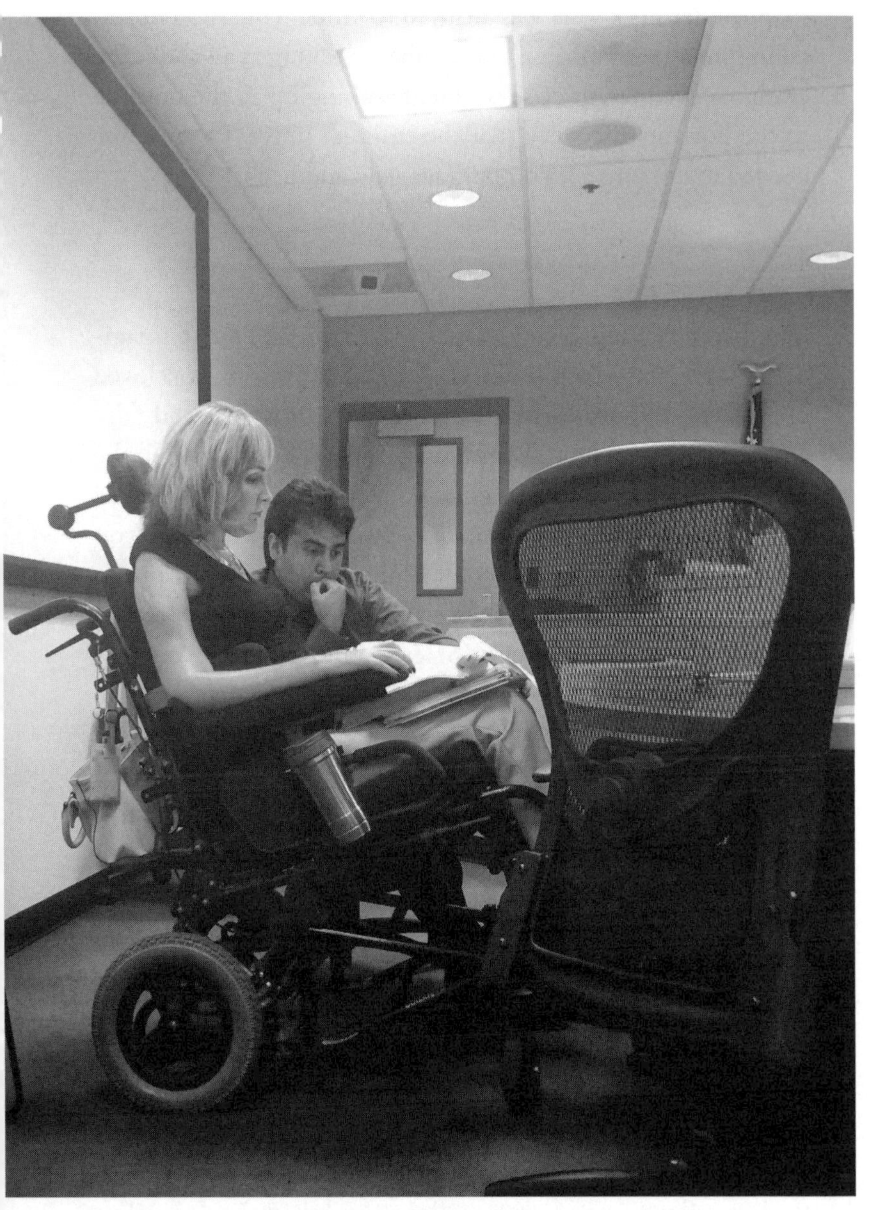

snapped her neck. She was airlifted to Good Samaritan hospital in Phoenix. She doesn't remember anything at all about the crash, or even any precise moment waking up in the hospital to the horrific discovery that she couldn't move. Or how she needed many surgeries on her face, jaw and neck.

★ ★ ★

Imagine surviving a catastrophic crash in the worst imaginable way. You can still detect alarmed expressions on loved one's faces, the too-serious tones of surgeon voices and false empathy of strangers. The florescent lights. You can smell the antiseptics and sterile linoleum floors, even the injuries and deaths around you, but little else. You want to die, but you can't even commit suicide, that's impossible because you no longer can walk or move your arms or fingers. You're forced to depend on someone else for every movement, every necessity in your life, except for your head movement and the thoughts inside of it.

Forget dreaming of the future. Forget it all. In this world you can't lift a fork to your mouth to feed yourself or brush a tickling hair from your face, much less reach out and touch another human being.

Then imagine somehow shifting that story – that self-narrative of utter defeat, isolation and loneliness – to something that's perhaps more complex and nuanced – a storyline mixed with a fierce yen to survive. It's not blind faith. It's not some god. It's you. It's all you in the center of an indifferent random universe ruled by chance and tragedy.

And then imagine telling yourself, and your skeptics, this: Fuck it – I'm going to go to college. And then: Fuck it – I'm going to go to law school.

That's what 39-year-old Ms. Schram did. She's a public defense attorney at Pima County Juvenile Court, and has worked in that capacity for seven years.

And she sometimes sees her teen self in kids she defends.

★ ★ ★

Butterflies with spread wings, enclosed in framed cases, decorate walls in Corinne Schram's quiet bedroom. It's painted in mood-lifting light pastels, and natural light streams in through big windows. A calico cat sleeps on a paisley comforter in the middle of her made bad. This central-Tucson house, which she shares with her mother and seven cats, is similarly airy and lazy, smells of flowers, and faintly of furniture oil. The Salt Lake City-born Schram has lived here since moving to Tucson when she was three years old.

She talks about life and her relationship to the world. There's an air of dignity about her, in her personal insights, in the candid way she offers them. That she's unable to move in a wheelchair, in the center of her room, is less a definition of who she is than it is a distraction and I can't pretend to even understand what it means in practical terms. Can't pretend to understand much.

Does she ever dream of living a different life?

"There's no point of having dreams of a different life because it's not ever going to happen."

Does she get lonely?

She nods. "Of course." A long moment passes. She adds, "Everybody does. But then, at the same time, it sucks never having time alone. My only alone time is when I'm reading or sleeping."

She needs caretakers. She needs her mother Katharine. In the first four years after the crash, until she received a personal injury settlement, it was Schram's mother who cared for her – the feeding, the bathing, the dressing, the driving, everything. Her father wasn't around much after the accident, and he has since remarried. Her one sibling, a sister who now lives out-of-state, was traumatized. "She went through years of depression and survivor's guilt," Schram says. (Schram has three much-younger step-siblings on her dad's side living in the Czech Republic).

Getting to law school wasn't easy. Schram enrolled at the University of Arizona, graduating with a B.A. in philosophy. She earned her law degree in 2007. She'd have a caretaker in class with her, or occasionally classmates would turn book pages for her. The writing part wasn't easy either, as voice-activation software was, and is, problematic. She took a full school load, "same as everyone else."

Her three years in law school weren't intellectually challenging, and she wasn't "gung-ho" about going. But law, in pragmatic terms, was something she needed to do, considering how quickly her settlement money was evaporating – caregiver expenses alone were costing at least $60,000 a year. She says, "I had to do something that I could potentially make money doing, as well as physically do."

And becoming a public defender?

"I didn't choose it, it chose me. I was putting out resumes and that's where I got called. Pima County. I never wanted to go into criminal law, but I knew that if I did, it would have to be on the defense side. I couldn't prosecute. I couldn't be part of sending people to prison for non-violent offences. Stuff I don't believe in. I couldn't prosecute somebody for smoking weed. And the whole system I just think is so wrong and fucked up and prison is so awful, I just couldn't be a part of trying to put somebody there."

Mom says her daughter was never a self-doubter and always stood by her beliefs. This analysis might help explain how mom dealt with the tragedy when it happened. But their interactions can get prickly. Their relationship is hardly *Grey Gardens*, but it hasn't been easy. Love is obvious. Mom, an intelligent, sprightly woman who looks a good decade younger than her 73 years, can finish Schram's sentences, and vice versa.

"We're close," Schram grins, "Maybe closer than we should be."

"She can be stubborn," mom says. She relates a story about how years ago her daughter refused a catheter so she could wear jeans in her wheelchair.

"It's not stubborn," Schram interrupts. "It's conviction."

"You're right," mom says.

★ ★ ★

Irving Talavera reaches into Schram's purse, which dangles from the back of the wheelchair. He pulls out a pinkish lip gloss, opens it and carefully applies it to her lips. She utters a quiet "thank you" as he returns the stick to her purse.

Dressed for court, Schram looks great in a black, sleeveless top with an elegant V cut, beige slacks. Her neck-length blonde hair shows lavender streaks on the sides, a subtle rebellion.

There's a stack of files piled on her lap, topped by her calendar book and a four-inch thick tome called Arizona Criminal and Traffic Law Manual.

"I usually don't carry a manual," the lawyer laughs, embarrassed. "It's for my depo hearing."

Schram's in the crowded waiting area outside one of many courtrooms inside the Pima County Juvenile Court building. There's a hearing for one of her juvenile clients. She has 35 active cases at the moment, and that's a lot. The Juvenile Court is woefully understaffed; too many cases, not enough lawyers and probation officers.

Talavera, Schram's assistant, flips her appointment book open to reveal the number of hearings scheduled for Schram that day. She'll tirelessly burn through five hearings in the next two hours – in and out of various courtrooms. Squeezed between the hearings are quick meetings with kids and their parents. She says probably 97 percent of her cases plead out. Few go to trial, and that's good; no one could handle even half that many.

Soon she meets with a set of bleary-eyed parents and their son, who has the gawky gait of a boy growing too quickly, filled of hormones and confusion. Their kid's welfare is important to them, as heard in their stiffly chosen words, seen in their concerned faces. It's a porous relationship. Schram reassures them: Their son deserves less than a six-month probation.

Talavera pushes Schram into the courtroom.

The prosecutor, the boy's probation officer, the judge and Schram go around about the boy's shoplifting and weed charge. Schram recommends a lesser sentence than the six-month probation sought by the court. The urine tests are clean, he's doing well in school and hitting his 6 p.m. curfew. Judge Richard E. Gordon agrees, delivers a lesser sentence.

This is a glimpse of her workday, in a week strictly limited to 30 hours. She's physically unable to work more than that; long wheelchair hours create pressure sores. Schram's empathy for the kids almost sparkles it's so palpable, but one would never get it watching her work. She's a pro. Such things are revealed only in private, where she's likely reminded of her teen self.

"I wouldn't call them lost causes," she says later. "I don't think any of them are lost causes."

November 19, 2015

LOOMING GRACE

Finely manicured fingers rotate like a miniature flesh-and-bone loom, looping and sliding yarn through a tattered selvage. Sinatra croons atop strings through concealed speakers, night music at 10 a.m.

After some minutes, the rug weaver rests. He shifts the 70-year-old fabric, a fetching cotton-wool Bijar accented in midnight blues and catholic reds, to continue stitching its edge. He talks meaning in the monotony of his work, and his Farsi-shaded English is spoken so softly it necessitates a closer lean to listen.

"Sometimes you really go somewhere, you go *into* the design. Sometimes it's 40 knots, sometimes it's a thousand knots." He lingers on that. His fingers move to his inner rhythms and it's so hypnotic I'm lulled into thoughtlessness. Time feels arbitrary here.

"Ninety percent or more is repetition."

He flips a corner of the rug to reveal the underside and its flattened random patterns of whorls and flowers. "There's a thousand different colorings," he says. "One side dark, the other side light." Another rest. "The challenge is matching the color. Especially the parts that are worn."

When the light side shows decades of wear and part of the soul of the fabric, of the million footsteps of people he'll never know, he'll match that color, too. His restorations rarely leave traces.

The perfectionism, unyielding patience. A relaxed relentlessness to a dying art and tradition. His monotony has meaning, he says, "like meditation." It's his *Vipassanā*. And Sinatra's lilt compliments the rug weaver's grace, and both efforts seem anything but possible.

★ ★ ★

He's Ali Shahinpour and he's perched on a low chair at a big table in the Asian Trade Rug Company showroom. Organized piles of rugs keep him cornered – carpets from Pakistan, China, Afghanistan, and his Iranian homeland, and Turkish, Persian, Indian, French, Navajo, contemporary and so on. Hundreds of rare antiques, flickers of art and the archeological. Practically every damn thing in here is beautiful.

On the floor beside him sits a mad, tangled mountain of

vintage silk, wool and cotton yarn, in soothing Middle Eastern colors. Mostly reusable threads, discarded from years of work, now essential to his color matching and repairs. Behind him hangs a large rug in pastel browns, taupe and red. A lovely replica of an antique he weaved himself. This chair, this table, this mad psychedelic mountain of yarn: his workstation, five days a week.

The slight forever grin suggests nothing can break his reserve. His bright dark eyes don't waver from mine when he converses. His fingers continue to move, though, and he explains lots in few words: The beauty of worn-in rugs, and silk sometimes makes the best foundation. How knots per square inch can vary from country to country, tribe to tribe. How tribal rugs from southern Iran have multi-hued selvages. He talks asymmetrical knots versus symmetrical, and how wool weft threads aren't twisted. Talks knot counts, quality of yarns and dyes and the sweet blends perfected hundreds of years ago. How so many Persian rugs came over to the states in the 1920s, and before, "to be aged." How the market for antique rugs, especially those from the Middle East, has taken a commercial dive after 9/11.

He's 55 years old too. He'd tutored with a master rug weaver in Tehran, and learned everything – from weaving and repairing to cleaning and wholesaling. An artisan trade, passed down from generations. This after surviving the Iranian Revolution of '79, after Saddam Hussein's invasion.

⋆ ⋆ ⋆

This son of military parents came up in Dezful, Iran, the sight of the biggest tank battle of the Iran-Iraqi war, and home to one of Iran's largest air force bases. "I could see the Iraqi pilots' faces – they would fly so low." He was a teenager in 1980 when Iraq invaded Iran, already weakened by its own revolution.

He relates Saddam Hussein terrors, the sickness and horrors of war-crimes. "Hussein blew up anything. He blew up hospitals and ancient mosques and architecture, and whole cities, and used chemical weapons, on women and children." The shock of seeing his blood-soaked father roll by in an ambulance. The shock of an Iraqi missile flattening his home, his family members huddled in the basement, terrified as the world exploded down in fire and dust and rubble above and around them. He endured the loss of friends and classmates, destroyed by bullets and bombs. During the invasion, the Iranian government gave families firearms for protection. "[The Iraqi Army] was bullying everyone. Saddam was not human." His family (parents, sister and two brothers) survived.

Ali did a stint in the Iranian Army in the early 80s. His voice, now full and slow, loses things in translation. (If only I understood Farsi.) He touches his cheek. Says, "this scar here," and straightens up. Touches his abdomen, "Right here, too." He reaches around his back. "And here." War wounds, bomb shrapnel, and he nearly died. "My back pain was very bad," he says. "I needed help to stand up. I had so much pain. Doctors in Iran didn't know what was wrong. That's when I got out."

An old Ali classmate facilitated an invite to a London-based doctor. It wasn't easy getting out of war-torn Iran. He tells of a risky exploit involving a "bicycle guy" in Abu Dhabi. Ali calls him "Nasir," which, in Arabic, loosely translates to "helper." Nasir helped Ali out of the country. He arrived in London broke, with a slight grasp of English. But he had the "friend who took care of everything." The doctor discovered

Ali's pain was, at that point, long after the wounds had healed. Said they were in his head.

Ali married an American woman during his year in London. She worked real estate, and the couple moved to Utah, where she'd worked before. He arrived stateside with several rugs and attempted to set up shop. But the demand for exotic rugs in Salt Lake City was minimal. Things looked bleak.

"It wasn't good for me there," he says, shrugging, fingers working.

One day Ali and his wife were moving into a new place and someone broke into their U-Haul in a mall parking lot. The couple were in the store. They lost anything of value including a rug that didn't belong to Ali. He only had it for repair, his only work. "I was responsible for it," he says. "That was 28 years ago and the rug was worth $16,500. That changed everything. That's when I moved alone to L.A."

He had an Iranian friend in Los Angeles who invited him to stay at his suburban home. He went to work for the outfit whose rug had been stolen from the U-Haul. That was his start in California – a recent immigrant who went to work for acquaintances and had to quickly learn the Los Angeles rug market, which was centered around La Cienega and Melrose. As long as you have a reputation you can earn a living in rugs, Ali says. Designers and dealers from all over the country began calling him. He rented a storefront and lived inside, and his wife moved out from Utah.

He was selling, repairing, even making his own. He opened House of Rugs, supporting, at one point, 26 employees. He trained each person. Profits grew. He tells of a German guy dropping $1.5 million on rugs in one day. One customer purchased rugs and built his home around them. The couple had twin children and purchased a comfortable house in the Glendale suburb of Los Angeles.

Then the marriage collapsed. "It was better for the kids if we weren't together," Ali says.

The day after his divorce finalized, Ali turned on himself. A festering depression deepened. The next day he was in the psychiatric hospital, and spent a month inside.

"I'm glad I didn't do anything to myself. But I was on a list that said I couldn't buy a gun for five years."

Asian Trade co-owner Kasra Massarat, who'd been sending Ali rug repair work through the years from Tucson, offered Ali a job. That was 14 years ago. He's been in Tucson since, a total reset. Left his business behind and his ex-wife kept everything back in Los Angeles. The afterburn of a California life.

His children visit summers and Christmas (now each are 19 and in college, the daughter on a computer science full-ride at Boston University. His son studies in Louisiana).

Ali and store owners Massarat and Tomas Almazan regard each other with respect, a kind of love. Ali met an Iranian woman here seven years ago. They married. He's done well enough to build his own house on the Northwest side. This rug weaver from Iran.

★ ★ ★

An hour or so later, Ali stands and lifts a heavy rug from a nearby stack, one tagged ready for repair. It's handmade lovely – yellow, cerulean and black – large enough to flatter any bedroom floor. He gazes at it a second or two, says it's only 20 years old. But someone had machined onto it an unsightly dirty-white fringe, and he grimaces.

When he first arrived in Tucson, Almazan told him if he wanted to find peace he should go walk along the river. "So I walked down and looked for the river. I looked for two weeks! There is no river. I didn't know you called a wash here a river."

"But here I found peace," he says. He begins to tear the fringe away. Those fingers like a concert pianist's, exposing so little effort, obliging his *Vipassanã*.

October 19, 2017

WAR MACHINES

Jack Martin trundles his acres as if on a private mission, pointing out war beasts with excitable affection. Watch close, his joy unbundles slowly – it's like he doesn't want anyone to see how much he loves his machinery. Middle-schooler enthusiasm isn't easy on a 71-year-old. Even harder after 41 years of salvage business in Tucson.

"They only made these half-ton Dodge carryalls for one year," he says, staying in hasty stride. "This one here's a 650 Kawasaki retrofitted with a diesel engine, made in California. It's going to Russell Military Museum in Zion, Illinois. They only made 440 of them for the Marine Corps and they turned them into Davis Monthan for destruction – but they decided to sell five. Almost everything gets destroyed. It's such a waste."

His salvage yard, Jack's Gov't Surplus Trucks, qualifies as high art, a repository of organized chaos. The visual equivalent of a Stooges song, you might say, tonnage and frayed edges equally metallic, muscular and organic.

Thousands of machines resigned to peaceful, perfunctory order: A half-ton World War II ambulance shaped in the cheery curves of a 60s suburban milk truck, rusted and sun-defeated in a bed of vicious buffelgrass; several Nam helicopters decorated with Vietcong bullet holes, emasculated with guns and rotor blades removed; a dozen multifuel engines lifted "from five-ton M54 Vietnam cargo trucks" provide cast-iron cubbyholes for desert creatures and their feral-cat hunters. Hard to imagine these vehicles once announcing brutal hostilities to faraway worlds.

It's 15 acres on four lots that smell of old rubber and juniper, out in the dusted no-man's desert where I-10 nears Drexel Road. A land of junkyards, forgotten trailers and colossal, high-voltage transmission towers. The tone is set nearby – miles of skeletal wings and tails form eerie symmetries behind tall chainlink, ghosts on Davis Monthan airfields.

It's lonely, and the silent horsepower deafens, but Jack's voice cuts through, conveying data and facts and numbers on pretty much any tactical vehicle, jeep, gun trailer, helicopter or chock block or winch attachment or axel or tire in sight.

Ask to repeat information if he goes too fast. He will, slower now, easily calling things into being in a dry, sometimes off-character melodic voice. He may stop to pet his goat, the one with no name. Sometimes goat-with-no-name follows Jack like an obedient dog down creosote-shrouded paths, between machines.

Jack is owner, overseer, mechanic here. He looks the part: a mechanic's stoop in a gun-metal gray tee, retro Civil War "US" belt-buckle, a cap ringed with dried sweat and the words Government Liquidation. Shoulder-tickling gray biker hair and matching beard. Sun-sketched facial wrinkles and watery eyes. Cast him in a horror film as resident sage – a *Grimm's Fairy Tale* elder doling wisdom to teens before they're slaughtered.

"Yeah, I know, I look like a biker," he says, shrugging, like an apology.

★ ★ ★

We're on his main lot, the sales lot. An antiquated military jeep, which sits a good 20 feet up atop a long storage bunker, hauled over from Davis Monthan AFB, makes the place easy to spot from Drexel Road. Behind that, in the front, sit motors, forklifts and military Humvees, *Mad Max*ian ephemera, and several ramshackle structures housing a garage and attendant sheds for storage.

Today, Jack's sole employee, his son Josh – a mechanic here part-time – works on a pair of ongoing restoration projects, military Blazers for a "lieutenant colonel from Northern California," and an out-of-state judge. Such work is the crux of Jack's business – the sales and restoration of military trucks for use by average joes, suburban alphas and collectors.

"One of these I bought at Davis Monthan – it was used by the national guard in 1984. It ain't got but 28,000 miles on it.

Thank God, that means there was no war."

Jack then leads up the path to one of his seven helicopters, a foreboding, house-tall Choctaw whose nose is shaped like the pregnant belly of a T-Rex. This particular copter belonged to Air America, operated in war-time Laos and Vietnam, got replaced by a Huey. Says Jack: "They started producing these in 1961, it has all the parts. I had 138 of them, and it took us three months to move them all. [William] Westmoreland's signature is on some of the paperwork." (He purchased them years ago from Bob's Airpark in Tucson, which is long gone.)

Scrapyards couldn't use them because they're mostly magnesium, almost worthless. So Jack sold most to a renter on one of his lots, who went broke in the 2008 recession.

"He was going to retrofit 99 of them," Jack says. "But he sold them as scrap. This chubby Vietnamese guy bought them and had them smunched up and shipped back to Vietnam. They were made into sparklers and firecrackers, because they're made out of magnesium. It was a real shame."

Between talk of firecrackers produced from war machines, and that some of his collection has starred in film (Kevin Costner's *The Postman*, for example), Jack talks about one of his daughters who lost herself in meth, who's fighting her way back to her own daughter, Juliana. Jack raises that granddaughter now, with the help of a nanny. He talks of Juliana's school performances, at-home shenanigans and age-old parental worries of daughter raising. His granddaughter breathes new life into him, as he breathes new life into machines. He says as much.

This Tucson-born son of a local milkman fell in love with army trucks after he saw the National Guard on practice runs. His love of wheeled machinery deepened when he began fixing things as a kid. "I had some tools. I put dual wheels on my Little Red Wagon."

"But I was a junker from day one," he adds. "My dad used to take me to the dump at I-10 and Grant. He'd be dumping stuff out of the jeep and I'd be putting things back in."

Jack's first car was a used 1950 Ford Business Coupe, "bought it for 20 bucks and drove it home." After graduating high school (in '64 from then-brand-new Palo Verde High), Jack worked for the railroad in Washington State. Drafted at 19, and stationed in Germany, he became a Radio Relay and Carrier Repairman, and was in charge of trucks. "We had 13 trucks in my platoon. Got awards and stuff for taking care of those trucks." Then his appendix burst, peritonitis came on, and he nearly died. "I love Germany, I cried when we left."

He returned to Tucson, hired on at Tucson Gas & Electric (now TEP) for seven years. He lived free, in exchange for nightwatchman work, at a local truck salvage place. He saved his dough, purchased a few trucks and, soon, several acres off I-10. Met his wife Linda and plopped a doublewide on the property. Had their first child, Josh, while opening his business in late 1977. The couple had three more children, two of whom found careers in the Army, and they raised Linda's daughter from a previous union.

The lot grew steadily, and at one point employed five full-time "until the economy tanked. Employees are like adopted children, you can't just hire and fire because business is bad. They have families... It's a huge responsibility."

Jack's wife died in 2011 after a bout with pneumonia, and he can't hide from the sadness. "I'd look at those dating sites, but I love my wife so much I can't do it." He still lives in their home, with Juliana, on seven acres out near east Saguaro National Park.

★ ★ ★

We climb into Jack's dusty-cabbed Dodge flatbed and roll over to one of his multi-acre storage lots, less than a mile away. This one's filled with walls of monster tires pulled off everything from six-ton trucks to 50,000-pound tank haulers. Tire walls form mazes where one can get lost. Jack hunts down a tire for another grey beard in a SUV. The customer could be his brother. After 20 minutes of hunting they find what they're after, the sale goes down.

Later, Jack lifts himself up and peers into the driver window of a 4x4 tactical vehicle – one of countless classic Department of Defense sell-me-downs for civilian use. "This one only has 3,000 miles on it," he says, "cost taxpayers $104,000! But it's old, from 1997, I think. You don't want to send our guys to Afghanistan in something this *old*."

Jack purchased this one, and so many like it, cheap, but won't reveal numbers. "I still get good deals," he says. One can drive this diesel beast off the lot for 15K. Hundreds of military trucks sit ready for sale to anyone. A buyer could roll away in a military GMC truck for $7,500, restored to dependability – a better deal than Craigslist or eBay.

His business is word-of-mouth, so he's fairly selective to whom he sells. He won't, for example, let an antiquated truck go for scrap metal. Maybe it's idealism left over from his military days, or maybe he only wants to preserve what's what, but, "If someone comes and wants to build a rat rod, I say out, out, *out*."

He's not the biggest fan of artists either: "They want everything free."

In the old days, Jack would stock up on trucks at military

auctions all over the Southwest and Southern California. But now the government and buddy contractors find their civilian buyers through online auctions.

And if ever a brand was forever flush with excess killing hardware, it's the U.S. military. The surplus is huge, and big business. The U.S. is the largest exporter of arms in the world. (The *New York Times* reported the U.S. made $42 billion last year selling aircraft, ships, armored vehicles, and missiles to foreign governments.)

The government's so-called 1033 program (which Trump insanely kicked into high gear) guarantees law enforcement agencies access to heavily armored and combat-ready machines from the Department of Defense. The military's harmless leftovers wind up in places like Jack's Gov't Surplus Trucks, or get destroyed.

"There's a place, HVF West, a contractor in Tucson, where you ought to see all the Humvees and trucks and bulldozers getting destroyed... I'm over here trying to put them together and they're over there cutting up brand new ones. It's such a waste.

"The internet has ruined everything," Jack continues. "Online auctions have made it easier for anyone to buy and sell, but the prices have risen steeply. My sources are my biggest competition." He cautions, "You buy online, you get as-is."

Jack gets by the old-fashioned way, and he knows it. Sweat and labor, and a certain kind of love. "Here, we're selling service," he says. "We get the trucks running. If it doesn't work you bring it back."

He pauses.

"I'm just a kid in a big toy sandbox."

★ ★ ★

A few days later rain falls on the dead-quiet sales lot. It's near dark, and Jack's in his tiny, fluorescent-lit office. Floor-to-ceiling: piles of documents and tools and heaving filing cabinets. Dozens of yellowed Polaroids stapled to one wall show trucks he's owned, a few featuring his sunny-faced boys in grins or bright jackets, posed on one of Dad's old things. Decades of spider-webs and dust mortared to the window kind of reflect who this guy is. Like what's set shouldn't be messed with.

In a moment he'll get up to let his dog Lucky out to roam the lot for the night.

"Ever get lonely?" I ask as we step into rainy dark.

He clears his throat. "I stay busy here so I don't have the time for that."

Talk quickly shifts like distraction to auto manufacturing. How after five years new cars are junk and junked, rarely parted out and wholly disposable. His acres are filled with things designed to withstand elements – the years, the rust, the wars. Machinery that's been around long enough – some pieces are among a few remaining on Earth – that it's only outshone by the desert sun.

"I don't have any money," he says, flatly. "The property taxes are so high I have to use every inch of 15 acres. I bought everything on payments. Never had money, only trucks."

February, 22, 2018

OUTSIDE THE BOX

There's something almost formal and studied in Del Hendrixson Jr.'s affect, not like he's been media coached or overschooled; more like someone who has dealt closely with the rungs of human existence. But if questions probe much, he deflects with queries of his own. When he quizzes this digit, it's the only time he seems insincere, yet to be the focus of his attention is flattering. There's his power. A born leader, more minister than Manson. "I just learned from my dad," Hendrixson says. "If you're not in control, someone else is. My dad was very powerful."

In the early 80s Hendrixson got popped for creating false birth certificates and Social Security cards for undocumented immigrants. He did a year in a federal pen where he'd become a monster who felt like a "garbage can. You learn to brutalize in prison."

Soon after jail the self-hatred peaked and Hendrixson procured an Uzi. He was, literally, going postal. But his mind got in the way; maybe murdering innocent folk at a post office wasn't such a good idea. To hear him tell it, it "could've been God's voice." A moment passes, and he adds with no blinking, "It was a voice, and a light" telling him to help others. "This message made sense to me."

Another pause.

"Look, I'm fucking crazy," he says. "I really am bonkers. But it's a disciplined insanity."

Instead of murdering people, he launched Bajito Onda, a still-going nonprofit ministry (minus the religious dogma) and foundation for community peace and development. It's a

Latino brand too, employing Chicano and prisoner artists, enlisting their designs for commercial purposes, with little offshoot startups like 420 Bake On Glass that creates proprietary glass-infused decals licensed to national bong and pipe manufacturers. Bajito Onda is funded through these operations. His client list now includes Procter and Gamble, Eagle Eye, Illadelph Glass and others. At 71, Hendrixson's a master printer too, able to "print anything on anything."

Raised in Arkansas and Texas, Hendrixson is a freakily ageless ex-con with a pleasing Southern drawl. Soft in the middle with snow-colored indoor pallor, sprawling tats and a shocking gray spiked coif. He also happens to have been born a girl. "If your brain doesn't match your body, oh, well. Everybody just get over it."

Hendrixson was walking fringes long before Candy Darling or jazz great Billy Tipton's transgender stories were widely known or accepted. He has an unpublished autobiography, *My Transgender Life, Confusion and Conquests*, that details his early life, a heady timepiece of 1960s and 70s mores, sex, and identity chaos. Late author Robin Moore (who penned, among other bestsellers, *The Green Berets*, *The French Connection* and *The Happy Hooker: My Own Story, with Xaviera Hollander*) helped Hendrixson with the book, which was actually published in the late 1970s on Moore's own imprint, but, for whatever reason, was never distributed. The book might see light soon.

Hendrixson's spirit has had to overcome a lot in life. And finally, he's been rewarded, he says.

The dark-skinned Hiracy is 31 and lovely like Lais Ribeiro's sister. She was a cop and banker in Brazil, owns a black belt in Brazilian jiu-jitsu. She was born to a tribe in the Ama-

zon rainforest. Through a friend, Hendrixson became her online English teacher.

"I'd been talking to her on the phone. One day she said 'I like you.' I was trying to teach her English. Soon she said, 'I really like you.' I said, 'We have to talk about my age,' and she said 'Why?'"

★ ★ ★

We're in the office of Hendrixson's smallish warehouse near Armory Park. The words "Bajito Onda" greet visitors on the front door and inside walls are filled with awards and certificates, prison art, pics of Hiracy, her two children, all seemingly happy. There's a pair of workshops with printing presses and a mad collection of more prison art in back, and ad hoc living quarters.

Hiracy's on Skype on Hendrixson's iPhone. Her English is pretty good, and his Portuguese is coming along. She's in Manaus, in northern Brazil, with her two boys, aged 9 and 11, who still live there. "Our goal is to get the children here," Hendrixson says later. "Until then she goes back and forth, three or four times a year. It's not what we want, but that's how it is right now."

Hiracy and Del are glued to one another, he says, and she nods in agreement. They talk as much as 30 times a day when she's away. When he first traveled to Brazil to meet her, she locked him in a room for a few weeks.

Jealousy. It's true, she tells me.

"When in the Amazon, do as the Indians," Hendrixson adds as a way of explanation. "She wanted to know what I was about. It was her way. She's very puritanical. I sat in that room and wondered..."

He adds, "Haters all over the world told her I was a womanizer. Now the Indians call me The Diamond; it's my skin color, I'm tall, and my hair."

Each other's names are tattooed on their person, and Hiracy lifts her forearm and knuckle to show me hers. They got her green card. The two were married by her tribe in 2014, and married here a year later. "Her uncles did a blessing over us there," Hendrixson says. "They had to feel our energies."

When he resorts to kid-voiced sweetnesses one understands theirs is at least love: "She treats me like a little baby. She bathes me. She dresses me. She's also powerful, and it's primal."

Hiracy grew up in a Tupinamba tribe and is considered royalty. She left the sovereign for college. Hendrixson says, "her father is connected to animals – his whole life is connecting to animals." She shoots her tribe now with a camera in the rainforest.

When Hendrixson boasts of his wife's life and intelligence, which he does often, it's like he's helping to define who *he* is. Her life ratifies his. He'll speak partnership in Bajito Onda and in the next sentence go personal: "our relationship is totally uninhibited."

★ ★ ★

When Hendrixson arrived in Tucson in 2009, he knew no one and his head was a mess. He left his Dallas office and workshop and printing machinery behind. He was done with Texas, especially Dallas, a place where "everybody dies. It's horrible there, all plastic... In East Dallas if you're not aggressive you're a victim. I got to Tucson and no one is aggressive. It blew my mind. I was more exposed to the world here. Bajito Onda was my whole world. No one knew about it here. Someone said, 'Do you even know who you are?' Bajito Onda was the vehicle for me to do something, but I never truly understood who I was."

He found help at La Frontera Center, a mental health facility. "Taught me how to be vulnerable. And it was hard."

Hendrixson's dad was a strict WWII colonel, and Hendrixson idolized him. He wasn't close to his mom and sister. They all disowned him when he went to prison. He lived in rural Mexico for a year and learned Spanish. But lived mainly in Dallas, where he "walked with snakes and rats" and "became one of the most violent people I knew."

Since prison, Hendrixson has helped people through his Bajito Onda. A 2005 *Dallas Observer* cover story tells of his rescuing lost and violent people from themselves, "and cleansing them and sending them out to live normal, healthy, productive, happy lives." Not much has changed.

He's still helping families deal with violent deaths of loved ones. Helping with gang members, drug addicts; he's helped folks reenter worlds after brutal prison runs. He's been commended for it, received citations from the Governor of Texas and international conferences for at-risk youth. He has spoken at United Nations conferences and at universities, and he has taken gang members to conferences on youth crime prevention. Started outreach programs in prisons and has given talks at law enforcement agencies.

And Bajito Onda has little chapters in other parts of the world, in Europe, Brazil and Mexico. It's a foundation, a way of life, he says. A loose-knit collective, internet connected. Cult-ish but not exactly a cult, nor a church. "It's more like DACA," Hendrixson says. "But an underground society." He claims the foundation has a half-million followers and fans throughout the world. The number's difficult to verify, but Bajito Onda's presence is evident.

Hendrixson's collection of Chicano and prisoner art is vast, boxes of the stuff. He befriended prisoner artists over the years, helped some with rehabilitation. Others are beyond reclamation, criminally insane, "but genius. It's not ugly prison art, it's art from the hands of prisoners."

Many murdered children and whole families. So some works collected on a table in his workshop stun in that train-wreck way; cellblock visions of turmoil and violence for the heartsick and the lost. The madnesses and sadnesses are transmitted. Thousands and thousands of hours of practice turn pencil-drawn scenes into symbols of street desperation. One shows a Native American's vision of death and faith and sex in images of lovers and mothers. Another shows a head and razor-sharp teeth and foul light floating from eye sockets, while the seven deadly sins are spelled out and float about mockingly. One brutal self-portrait in pencil is surrounded by symbols of human struggle and peace, and the equally unattainable and heavily sexualized female form, and it's pure yearning. No one else on Earth could do these works.

"When you're in prison, your mind is free but your body is frozen," he says. "It's the opposite when you get out. I was insane when I got out of prison – a total piece of shit."

September 21, 2017

UP IN SMOKE

Meet Skip Blum. Little serpents dance in the air above his head.

He's lanky and old and could be one who road-managed Little Feat back in the 70s or that guy who'd travel to the Hamptons and Florida with an ounce of blow in his briefcase talking endlessly about the recording studio and record label he owned that nobody had ever heard of. Maybe they were the same. (Wait. Skip says he *did* sell ounces of blow in the Hamptons and down in Florida.) Or maybe he's some Coen Brothers caricature, a walking, talking allegory for the decay of the classic rock 'n' roll era and its attendant sensibilities, what's left of its rock-star scheming, its endless cash cows, its cocaine cowboy casualties.

Anyway, "I passed my nine lives," Skip says, exhaling another serpent of meth smoke. Then he picks up a guitar and strums along to The Kinks' "Celluloid Heroes," a semi-tender rock 'n' roll epistle to failed dreams if ever there was one.

He stops playing and dumps what's left of his meth out on a little desk and pinches a few more translucent chunks and drops them into the glass pipe.

"I'm not like these people around here," he says, lifting the thing to his mouth. "They smoke this shit and they can't stop; on and on for days. I only smoke a little, and then I play guitar. I sleep a lot, every night."

He places his lighter under the bowl, sparks a flame and sucks. The flavored vitamin water in the low curve of the pipe bubbles ("adds a bubblegum flavor") and the meth vapor curlicues, passing between his lips into his lungs, ballooning his

blood vessels, and his heart and nervous system kick into overdrive and serotonin rushes his brain.

Yet he just sits here. No inner-animal unleashed. No bizarrely contorted countenance. High or not, his thin white face stays blank, as if chiseled into a tree trunk. Dude would make a kickass three-card Monte man.

In fact, little vitality pumps through Skip's limbs, not like you'd expect after a long pull from the pipe. For one thing he's suffered a couple of strokes in recent years. Amazingly, he sucks an inhaler for chronic pulmonary disease and talks of collapsed lungs. I ask him if the meth is such a good idea.

"It can't really help," he says.

Then he muses leisurely about his favorite music, talks about playing with Dire Straits decades ago (uncredited, but he produces evidence of it), a stint living in Jamaica ("I was a white Rasta") where he befriended and jammed with reggae star Justin Hines and smoked the kind of weed that guaranteed you wouldn't get up off of the street. He relates tales of traveling to islands with Dick Clark and his wife, and of old friends, like actors Melissa Gilbert and Bo Brinkman and how they loved his Manhattan apartment so much they purchased the one above his. Other yarns involve bit players and East Coast has-beens and urban-legend thugs.

He leafs through squeaky pages of a photo album that show his family's spread on Long Island's gold coast (Muttontown), one of America's wealthiest blips. Yellowed snaps show fresh-faced, long-haired Skip with horses and German shepherds he raised, and his mom, dad and two brothers, an ex-wife and daughter. He points out shaggy-headed musician friends who died young. He tells of a cousin, a higher up in the Jewish Defense League, who was gunned down in New York City.

Skip knows his life's narrative is listener-friendly, and it comes in fits and starts. The visuals help but he can't remember much. He has no memories of childhood or high school, for example.

Why?

"You'd have to ask my psychiatrist."

Let's back up. I met Skip through a Lyft driver who said he was a living Scorsese script. The mob connections and he smoked through two mill worth of cocaine.

I drive Skip to the Walgreens on Speedway and Craycroft. Though his face looks like what might result if you combined Joey Ramone with Howard Stern, with added hard road, and his speaking voice sounds like Winnie the Pooh's Eeyore with a light Bronx patois, he strolls into Walgreens with an air of one who once had lots of money, like an old English rock star who's been hitless too long, sequestered in some over-mortgaged countryside estate. With his cane and flowing gray mane there's an almost diva-like grace and eccentricity – that particular kind that only money and privilege and age can cultivate. Yet the 63-year-old wears ratty blue jeans with worn knees, a tired green shirt, and carries a camo backpack.

Dave, the grinning man behind the register, says "Hey! Skip! How are ya today?"

Skip steps past him. Makes no eye contact, says, "couldn't be better."

Dave looks at me, chuckles, and adds, "Skip pays the light bill here."

I follow Skip as he negotiates the aisles, sometimes the same one three times, comparing prices and collecting things: A box of cookies, hydrogen peroxide, crackers, flavored water, gum; "snacks" to fortify his body so he won't faint. He collects a script he called in earlier. He takes pills for his anxiety disorder, for his cholesterol, for his depression, and so on. So many pills.

He's had the anxiety since he was a kid. And there are skin problems. Forearm scars from cancerous operations, and the cancer's still in his body.

The strokes he suffered landed him at Campana Del Rio, assisted living for the elderly. Skip laughs at the inherent futility of that: "I'd wear nothing but my cowboy boots and underwear around the place, in the front, the dining room. I'd play my guitar through an amp in my room. It was me and all these 90-year-olds. Of course I got kicked out of there."

Skip strolls aisles talking mob. "They're still around. It's bullshit that it doesn't exist, there are crews in Tucson." Says the FBI popped him once and let him go. Did jail time for drugs too. Says he's not allowed to know how much money he has or where it is. Dad left an estate, life insurance, that's all he knows. His condo is paid for. His brother handles his finances. He never sees his two grown daughters either, both born in New York City. The coke freebasing made them disappear. Wife too. "I miss them all the time."

We hit Headhunters tobacco shop on Speedway, then Rainbow Guitars on Campbell. Everyone knows him. And as the day progresses, more things about Skip stand out. He's perpetually self-deprecating and fiercely intelligent. He once earned his teaching credentials on the fly and taught fourth grade for six months in Tucson, to jumpstart a normal life. Didn't last.

The Bronx-born Skip has two younger brothers. Dad hit paydirt working for a Rothschild in finance, made a killing in banking. After high school Skip split for Israel, busked guitar on the streets of Tel Aviv, on the Dead Sea coast, and weathered bombings during one of many Lebanese-Isreali wars. That was the 70s, during the rise of the PLO. He ran out of money, stranded in London.

Hey dad.

He later graduated from Syracuse University, degreed in

marketing and advertising, and earned a masters from Florida's Hofstra University. He declined mad job offers to work in a bowery leather shop and live in Little Italy when Blondie, Ramones et al were breaking Manhattan. He was a China Club regular, sometimes the Mudd Club and CBGB. He got involved with a recording studio because he wanted to be a rock star. Made a tidy fortune heading up a giant limo company "owned by the mob."

Two decades ago Skip landed in Tucson and holed up in the Catalina Foothills.

★ ★ ★

There's drug-dealer futility beneath the surface of Skip's boxy-anonymous condo complex near Wilmot on Tucson's east side. Waning afternoon light through smudged windows gives his sparely furnished place a suffocating despair. Like heartbreak. The phone rings and Skip learns cops nabbed the guy who brings meth into his complex. "He got caught with $100K in cash," Skip says. "Eh, they're all going away sooner or later."

He shows me his extensive collection of custom-made knives he uses for protection and how his place is fitted with bulletproof windows. "I've been ripped off too many times."

He asks if it's cool if he smokes some meth.

The smell makes my heart skip, years of meth sobriety feel inconsequential, perfunctory. I want into that festering, shuttered world, to never come up for air. This is the first time I've been around meth since I managed to quit it, and my entire body screams for it. Frightened, I feel nauseous. It's no wonder sad people adore crystal meth.

Defined and discounted by his mistakes, Skip's long past the point of shaming himself because of the drugs. His power never outweighs his pain, never allows for the acceptance of how things will never likely go his way again. He's regretful, contrite. Even while high. That's what amazes. He just wants to get by. I feel only tenderhearted toward him.

"I've tried to grow up," he says. "I haven't been able to. I'm just a fuck-up. I'm still here because god won't have me up there. I'm alone a lot, and I wake up scared all the time. I got scared when my parents died; who was going to take care of me? I still don't know what's going on in my life, like where I'm going to be in 10 years. Music is my life, but I have no goals, nothing to look forward to. I get depressed."

Before I'm out of there, Skip cues up a cassette demo of a New York City band he was in years ago; tunes he co-wrote and played guitar on. We're in the spare bedroom, filled with lots of cared-for acoustic and electric guitars on stands, a few vintage Fenders and Gibsons.

Blum can't remember the exact recording dates, sounds like late 80s, early 90s. The tunes are written, performed and executed well. One's like a classic-rock radio hit, would've sidled up sweetly to Night Ranger's "Sister Christian" – big guitars, chesty vocals, syrupy pathos.

Skip sings along: "I just might make it out of here, I just might..."

June 2, 2016

A LOVE-STOKED WORLD

It is easier to build strong children than to repair broken men. – Frederick Douglass

I turn him upside down and hold him there and soon he begins screaming. But it's closer to a cry, I guess, with some cackle in there, and if you didn't know any better it's probably what it sounds like when somebody's getting stabbed. His face is turning all red.

"Abajo, mamá, abajo. Caer!"

Three different words, something about falling and mother. I'm a Spanish-illiterate idiot, but I get that much.

We're on a big rock above Tucson and a strong westerly is about pushing us backwards. Cars move slowly through Gates Pass below, a lightning-streaked wall of blackness falls over the Tucson Mountain peaks, and the Old Tucson movie studio down in the basin is whelmed in monsoon dust and rain. Too-green saguaros, bloated on so much recent rain, stand tall against it.

So alive, electric, like this upside down three-year-old named Reece. When you're never around a little kid and then you suddenly are around a super-intuitive one, it's like they're from asteroid B-612. I vividly see my own inertias, and ugly fictionalized inner-narratives and self-hatreds and I sense how all of it is pretty much killing me. Man, I don't want any kid getting a whiff of that stuff.

He's just another boy against the world, a white Yankee with corkscrew blond locks and big soft green eyes whose first language is Spanish. A kid who doesn't yet understand intolerance and racism and fear and beliefs ruined by too much self-belief, or not enough self-belief. A kid not ruined by debilitating inner needs to have someone else make him feel authentic, or that first kiss with a girl (or a boy). No starry-eyed dreaming on bright handheld screens.

I lift him right side up and set him down on the giant rock, and in that moment – like how sometimes you can think 17 ideas in the time it takes to stand up straight – I think how lucky Reece is to see in his every sightline a world of a million different marvels and discoveries beyond the surface of a desert storm and skylines.

I think of how there's no room for the mean reds in this boy, and how it's impossible to imagine Reece ever hating what he sees when he sees himself. Maybe I'm a sentimental fool, but common sense says that when there's nothing feeding his potential sicknesses there'll be no unhealable hole in Reece's chest as he grows up, therefore no fists jacking in all-white centers of Donald Trump rallies or bloody alcoholic screams from state-paid beds. No lost years ripped straight from the real world, floundering, forgotten and wasted.

But how quickly beauty vanishes. I think of how Reece has yet to give shape to real live boogeymen, to that avarice-drunk mook Trump, whose gift to the world is his ability to release festering hate from constricted minds like a pressure valve. Reece doesn't yet see the solipsistic ugliness in the Donald, or anyone. So maybe Reece will never be aware of what it feels like to be embarrassed of your own skin color, embarrassed of your own gender. It's fact that Reece, like me, would rather see Donald Duck as U.S. President than the Donald.

I think how hate's learned, and of little boys and girls whose curiosity leads them directly to the hems of strangers,

how they can fall instantly in love with them, or be perplexed by them, but either way enlightened. Reece's eyes sparkle in the presence of strangers and he approaches them with curiosity – observation without judgment – and I'd watched him befriend the Latino kids leaping on these giant rocks, and embrace and follow a man named Sticky dressed as a saguaro cactus, and feel sorrow for the homeless, and so on.

Reece is already beginning to learn the stories of others, inherently. When you learn stories of others you learn empathy, and then how it can feed and define you. I didn't understand the value of any of that until years and years later. So in Reece I can see that there is no devil, not one that I know, not one that I don't know. Is that possible?

I think of a boy fueled on love, who doesn't eat animals because he loves them. He's lucky too because he'll likely never know welfare birthdays, and his refrigerator is always filled – there's that. And he has a real home and a remarkable mother who teaches ideas of love and art and song and literature and things like how Black Lives Matter is only a bare minimum in humanity's gaze. Reece is never his mother's down time. Back at his home in Los Angeles, Reece, I'm told, helps care for various barnyard rescues and has an adopted turkey named Joanie, and of course he was horrified the first time he saw a spitted turkey at the grocery store.

Reece makes me think of other men and women who abandon their own children. I'm no parent but wonder who could abandon something like this? What cruel, selfish lives deadbeats must suffer.

I now know his mother. She's a Los Angeles-based novelist who contacted me out of the blue one day to edit her novel. And she was in town so we could finish the first edit of her book, which we did. She brought Reece and that's how I met him.

Now we're in the dirt between rocky formations above Gates Pass and Reece is on his knees building a house from stones and things, and he buries sticks for the plumbing and electrical lines, digs holes for a bathtub, toilet and sink, for animals to drink from too, and clears a road to and from, and it turns into visual storytelling. He's reproducing mental images of the bigger idea of home, and there's self-reflection. He occasionally breaks into a song by The Smiths and one by the Chris Robinson Brotherhood, in little-kid English, but the melodies are there.

Make the world stop. Make it radiate love so pure that it overpowers blind hate. Maybe that sounds corny as hell; maybe the gauzy innocence of a boy makes me a harebrained optimist. But this kid inherently chooses love over hate and anger, and I think of people I know, ones who nearly died prematurely. They're jaded but still generous of soul and can talk of love and hope even after having gone to war battling wrenching addictions, or after suffering poverty-riddled childhoods marked with molestation and beatings and hatred. They talk of this stuff without hiding behind irony or sarcasm or pseudonyms. It's learned spirit and hope, and they're not so busted up anymore, but they had to go to battle for it because it wasn't inside of them. They're in the fringes and minorities, but they're brave ones. Reece already has it in him.

Later that night Reece is strapped in his child's seat and he makes up a song, playing a guitar he made from straws. Sings a ditty in Spanish about a guy under a table who's sad because the wine is gone, or spilled, or something. Great song.

Then we arrive at a record store, Zia on Speedway.

"Por qué la música de Kid Rock es muy malo?" he asks.

Mother says her son wonders why Kid Rock's music is so bad? Reece has yet to ask a stupid question. I begin to say something bloated about how Rock's a talent-free hack who rode the backs of gifted, black Detroit rappers to fame without giving them any credit, but I stop myself. Instead, I tell him that all he has to do is listen to the music. He'll hear no soul there. But he already got that.

He walks out of Zia with Harry Nilsson's *The Point*, so far the best adult kid's musical parable ever. It'll reward Reece with meanings for years.

For years.

Reece will likely live to see the year 2100. Think of that: a year that very well could be fraught with political insanity and social insanity, but absolute scientific amazement. Reece, a thigh-higher who inadvertently teaches that rewards are everywhere, and if you can't find them, you still have to look for them, or perhaps you're dead.

But he'll make bad choices too, get lost, and drunk or high or whatever, maybe wind up in dark places, and his heart will get shattered and burned. He'll stumble, fall, but he'll pull himself back. He'll be able to pull himself back because his mother understands the truths and she's setting the boy up on solid ground, overseeing valleys of sun and valleys of rain.

August 11, 2016

THE RUNWAY

It's so sweetly rhythmic and fantastic. It must be the greatest Woody Woodpecker laugh on Earth, even if it smothers Paul Simon's crusty-sweet "Me and Julio Down by the School-yard" and inspires at least one set of nearby eyes to roll. Mark Torres fully owns that chortle, and more: His short, thick graying coif rises into a mini version of Woodpecker's 'hawk. So, yeah, the other barstool lollygaggers call him Woody.

Back in the 1980s, when Woody was a student bused to Catalina High School, his nickname was "Twelve Pack." Was considered a legend. He's a freelance plumber now, lives walking distance from here in the same neighborhood in which he grew up. Even when not Woodpeckering, Woody still shudders with delight – his grin is as perpetual as the Bud Light on the bar before him. He's instantly likable, outwardly gentle and it's easy to sense he might've been unnecessarily fucked with over the years, and that maybe he never relied on the kindness of others for anything because there was no kindness from others.

"That guy," Woody says, laughing, pointing to the bar's grey-haired manager Tim Smith, "treats me better than my own family." Woody says most everything with a laugh – even the woeful stuff. Maybe he knows the secret? Either way, it's easy to see how one might feel protective of him.

★★★

It's Friday night at The Runway Bar and Grill, which sits on a dusty, dispossessed stretch on Alvernon Way south of 29th

Coors
LIGHT
BUD LIGHT
Budweiser
Coors
ORIGINAL
STEINIE
Lite
12/1 LITER

Street, a piece of Tucson that doesn't exactly relish much of its own history. In fact, decades ago, a Douglas F4D Skyray fighter jet from Davis-Monthan Air Force base lost control and exploded into a Food Giant supermarket that sat across the street, killing four people and destroying the store and nearby homes. The crash might've set the area's aesthetic tone, which now includes a used car lot, an abandoned gas station or two, a tire shop, a few vacant storefronts, dirt lots and a fairly spectacular-looking tattoo parlor.

Yet, the lounge inside retains mirthful details, such as pink and blue trimmed walls, and a warm magenta hue saturates its two rooms. There's a glorious-sounding jukebox, TVs of various shapes (tonight showing wrestling), ancient gumball machines, framed photos and well-crafted models of WWII-era fighter planes, a pair of pool tables, and an outdoor patio. There's a 60s-vintage menu showing Korean dishes such as bulgogi, as well as tacos, and chicken strips with fries, all prepared in the back kitchen. Taped to a wall mirror below the menu are snapshots of jolly Runway inmates, including the storied Professor and his pool-cue bud Damage, two brotherly gents who survived wars and hiccupping livers but not cancer. Gone forever but still mourned here.

There are no chirpy undergrads or self-styled artiste fringe-dwellers in Warby Parkers here – it's too far from downtown, and, anyway, hunting for renditions of the loser experience is passé; too many drinking-driving horror stories put an end to that dreadful pastime.

These are beer-swill floor finishers and housing inspectors, one-legged bakers and disability recipients. Its air is tinged with the tangy scent of functional alcoholism, wrapped in a warm misfit-family glow and warmth. It's a cozy corner bar, a backdated scene from a waning watering-hole culture heading the way of drive-in movie theaters.

It's easy to feel terribly rustic about The Runway, because it's easy to feel terribly rustic about a corner old-man bar whose regulars move through the world like how a lot of us do, in a state of lasting resignation and bafflement, in the way of the heartsick and battle-worn. For me it mirrors what it's like to be a grown-up in the deepest sense; that is, realizing but perhaps not admitting to myself that I understand what it feels like to be hopeless.

★ ★ ★

Woody's barstool bud is the broadly built, glabrous-headed Dave Gonzales ("with an 'S'!"), a former baker. He lifts his left pant leg at the ankle to reveal a prosthetic limb, which he lost to health problems. He's been back in town for a couple days, in from New Mexico where his mother had just died.

"We're barflies," Gonzales says, and tonight he's helping to break-in the new bartender, a pretty, big-eyed 25-year-old named Teti Moniz.

"She's a rookie," he adds. "But it's obvious she'll take no shit from anybody."

She bites her lip, smiles. She's never tended bar and it's her second night, and Tim's training her with fatherly patience. He hopes she'll bring in a few customers because, he says later, the bar just isn't making it, not like it did.

Tim, a retired Air Force man who was born on a Massachusetts farm, is a former hurricane hunter who flew on crews into typhoons for study. He now teaches weather forecasting fulltime at Davis-Monthan base while manning The Runway soberly each night including weekends. He looks tired, but is thoughtful and intimidatingly articulate.

Tim met his wife, Runway owner Huicha "Lee" Smith, bartending at Fort Ord military base in Monterey, Calif., where he was stationed. Born in Korea to a military pop, Lee moved stateside after marrying an American who fathered her three kids. The guy was severely abusive, charges were filed, and she took her children and fled.

Tim married Lee after a three-year courtship, wound up in Tucson upon his '95 transfer to Davis-Monthan. They joined a local Korean Baptist church, and through an acquaintance there found this bar, which Lee scraped and borrowed to purchase in 2001. The two previous Runway owners were also Korean.

Tonight the bespectacled Lee's slouched at the end of the bar tapping languidly on her tablet. She's been here most of the day. In conversation, her percussive Korean accent gives her voice indelible authority, reinforces an idea that she's a tough family matriarch. Get talking and she softens. Her seven grandchildren take up time she'd otherwise spend working on her art. A framed portrait she drew of her son hangs in the bar. He took ill and fairly recently died and the drawing is a tribute. He worked here sometimes, she says, and the regulars all loved him. She loves the regulars too. The Runway stays afloat on them. "The customers don't pick us, we pick customers," she'll say, adding how it helps to have the man upstairs on the Runway's side.

She offers a story: One day a gent in a ski mask entered and pulled a gun on her. "I didn't know who it was," she says. "But I just shouted, '*Jack*! Put down the gun. You don't want to *do that*.' I don't know how I knew it was Jack; his name just came out of my mouth. It was god talking."

Jack, a onetime Runway barfly, set the gun on the bar, removed his mask and apologized. Lee never called the cops.

"It's the only robbery – or attempted robbery – we've ever had," Tim adds. "People do desperate things when they're hungry."

The couple form relationships with patrons, feel protective of them. Tim, for example, hires Woody for Runway plumbing needs. When Lee took ownership, The Runway held steadfast to the blue-collar tradition that saw regulars cashing Friday work checks at the bar.

But the bar's business waned significantly. Tim says they wouldn't make it if he didn't teach fulltime. "Stiffer DUI laws. Culture changes. The revitalization in downtown may have hurt our business too."

More, the Runway suffered incidents that, Tim says, were beyond their control. The Arizona Department of Liquor Licenses came down on them a few years back when the bar hosted hip-hop shows; someone pulled a gun in the parking lot, patrons smelled of spliff. There were other small infractions. The fines cost them nearly $8,000.

"We 86'd drug dealers when we first bought the place," Lee says. Her voice rises. "And I had death threats! I'd say to them, 'You're gonna come over here and kill me? Come on then!'" She shakes her head. "Of course they never showed *up*."

Potential killers steered clear. There's no undercurrent of menace or casual aggression detected here. Not now. But there is magic tonight.

Greg Rhetta's a gray-mustachioed guy, late 40ish, in town from Vegas. His third in as many nights at The Runway. His talky charm suits the corner bar milieu.

He slides a novel from his leather messenger tote, which also contains another book and four decks of cards. He instructs me to go stand in a corner of the bar and select a single word from the book's 300 pages.

"Handkerchief" it is. I close the book and return it to him at the bar.

"Think of a word that begins with the letter of the word you chose from the book," he says.

"Hammer," I say.

He pulls a pen from his tote and scribbles on the back of a business card. It says "Handkerchief."

There's stony silence. "Jesus Christ," I say.

And like some black Elvis, Rhetta says, "Thank you very much."

Maroon 5's "Sunday Morning," comes on the juke and Rhetta sings along in perfect pitch, adding a honeyed harmony. He's been harmonizing the night with about every song played. He deserves another beer, on me.

Woody goes on about his dog. "Know why I call him Chance? Because I took a chance on him..." Then that Woodpecker laugh of laughs follows us through the door, out into the precise hum of the windy Alvernon night. The colorful blur of tattoo parlor neon, the darkened tire shop, the spectacular Runway sign.

January 28, 2016

BAD ART, KILLER PSYCH

Steve Purdy pumps a clinched fist and rocks in his desk chair to a loud YouTube video of a Tucson epic-rock band called Ashbury. It's as if they're transmitting mystical currents. With outward, kid-like energy, he shouts, "These guys are huge in Europe and no one knows who the hell they are in Tucson." He points out the guitar heroics of Randy Davis, a dude who looks straight out of Jethro Tull circa '74: "Just look at him! Just listen to him!" One needn't be an Ashbury fan to understand their brand of sonic truth, so persuasive is Purdy's energy.

It's funny because Purdy's a ringer for your old stoner uncle who still talks fondly of, say, Quicksilver Messenger Service, Ken Kesey and Peter Max. He looks like pre-liver-transplant Gregg Allman: Tender blue eyes, which can stubbornly take hold of your own when he talks, a bit of a gut, and long, gray-yellow hair slicked back into a ponytail, and a matching beard. But the 68-year-old Steve Purdy is beautiful, and here's why: When he gets going he's a charming raconteur with all the eye-sparkling, air-guitar-playing passion of a 19-year-old music nerd living in his parent's garage. He's also a mad collector of gloriously bad thrift-store art, and proprietor of a rising boutique reissue record label that mostly specializes in unsung, vintage psychedelic bands.

With his record label and art collecting it's like he's excavating bones that shaped his boyhood, and when the conversation shifts from Ashbury to an idea of eternal youth, and his recent high-school reunion, which he didn't attend, Purdy says, unambiguously, "I see guys my age and I'm shocked because they're just so old. It's terrible."

The digging keeps him young. This married father of three grown children offhandedly calls himself the "world's greatest digger," and if someone were to ever compile a list of such, maybe Purdy would make the Top 10.

At least once a year he travels the country mining and discovering pop-culture gold, and can talk endlessly about scouring radio station attics in Illinois, garages in Montana and living rooms in Gallup, New Mexico. For example, he recently unearthed an unreleased album by a super-obscure early 80s Detroit punk band called The Gerbils. He dug the master tapes out of an El Paso garage. Another time, by sifting through a collection of 70,000 45s that belonged to a retired radio DJ, he found a garage-rock holy grail, a '68 single on Stanco Records by a forgotten band called the Graveyard Five, one of less than 10 in existence, worth thousands. The 45 was boxed away in a 1953 Dodge van (an old mobile X-ray vehicle) that had been parked for decades amongst giant weeds in this DJ's backyard. (Purdy managed to track down the rights holder to the songs and he reissued the 45 on his label.)

Purdy's home office on Tucson's east side could be a bedroom belonging to that kid nerd – a simplified extension of his mirthful psyche. Dusty, palely lit and smelling of old record jackets and incense, it's crammed with collectable records, vintage rock posters he pulled off telephone poles in the 60s, thrift-store discoveries dirt-shoveled into open boxes, and extraordinary amateur art, which ranges from what could be described as demented landscapes and acid-trip fantasies. Purdy lifts one purple-hued piece from a stack and it depicts an alien-looking bird-boy wielding a skateboard, which he cleverly calls, "Tony's Hawk." It's one of hundreds and hundreds he has collected, puntastically named, and shown at galleries.

Since 2012, Purdy has co-curated three showings of his collected art, unearthed in thrift stores, swap meets and dumpsters, in Tucson and around the country. The shows, called "Tales of the Trash," play to enthusiastic crowds in Tucson and Bisbee, and he's taken on a show partner in trash-art collector Mark Bloom. They create swag for their gigs, including posters, T-shirts, magnets and postcards of some of the art. "We sold a bunch of it," Purdy says, "and I had no intention to make money."

In fact, Purdy's been a devoted collector of records and things for 40 years, an obsession that shifted into a business of selling vinyl. That led to Purdy starting his record label, Lysergic Sound Distributors (L.S.D.), about nine years ago. Purdy runs L.S.D. with assistance from his son Trent, who's an accomplished bass player and an archivist at the University of Arizona library. Trent might be a chip off the old block. "He got a Master's in archiving," dad says, "so he's not fucking around." L.S.D. has so far released five, limited-edition LPs, one EP and a single, selling more than 10,000 pieces internationally. To vinyl fetishists, reissue hounds and psych freaks, Purdy's doing god's work.

One of Purdy's "discoveries" was Tucson band Ashbury, whose story is similar to Detroit folk legend Rodriquez. See, Ashbury quietly, and almost mythically, amassed a huge, overseas following on the strength of their long-forgotten, self-released 1983 album, *Endless Skies*. The album's now considered a stone classic in European hard rock circles, some metal critics agreeing that it's one of the best albums *ever* recorded. The band, led by brothers Rob and Randy Davis, didn't know of their overseas popularity until a few collectors began trying to

GREYLOCK
ARIZONA

locate them in earnest.

Purdy fell in love with *Endless Skies* in '08, discovered the band had an uncommonly huge (and growing) fanbase "screaming for a copy" of their original vinyl album, which had been bootlegged myriad times on cassette, CD and vinyl in Europe, Japan and Canada. He couldn't believe Ashbury was from Tucson, and he couldn't find anything out about them. Through a chance connection at a local recording studio, Purdy found the two brothers living in a Tucson trailer park.

Ashbury couldn't get arrested in Tucson, not now, and not when they released their album in 1983. And this band likely wouldn't be headlining European festivals in front of thousands if not for Purdy. The brothers tell me they were already aware, and shocked, of their growing overseas popularity, and they had signed a deal to get their album legitimately reissued. But they really had no intention of putting the band back together. Purdy, and Tucson's musical man for all seasons, Al Perry, helped persuade the bros to reform Ashbury. It paid off. The brothers now support themselves solely on their music.

"Steve, and Al Perry, helped us a lot in other ways, too," Ashbury singer Rob Davis says. "And right now we have offers on the table to play from every country in Europe except Luxembourg."

Another angle to this bizarre little yarn: the siblings now play acoustic sets at Tucson eateries, covering songs by Eagles, James Taylor and others, calling themselves Davis Brothers/Ashbury.

Purdy grew up in "deep" southern Illinois with "the craziest fuckers ever. Nothing back there but cornfields, oilfields, hillbillies and bikers – real bikers." He cut his musical teeth as a lead singer in a couple of bands. Dad was a straight-arrow school administrator who "wasn't crazy about me playing music in the late 60s." Mom was a singer who had recorded a few records (78s) in her day and was a little more accepting of her boy's musical inclinations. But Purdy stayed in school and graduated from Kentucky's Murray State University, did grad work in accounting and finance, and soon honed his entrepreneurial skills on side ventures, like a video store and a poster and T-shirt company.

But, he adds, if not for his wife he would've been dead "years ago." He declines to elaborate. Instead he chuckles that he didn't always look like "Greg Allman. I wore a suit and shaved. Had to. I had three kids. I was vice president of a commercial bank in Illinois before I moved to Tucson 30 years ago. I wound up owning two insurance companies here, including an Allstate agency, which I sold. You've got to put your kids first. And it worked."

The house Purdy shares with the lovely and accommodating Arlene (they've been married 40 years) is filled with folk art, plants, settled-in couches and chairs. There are three cats and a long-haired Chihuahua named Nimi who never barks and whose feet make no sound when she moves, like a dog ghost. Purdy tours the storage areas – the bedrooms that once housed their kids – and they're stuffed with more records, found objects and bad art. He shows off items that'll end up hanging at a forthcoming "Trash" show, or sold on a website, or released on his label, such as the cover art of a forthcoming LP by should've-been-giant, late-60s Tucson psych band Greylock Mansion.

Because vinyl pressing plants are now overrun with orders, the self-titled Greylock LP, which consists of single sides and unreleased songs, has been delayed. But Purdy is patient. It took him three years to even get permission from Greylock leader/singer Merl Reagle, who died in August, to release the tunes. Yes, that's the same Merl Reagle famous for his crossword puzzles, and who was portrayed as himself on an episode of The Simpsons.

Purdy spins Greylock on his office turntable and the guitars burst through the speakers sounding like dull hacksaw blades across pipes, and organs swirl heavenward, like The Doors, but heavier. It really is glorious, hard to believe the band was an obscure teenaged combo from Tucson. Purdy's all kid nerd now, arms flailing, commanding I listen to this "insane" vocal and that "god-like" rhythm. It's a cosmic libretto where Purdy loves to live, a beautiful place that's discomfiting at first. It's where no one ever grows old, but they do get more wrinkly.

October 29, 2015

STICKY SUMMER NIGHTS

The woman in the red and white sundress behind Sticky falls to the concrete, and a disturbing voltage surges through her limbs. Legs kick, body twitches. The two dozen sweat-soaked baseball fans in the same concessions line – tired dads, tubby teens, blue hairs, and jumpy children with festive stripes painted on their faces – are stunned into do-nothingness.

It's the Fourth of July, the sun's still out and it's stupid-hot. Too much beer, bad things happen. The paramedics are onto the suffering woman in seconds, pushing people out of the way. Sticky, who's dressed in a thick, padded green nylon saguaro cactus costume, winces in sympathy for the woman but moves into action, diffusing the grim with a hype-man's chutzpah and a strange high-pitched laugh. He bumps knuckles with those who recognize him. Half pirouettes for a scrum of tiny kids, saying over his shoulder, "I'm a giant pickle from behind." Then he turns and faces them, arms held up in U formation, and shouts, "and a cactus from the front!" Kids hop in place and laugh. He leans over to apologize to a woman in a wheelchair for shouting too loud while ruffling the hair of a wholly captivated tow-headed boy. Few notice the seizure victim being gently lifted to a stretcher, and wheeled away.

The bespectacled, soft-as-dough Sticky is Ken Weir, volunteer mascot for the indie pro baseball outfit The Tucson Saguaros. This evening is the team's biggest home game of their three-month season, and they're kicking ass on the Monterey Lumberjacks. The crowd represents a cross-section of Tucsonans – multiple ethnicities, colors and shapes – and numbers in the thousands, many here for the post-game fireworks. On most home-game nights the crowd numbers in the hundreds, or less.

Sticky moves through Kino Sport Complex with celebrity verve, adored by everyone – from the popcorn lady to the uniformed security folk, from concession attendants to the hardcore Saguaros fans, to the sugar-fueled kids barely old enough to grasp the idea of baseball. (Theirs is fussy infatuation; they beg obliging parents for pictures at Sticky's side, or trot selfishly behind him around the ballpark like he's got the magic flute, frustrated parents in tow.)

How strange and addictive it must feel to be greeted by grins everywhere you step. The adrenaline rush, Sticky says, makes it worthwhile, and therefore the heat doesn't get him, even in his summer-suffocating nylon costume. He donates many hours weekly to the Saguaros, beyond live-game action, so no one can say he doesn't suffer for the team, or the kids.

The Kino is his stage, pure theater, of course. That and a love for hometown baseball.

★ ★ ★

The well-organized Saguaros play in the Pecos League, an indie alliance launched in 2011. Last year was the Saguaro's first season. It's not associated with major or minor baseball teams, yet pro scouts occasionally attend Tucson games, and some players have moved up to bigger teams. The league features a dozen startup pro outfits sporting killer names like The White Sands Pubfish, The Bakersfield Train Robbers, The Roswell Invaders, mostly from dust-up Western towns. Last year The Tucson Saguaros won the league championship and had a record of 51-14.

It's a hard-knock life for the young players, who show unyielding hunger for baseball, for any potential to move up, however slim the chances. Players are paid little and pay their own expenses to games, with help from a booster's club. When teams travel, players often stay with "host families" who also feed them. Part of Sticky's unpaid work is seeking such kind folks to host the visiting teams.

Kathie is Sticky's wife and they've been married 33 years. She's front-office, oversees the Saguaros ticket and merch sales. She's a smart, self-deprecating Texan, and the team's sole paid employee – part-time, ten bucks an hour. ("I put in a lot more hours than what I get paid for.") The 58-year-old says "dude" often and it's never off-putting, mainly because she colors conversations with proud talk of her two children and three grandchildren.

Sticky mostly grew up in Utah, the oldest of seven in a Mormon family. He and Kathie donate dozens of hours weekly to a local LDS church, where Sticky's the first counselor to the bishop in a congregation boasting hundreds of families. He works full time too, and recently began a new clerical administration gig at Davis-Monthan Air Force Base. He had the same job at the VA hospital here, and before that spent nearly two-dozen years in the U.S. Air Force, which had the family living in Germany, Alaska and then Alamogordo, New Mexico. Kathie will talk about the frightening cold and back-break challenges of raising children in America's last frontier, days when the sun rose for an hour at best, school recesses at 38-below in the dark. The Weirs moved to Tucson four years ago and started last year with The Saguaros.

★ ★ ★

Several days after the July Fourth game, we're at the historic Bisbee Warren Ballpark, the oldest operational ballpark in America, a lovely, half-decrepit wood and concrete structure built in 1909 for miners and their families. (The Saguaros call Kino home, but play Sundays here, and this game against The California City Whiptails is their last Sunday of the 2017 season.) We're informed no concessions are available at Warren, and to head across the street to the convenience store ("but be careful bringing in beer").

The announcer's steady radio voice on the tinny PA: "Leading off in the sixth, it's Josh Freeman!" Scattered hands clap. We also hear Sticky: "Go, Josh!" Then he rattles off his raffle-ticket spiel, "One dollar, or six for three. You get a $70 jersey, a hat, or a baseball. Three chances to win."

Kathie's arranging jerseys for sale on the rickety merch table just off to the side of the stands. More than a study of baseball fandom, this is family, and the Weirs seem inexhaustible, intent to cultivate an aura of goodness around The Saguaros. Your parents on a good day.

Kathie shakes her head, making sense of her husband: "Ken is the host-family finder in Tucson, he's the team mascot, he's the guy who picks up players at the airport, he gets griped at, he makes everyone laugh..." She adds, "And we're not coffee drinkers, we're Mormon."

There's usually a dark side, Kathie agrees, to any happy-all-the-time persona, one loud in laughter. Her husband doesn't have a dark side though. Even she's surprised at that, and grateful. She knows depression. Her flight-attendant brother was supposed to be on a United flight lost on 9/11. "He had survivor's guilt and went into deep depression, which lasted years." She looks to her husband over in the stands, in the saguaro getup, his face poking out from its sea-green enclosure – this ageless mix of the Jolly Green Giant and Michelin Man – offering up his song and dance, hustling raffle tickets to every last one of the fans in attendance. "He doesn't get depressed," she says. "Not ever. But he gets tired; he winds down hard."

Out of costume Sticky could be dad-guy in flip-flops with a sunburned forehead, flipping chicken breasts on a backyard barbeque. Kathie adds, "Oh, just add the letter D to his last name."

Sticky converses in Spanish, which he learned living in Columbia for two years on his Mormon mission. He went at 19, and never lost the language. "It's a right-of-passage," Sticky says of the Mormon tradition. The irony isn't lost on him that the ubiquitous Saguaros logo resembles a crucifix and thorns.

He nods, "Yes it does." Mormonism is like their baseball, in a sense.

"Do I believe?" Kathie says, "Is this something I want to do? Yes, I want to do this because I want to do this. Our son no longer comes to church, and it doesn't matter. It's OK. We love him whether he comes to church or not. It's personal," she adds, saying "it's like anything, you have to figure it out for yourself."

She laughs.

"We never stop. I just love the people part of this." She pauses, "But we don't know about next year."

"Who knows if we'll be a team next season," Sticky says later. "But I couldn't leave this if I wanted to."

A Saguaro player appears at the merch table, hunting down his cracked bat, which he's looking to sign and hand to a fan. Kathie hasn't seen it. When he steps away, she says, "It's a shame these boys have to buy their own bats."

★ ★ ★

James "Cowboy" Gilbert sits up at the top of the rafters, is gentle and talkative in a cowboy hat, pearl-snap western shirt, bushy mustache, leathery skin, glasses. He has a frank, unapologetic way when he converses that recalls an older era, some romantic time, when civility wasn't dated. He occupies the same seats in Bisbee and Tucson, and hasn't missed an in-state Saguaros game this season. He's likely The Saguaro's number one fan, even went to spring training to meet the guys.

One night after a game at Kino, Cowboy took me out to the parking lot to show off his in-progress restoration of a '52 Chevy, and he talked of it with the desperate sunniness of a lonely guy. His wife promotes the Freedom Celebration Tucson car show each July 4, filled with hundreds of street rods and classic cars, and best in shows. She accompanies him to one Saguaros game a week. He's a mostly retired mason and carpenter, and he's built things all over Tucson, hospitals and homes, schools and ranches.

His Saguaro team fandom is giant, took hold when he began attending games last year. He knows Sticky and Kathie, and he's part of the family now. The Saguaros even invited him to throw out the first pitch the other night at Kino.

"Oh, man, I was nervous," he says. "I one-hopped it to home plate. The team came out of the dugout to congratulate me. I tell ya, what a highlight in a man's life. If only my father were alive to have seen me throw out that first pitch."

His eyes scan the mostly empty seats at Warren, and he adds, "I'm having a ball. This is my year."

Because of The Saguaros?

A slow deliberate nod. "Oh, yeah."

Jinks is here. Gray hair, chesty laugh, hunched over some. If he looks like a long-retired mail delivery man it's because he is. Worked years for the Bisbee postal service. A Bisbee original whose dad worked in the mines.

Cowboy met Jinks at Saguaro's games here this season, and already they inhabit each other's spaces with the kind of trust earned in long-time friendships. "We just got to talkin'," Cowboy says, "got to chasin' balls."

"Now we've been trading balls." Jinks adds.

Jinks pulls out a pair of photo albums and hands them

over to me. Filled with pics of Bisbee rugby players and a local baseball team dressed in old style uniforms, the albums betray a deep respect for sporting tradition and Bisbee.

The game ends as Sunday evening's coming down. The Saguaros whipped the Whiptails 8 to 4. The several dozen fans move slowly from the stands in that sluggish and hollow post-game way, like they've been cast uncomfortably back to themselves, headed for some Monday reality. As they gather around cars parked on the street, we hear Sticky's percussive laugh again, far away on the other side of the fence, echoing out to the empty field.

July 27, 2017

DESERT DUST TO DUST

The bespectacled guy wearing the beret with the angel pin introduces himself as Boothill Saloon. He unballs a full-length vintage leather coat from his dirty gym bag, slips it on over a black T-shirt and dark shorts and models it for me. Makes him look like Youngblood Priest, only white. He's debating wearing the coat out on the street. Says, "I'll get the dirty looks."

Swampbox humidity winnows fleshy body parts, offering scant protection from the heat. It's the hottest goddamn day on record in Tucson, and Boothill's on foot. I tell Boothill that Youngblood was a badass who'd wear it outside.

Two minutes pass and Boothill has fired off a dozen non-sequiturs. I learn of his goat-killing Pitbull and military-grade crossbows, of booze-injected oranges and the tattoo etched on his right underarm below his elbow, which he proceeds to proudly show you, but not long enough to decode anything save a blotch of blue, crimson, and black. "It's a tower," he says. "I got it before the towers fell."

Then he laughs in that disapproving way that says I'm from some straighter world and therefore incapable of hearing his wisdom and lingo from the street. He launches into another round of sizzling non-sequiturs and I sense his alarming fondness for the Vietnam War, and suddenly understand his many war-inspired tattoos. He's a Nam fanboy. I learn he's 58 years old – but he appears older – and how he regrets being too young to have served in Nam.

His name really Boothill?

That disdainful laugh. "*No*!"

"Walter Caho!" he adds, stuffing the Superfly leather back into his bag. "Lived in Tucson my whole life." He loses interest in me and turns to the register. Fingers a vintage President Nixon lapel button while purchasing a $6 necklace of fake turquoise. Says, "I'll give it to a gal or something." I imagine the gal.

"Boothill is a killer name," I tell him. I'm sincere in saying this.

"I'll be back tomorrow after I get a tattoo," he says to me and store proprietor James Golden. Then he collects his red-stained Styrofoam Eegees cup and street-ready bag, pushes open the front glass door and steps into sunbaked misery. In that light, in one telling, bizarre instant, I recognize in Boothill how desperation of desires – love, money, hope, security, whatever – had taken its toll. I feel pity for him. Wonder at what point do I myself surrender? At what point do I realize that I'm left to flounder in that invisible part of the world haunted by the unwanted? What point do I choose that place because no one expects anything?

Golden's patient indulgence of Boothill had passed. "Fried, died and laid to the side," he says, and I feel guilty for laughing. But I laugh more. I must laugh because it is suddenly so obvious how everything big and small that sits on either side of the smudged glass door of Desert Dust Thrift Antiques and Collectables, on Alvernon south of 22nd Street, is dying. Such a fact has never been more profound than on this 116-degree Tuesday. That's what Golden is really talking about.

Golden is Desert Dust's proprietor, equal parts swap-meet crank and Tennessee gent. His slight southern honk – rounded off, and expressive, jammed with one-liners ("this town is full of liars not buyers") – soothes. Hails from a long line of raconteurs and moonshiners. The mountain people, he says, "the ridgerunners. They come from the Scottish, the highlanders." He laughs: "I'm still that way. As long as I got two goats and a bottle, I'm OK."

Golden stores rolling tobacco in his shirt pocket and a holstered sidearm. He's thin with deep-set eyes and not too tall but looks like he could brawl with the best of them. He knows martial arts too.

Anyway, his Desert Dust is dying. Too bad. It's mind-boggling, a fantastical dusty surplus disorganized in orderly ways on shelves, floors and ceiling, a million and one pieces from your mom or grandmother, or what your eccentric uncle would use to populate his strange world – the sentimental symbols of indignities and joys, the tattered, the insignificant and the bountiful. It's like walking into the startling insides of someone else's stoner head – the deranged Santas and dusty Star Wars curios, distressed gargoyles, pistol BB guns, toe jewelry and Empire-era rockers, and glitter-heeled boots and 15-cent books and Reagan-era clothes and Lovin' Spoonful 45s, all hand curated, and priced as such. I could live here. I could die here, too.

It's like many in Tucson, big Going Out of Business sign slung across the front of the forlorn cinderblock, soon to be joining the hundreds of other empty storefronts that populate so much of Tucson east of Campbell Avenue. Golden doesn't reckon the Tucson economy is coming back anytime soon, not the real-world economy, anyway. Too hard for him to keep the doors open.

The man who hustled years in local swap-meets, on used car lots, in auction houses, who sold shoes, and who raised three daughters (all have helped him in his shop) with a good business sense and transmissible entrepreneurial spirit, who says he hasn't had a "straight job in 20 years," opened up this place in 2007 with "ten swap-meet tables full of stuff, a few show cases and a credit card with a $15,000 limit." That first year was his best business-wise.

I learn of Golden's dad, a huge inspiration for him and his two younger brothers. "Back in those days they called him a cripple – he had a fused hip bone – before it wasn't PC. After I was born [in the late 50s], my dad was driving a cab trying to make a living. Then he went to school to be a watchmaker in Decatur, Alabama. He could clean and oil 36 watches in a day. Ten and $12 a pop. That's a lot of money in those days."

By the late 70s, Golden was doing the books for his Pop's watch and jewelry business. Townspeople called dad the Golden Boy, the cripple who overcame physical and class odds to open his own jewelry and watch place in a Tennessee blip still run by Klansmen, a good-old-boy network of bankers and politicians. "Corrupt as hell. But my dad knew business. They had nothing on him. And they thought we were Jewish."

He pauses. "You can't cure stupid."

Golden himself got called a "n****r-lover." The shock of that word makes me wary. He wasn't supposed to associate with black people, and this was the 70s. "The Klan was everywhere still. Hell yes, I had black friends. You'd drive by the grammar school on a specific night and you'd see pointy hats and tommy guns. It was like Mayberry only with an evil slant to the people. But sometimes growing up white in the south wasn't easy either. You just had to be there."

He speaks of his great-great-grandfather "killed six months before the end of the Civil War." He talks of government plots to conceal John Wilkes Booth's death and escape and how in Tennessee's Franklin County Courthouse, "it lists my great-great-grandmother married a John Booth. My family claims they went off to Texas."

He'd split Tennessee for the Florida panhandle in the early 80s, taught taekwondo there, did security in bars, but returned home. "I had people from the Klan come down to Florida looking for me," he says. "I picked up a 30 cal. M1 Carbine with a jungle clip and went back to Tennessee. Then the Klan boys tried to kill my parents. They burned their house down." Golden wound up in Tucson indirectly because of the Klan. His youngest brother married into a family with Klan members, and wound up trying to protect a child from them. FBI got involved. Long story short: the entire family packed up and moved to Arizona in a caravan, 37 years ago.

He now lives in a trailer west of Tucson. His brother and his mother each have their own trailer on the same acre lot. He has a wood-burning stove for winter heat, scavenges the wood. Swamp cooler for summer. Says he'd rather be a survivalist on 10,000 acres, away from the numbers where no one expects anything.

"We're all hunters and gatherers," he says. He looks at me like he does anyone else and says I'm hunting and gathering. Fodder to sell to a publication. "Prostitution isn't the oldest profession," he continues. "Pimping is. Buying and selling. It's all commodities." He looks around his dusty shop. Adds, "It's like the stock market, only a smaller scale."

Golden's tired of operating a thrift/antiques store. Another reason to close up shop. "I may go to Denny's and drink coffee all day. I may be on a trail in the mountains and wind up in Argentina. I may just go fishing. It may take me six months, it may take me a year – I'm going to get rid of everything in here."

Is he ever surprised what people will pay for here? "No," he says, "Look who they voted for."

He communicates his politics with gestures of politeness and civility. When he talks of the government and Trump and the media he bundles them together into some vague vessel of tyranny, convinced they're on the long con. I choose not to argue. I understand whatever inner need he has to be away from the numbers.

Ulli Malcolm is an older white-haired woman with a wide smile and German accent who recently moved to Tucson from Las Cruces, New Mexico because her husband, who worked "in missiles," just retired. She purchases a wooden box display filled with a dozen or so aluminum Christmas tree ornaments.

Don't know why but I remind her it's the hottest day of the summer. Hardly relevant; she's happy with her discovery. Ulli and Golden joke: A public hanging of Washington folk and the unyielding virtues of Rooster Cogburn.

The dusty register rings and Golden offers up a total including the everything-must-go, 30-percent-off discount.

"I just can't believe this place is closing," Ulli says before stepping out. You wish it weren't so.

June 29, 2017

TAO OF ARTHUR

Alone in the world and full dark is falling soon, and he listens to the stupid cars and trucks pass by, their low rumble, the severity and austerity. He leans in toward the traffic from just behind the curb, absolutely motionless and expressionless. The tortured pistons, the sonic crush of city buses, the precise whir of hybrids, all create a hypnotic drone, but the birds chirp counterpoint during lulls. Melody is everywhere, and he gets it, for hours.

The wind rustles eucalyptus leaves and palm tree fronds overhead, lifts his sighs away, to somewhere far beyond that one barking dog. The wind runs through the thinning platinum hair on the sides and back of his shiny black head. It moves the dirty gray fleece draped over his straight-backed, soft-in-the-middle body. He tastes dust, car oil, exhaust.

His dark eyes stay mostly motionless too, as he sees obdurate cityscape of wire and poles, bowed chain-link and high cinderblock fences, sometimes a roadside altar to the dead. He's set back from the road on Swan between Fifth and Broadway, in front of the Poet's Corner neighborhood, where it's easy to imagine all the dreams, hopes and money long ago pumped into this area. He searches for beauty on streets designed solely for automobile comfort. It can't be easy.

At first glance he appears feral, frightening, but easily frightened too, long dismissed an autistic pity case. After some time, I became obsessed with him. It's like he's exuding a secret, like he's communicating with the dead. Maybe he's beaming himself elsewhere. Or maybe he's contemplating some deep-seated hurt involving dead loved ones who maybe

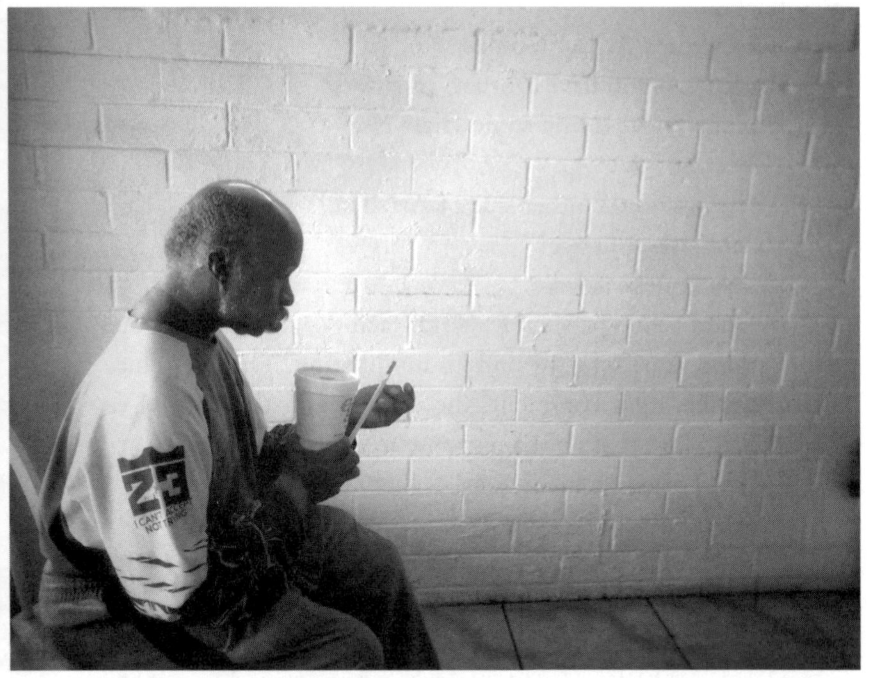

once attended Rincon High School, which he stands and faces, motionless for hours.

(I've seen him many times, in the same exact spot – different week, different time. Sometimes I'd spot him a mile away, still leaning forward slightly, and completely motionless.)

I brought him lunch a few times. I'd hoped to hear his story or learn what his secret could be. I'd edged around his silence for hours, getting little from him, but understanding more, and I took his silence as a respectful way of saying he'd rather be by himself. It felt rude and insensitive to hang around him long, like pestering a praying man. But watching him inspires dreaming. One day he got to talking, saying very little, but enough. It was tentative, free of inflection, and never with eye contact.

His name is Arthur Conlee.

I ask, "Do you have brothers or sisters?"

"Yeah. They're, um, somewhere else."

"Parents?"

"They're on the other side of Arizona."

"Can I ask your age?"

"Um. I guess 38."

A good while passes. He stands facing away from me but into traffic. Cars whiz by and it's humiliating. Then he reluctantly offers up a comment, the only one in the hours I've spent with him that's not a response to a question.

"I kind of enjoy life."

"That's enviable," I say.

"That's what I do. Ever since I can remember."

More times passes. He adds, "I go with the flow."

I reach my hand to shake his and he jerks his right arm back and his entire body turns away. He's embarrassed, shamed. Me too, for thinking it strange. He lives mostly on his inside. I get that, and it makes me more of a fan of him. I feel a sudden, boundless tenderness for him.

I get his address, and he says it's cool if I come by at 2 p.m. the next day.

★ ★ ★

When I arrive, Arthur's sitting on a dinette chair placed in the middle of the floor, waiting. He's wearing the same clothes as the previous day; they hang off him like the unloved garb of a big brother's hand-me-downs.

He lives in a boxy but spacious two-bedroom guesthouse,

clean and sparse. It's situated behind a halfway house near Fifth Street and Swan Road.

Place smells earthy, of sparingly showered bodies and cooked carbs. An episode of *Bonanza* flickers on a TV atop the refrigerator. Someone in another room stirs restless under a brown blanket in a bed. A closed door hides the second bedroom. A pink, hand-scrawled placard above the kitchen sink reads: SHOWER: Tuesday, Thursday, Saturday.

Arthur is hardly living on juice and Dumpster swag. Somebody works hard to keep the dust and dirt and dread out of the place. ("It's a pretty nice home," he says. "Some days there's really something to talk about.")

I tracked down Ruth Dempsey, whose company, Dempsey's Adult Care Homes, owns the residence in which Arthur resides, as well as a number of other such places in Tucson. She explains that Arthur lives on Social Security benefits, and a monthly government stipend of $60 for toiletries. A caretaker arrives daily to cook and clean for the three folks living there, reminds them to shower.

"We help people with low incomes," Dempsey says. She herself was raised an army brat in Mexico, moved to Tucson to train as a nurse.

People come and go from the homes and care that Dempsey's company provides. She has helped to look after Arthur for 15 years, after he arrived in one of her homes from a Tucson health center. She's emotionally invested in his wellbeing, and talks about him with personalized detail, avoiding the programmed syntax of a jaded caretaker. There's love, laughter and concern. In that 15 years, she says, they've attempted to locate Arthur's family but "there was no one." And he suffers from haphephobia, a fear of human touch.

"His sickness keeps him away from people," she continues. She says Arthur hasn't really changed in 15 years. "He just likes to walk, and stand. It's what he does."

She doesn't attempt to explain his behavior. Arthur just is. He's on time for his meals, and for bed sleep and rest.

"He doesn't try to make friends, really," she continues. "I only had one complaint about him in all these years. A neighbor said he was standing in front of his house." She laughs, "I told Arthur, 'you can't stand right in front of people's houses.' And now he doesn't."

"And the other day I watched a woman give him popcorn."

* * *

Back out on the street, processions of cars shimmer in sad November afternoon half-gloom. Arthur's leaning slightly into all of it from the side street along Swan Road. He's not addicted to a screen assigned to a satellite hanging far above the Earth. He lives in the moment, addicted to his surroundings – the shadows growing taller, the sounds from front yards and alleys and ditches, and kids trudging home late from Rincon High School. He's really watching time, as some might say, from the edge of lunacy, which is I always figured, the very best vantage. I say he has better sight and listening skills than most anyone I've ever met.

Who gazes that hard anymore? I try to always do that, meditation. So I'm watching a man stand completely still, watching time move for long stretches, trying to see what he sees.

"Everything changes," he says, "in every second that goes by. That's beautiful. But it's really nice. This is basically what I do. I look around. Just outside looking at the scenery."

I catch confused expressions on faces in passing cars, probably like mine the first time I saw him. One approaches and slows, eases slightly over toward the curb. Its driver hits the horn and a tubby white blob of a face with small eyes nudges out from the passenger window and shouts disturbing racist horseshit at Arthur, and speeds off.

But Arthur doesn't budge. He doesn't seem to care, doesn't even appear self-conscious. But I know he hears it.

Does racist shit happen often?

He shakes his head. Then he turns and moves cautiously up the gravel-strewn street, hands in pockets, looking down ahead of his feet. He stops and turns to face the street again, leans in almost enough to fall over forward, and stands tree-still. A half hour passes and he adjusts his stance, but only slightly.

November 16, 2017

WAITING FOR THE MAN

Incessant birdsong, traffic din and distant baseball kids create a melancholy jam, giving the grassy Santa Rita Park a Sunday-at-dusk quality all day long. The song evokes lost or unreachable worlds, a soundtrack for veterans of ugly wars waged internally or in far-off lands, or both. Worlds ticking free of time.

Park lethargy is easy, especially when a dozen or more homeless heads rest beneath trees, on backpacks or heaps of personal things. Hearts beat slow, and slower still, except those pumping at G speed.

Two abandoned swimming pools, framed by a dun-colored pool house and tall, pad-locked chainlink, sit in the southeast corner of the park. The pool house provides a shady spot for the lanky Orly Tyrone Williams, where he runs his own makeshift bike repair shop.

He has many spray oils and tools – crescent wrenches, various hammers and screwdrivers, crank removers – spilling from out of a backpack and oily grocery plastic. Nearby, wobbly and ramshackle inside a cluster of shopping carts, covered with a blue tarp, is his life's loam. He sleeps under stars in the dusty, brome-heavy wash, over across 22nd Street, between industrial walls and chainlink and railroad tracks.

Orly's from Monroe, Louisiana, and he's been outdoors, surviving, about four years. Has three daughters. His lot couldn't have been so easy. But it is easy to uncover wrongs about people, and I later discover that since the mid-90s, Orly's been arrested for possession and sales, a theft charge or two, failures to appear, possessing a firearm, etc.

In 2011, a South Tucson drug deal went south and Orly took a bullet straight into his heart and by some miraculous fluke he survived. Cops nailed the shooter, who got 12 years.

Yet there's unjaded sparkle in Orly, minus born-again insincerity. No shifty eye contact, no stiff movements when in my presence, no sensation of powerlessness evident in his stoop or grimace. That or his formality is a ruse. He has the quiet calm of a southern gent, or stoner. He offers water to drink; it's all he has. Could be he's grateful, like he says, and that all grief is relative. Don't know why I find that hard to imagine, maybe because I have an actual bed to sleep in at night.

He sometimes slips into a street-preacher mode: "Tucson is a beautiful place. It's how you live. If you live with a criminal mind, you're going to make Tucson a hell place. If you live in a positive mind and do things positive, you're going to find those positive people. And those positive people will be your anchor in life."

I know Orly is 55 years old and arrived in Tucson as a child because "mom wanted a better life for us." Jim Crow was still easily felt in Louisiana then. Real opportunities for black people, he says, were limited to work with the city sanitation department. His home "broke" when his mom died in '84 from multiple sclerosis. A heart attack took his dad in '98.

"I had the best parents you could ask for," he says. "My mom and dad probably wouldn't approve of me living outdoors. There were times when I was a boy in Louisiana I used to go sleep in the woods. I'm just a nature type of boy."

So now he peddles neighborhood streets on his Mongoose, sorts through junk piled on curbs where he "might see a bicycle frame in there." He hauls his treasures to his camp in the wash and then to the park to work on. But it takes time, he warns, and you don't take parts with filed off serial numbers. You don't steal bikes. You have to hunt shops and trash for missing parts. He often hits BICAS (Bicycle Inter Community Art and Salvage) for them. The mechanics of building and fixing are easy with experience, and he's done it since childhood. "It's like they say," he says, "'you're once a man and twice a child.'"

People roll bikes up for him to fix. He builds bikes for children, college students or people fresh from prison who need a job. "And I help them out. They always like to pay me, and sometimes I accept it because I really need it, mainly to buy parts for other bikes."

He gets meals at soup kitchens and in the graces of "real good people who feed the homeless at parks." Many of Orly's tools were donated too, by acquaintances and passersby. "They see what I'm doing, and they say, 'I got some extra tools you can have.' So they'll return with tools. I'll take them and lubricate them, get the rust off, put a little sandpaper to them, and they're new again."

Orly sweeps the dirt from the oil-stained concrete of his shaded area, flips a bike over and stands it upside-down. He unlocks its rear quick-release, yanks the wheel free, grips it by its hub and spins. No damaged bearings and the wheel is straight, so it's a good find, he says. He slips the rear wheel back into place and returns the chain to its ring in one swift, honed movement.

His girlfriend strolls up, baggy shorts, T-shirt, knee in a brace. I don't get her name because I have somewhere else to be, but Orly's talking family and life, says he trusts my ears. He tells me he's in this location every day until sundown. He made a point to say "every day" twice. He wants to talk his life. I'm down.

★ ★ ★

I return the following day to resume my hang with Orly, and after searching the entire park he's nowhere to be found.

Dust and grass rise behind the wheels of a little municipal truck rolling around the park. It's like a glorified lawnmower, greenish with the City of Tucson seal emblazoned on the side. A Latino groundskeeper in a sweet boonie hat mans the thing. He's been on the job 18 years. We talk. He tells me his name too but warns I can't use it because it'd cost him his City job.

OK.

The groundskeep cleans the park bathrooms "meticulously," otherwise his grandchildren who visit him on the job couldn't use them. No way. He keeps grass cut too, trash picked up, not only here but at other Tucson parks. He says I wouldn't believe the stuff he's seen. He is acquainted with Santa Rita stories – the homeless, the drugs and the torment. But he's got a heart. Shows interest in the well-being of others. Knows of Orly too. Shakes his head: "If he's not here today, he's in jail. He'd never leave his stuff without somebody watching it."

Orly's shaded area at the abandoned swimming pools is telling. There's a single shopping cart filled with remnants of good intentions lost to some authority – discarded clothes in homeless-ready pastel colors, a brand-new unused 2018 calendar datebook with a kid-happy polka-dot cover, a box filled with mushy, unopened microwave burritos. Orly's dollar-store broom leans against the wall. Fifty feet away sit his shopping carts with the blue tarp, two bikes chain-locked to the heap. Behind that, the train.

* * *

Dealers on mountain bikes and old 10-speeds. One wheelman looks like Hunter S. Thompson in a poly buttondown, khaki trou, gray on the fringes, pole thin, and he's selling G. I'd guessed weed, but I'm so out of practice. G is meth, easy as shit to score here. I find it hard not to, and I could easily redouble at least one fading addiction. So the old blue bird of depression kicks in with that brassy Tucson light that so effortlessly illumines dying things.

But no one here on this weirdly cool May morning considers me a cop, just some addict, likely. Certainly not one of the Veterans on Patrol, those who live in tents across the park at Camp Bravo, the homeless shelter mostly for war veterans, some of whom patrol the park evenings. They're into Jesus and sobriety, the Stars and Stripes, and are often sidearm strapped. Most homeless folk shrug at them.

So, some things don't change, and it's easy to make friends. Good thing. I'd always found some comfort and camaraderie with the homeless, more than with most other people, really, except the times in my life when I actually had no home. Then it was all fear and suicide shakes and alcohol. There's really no explaining the sadnesses. Still, I've never met anyone who preferred to be homeless. Never. Even if they claimed they did. That's just ignominy talking.

I wait for Orly in the park and meet Julio Sarmeinto. Offers me a rolled smoke, end wet with spit. Just rolled it. If I want G, he knows who's holding. He unwraps two bologna sandwiches from plastic baggies, eats while tearing pieces off for the birds. Plaid shorts and blue T-shirt, black shades, dusty rat's-nest hair, very rock 'n' roll, a young Link Wray.

He tells of his pal Lionel, murdered nearby a month or so back, in the wee hours at a nearby convenience store. He points in the direction of the market: how it happened there, how it was over $20, how he saw Lionel the day before. Says Lionel was the kind of dude who always volunteered to feed other homeless.

His buddy, Richard Marcado, nods off a few feet away. His arms rough with too-scratched mosquito bites and things. He's old Tucson hippie, white bandana around his neck. Born (1956) and raised here. He wakes up and talks legends like John Wesley Hardin. He's got Robert Palmer on a little hand-held radio, the kind you never see.

Julio was born in Ciudad Juárez, Mexico, moved to El Paso as a pup. At 16 he was born-again, the family following mom's lead. It didn't sit so well; Julio was all Black Sabbath and Alice Cooper. He graduated from the same high school that gave us Sandra Day O'Connor years before and he's proud of that. The U.S. Navy was where the action was for the El Paso 19-year-old, and he served 1985 to '89. First stop, San Diego. And the cold war, man. On an amphibious assault ship. He didn't know what shit was going on when he was 19, how Russia had invaded Afghanistan, the Black Ops in South America. Blew his mind. He went all over, Hawaii, Philippines, Australia, Japan.

Later he drove trucks, interstate. Married, bought a house with a mortgage and two brand new cars. The American dream lasted an entire decade. Pulls on his smoke, pushing his hand through his thick black hair, "We all age differently." His involved escalating OCD issues.

The divorce gutted him. Short jail time (weed, resisting arrest) ensued. He landed in Tucson four years ago, looking for a relative. He's a learned guy and talks varied subjects, from the Jewish Torah, Old Testament and the Dead Sea Scrolls, to getting connected to yoga and the laws of nature, and then crystal meth. He's partial to G, only discovered its joys a year ago. Yes, it connects you to worlds far outside your own. Then it doesn't. He hasn't yet done enough to strangle himself. He knows. I like him a lot.

Later on, Carolina Richtie (or Carolyn Magrit), lit-up energy, long hair, rock 'n' roll hippie with her own business card – a personal production company specializing in everything from pet sitting and lifestyle coaching to "Kaos" piloting. She's from Los Angeles, Northern California and New York.

Makes a beeline for me, shouting she knows me.

"Do you?"

Says I look like Max's Kansas City. She was in New York then. "CBGB's too, and Warhol." People have said things like this to me since I was 15. Carolina feels familiar, for a moment. Like an aunt or older sister from another life. Her broken down pickup sits with its engine hood up in the parking lot. She's been stuck here with a busted ride for a few days, nowhere to go. She introduces me to Billy. "Billy from L.A.," he says. Billy has the magnetism of an undefeated street battle-rapper, but with a tender underside of personal tragedy, which makes him approachable. I'd buy his records if he'd made any.

I ask the two if they've seen this guy Orly, who fixes bikes at the abandoned swimming pools. Billy's seen him, but it's been a few days. Come back tomorrow, he tells me. "He's not going anywhere."

I return again the next morning. I see Billy and Julio down by the baseball field, but no Orly. Carolina's pickup is gone. I walk around aimlessly before settling at a picnic table under a wondrous tree, waiting for my man. Kind of like the old days, but minus lots of friction. Here come the melancholy jams.

May 31, 2018

ACKNOWLEDGEMENTS

This book couldn't have happened without Maggie Smith, Mari Herreras, Jim Nintzel and John "Cal" Freeman. Also, Todd Swift and the literate true believers at Eyewear Publishing, as well as Jason Joseph, Chelo Grubb, Jaime Hood, Tyler Vondrak, Casey Anderson, Logan Burtch-Buus, Danyelle Khmara, Louie Armendariz and everyone at the *Tucson Weekly*. Can't forget Billy Sedlmayr, Alan Fischer, Jeremy Voas, Doug Coombe, Jason Schusterbauer, Patrick O' Connor, ML Liebler, Tammy Allen, Clif Taylor, Lowell Rottenberg, Matt Cole, Curtis Endicott, Al Perry, Gabriel Sullivan, Dan Stuart, Ellen Berman, Tim Gillis, Alan Colombo, and so many subjects who gave up their stories and battle scars, for better or worse, as well as the *Tucson Salvage* readers who made the column popular enough for this book (and documentary) to happen at all. And all the lovely 22nd Street urchins.

Mi familia: Reece, Julie, Marcia, Mary, Barry, Stuart, Howard, Travis, Tulah, Blake, and Moose. Nora Herrling and Stacia, Faith and Kevin. The George's: Lois (ma), Don, John, Terry and David. And Robin Johnson.